RA

D0261362

Dun La
DUND.
Inv/99   Price IRf24.11
Title: Wellington & Napoleon
Class: 940.27

WELLINGTON

AND

NAPOLEON

Clash of Arms
1807–1815

Other books by the author

The Hundred Years War
The Wars of the Roses
By Sea & Land (The Royal Marines Commandos 1942–82)
The Raiders (The Army Commandos 1940–45)
The Desert Rats (The 7th Armoured Division 1939–45)
D-Day 1944: Voices from Normandy (with Roderick de Normann)
The Road to Compostela
Armageddon: The Defeat of Germany 1945

WELLINGTON
AND
NAPOLEON

Clash of Arms

1807–1815

ROBIN NEILLANDS

JOHN MURRAY

© Robin Neillands, 1994

First published in 1994
by John Murray (Publishers) Ltd.,
50 Albemarle Street, London W1X 4BD

The moral right of the author has been asserted

All rights reserved
Unauthorized duplication
contravenes applicable laws

A catalogue record for this book is available from the British Library

ISBN 0-7195- 5151 X

Typeset in 11.5 on 13 pts Baskerville by
Pure Tech Corporation, Pondicherry, India
Printed and bound in Great Britain by
The University Press, Cambridge.

For
Nigel Massey
of
The 45th Foot

Contents

Illustrations

(between pages 140 and 141)

For kind permission to reproduce these illustrations, thanks are due as follows: 1 and 2, National Portrait Gallery; 3, 9, 11, 15 and 28: Anne S. K. Brown Military Collection, Brown University Library; 5, 6, 12, 13, 16, 17, 18 and 20: Collection Philip J. Haythornthwaite and Cassell; 7, 19, 22 and 23: Hulton Deutsch; 14: The National Trust (Plas Newydd), photograph Courtauld Institute of Art; 21: Mansell Collection.

Maps

Acknowledgements

A great many people helped me with this book, so thanks to Dr David Chandler of the Royal Military Academy, Sandhurst, doyen of experts on the Napoleonic Wars, and to Captain and Mrs Snook of Holts Battlefield Tours for an informative visit to the battlefields of Spain and Portugal. Also to Nigel Massey at Waterloo, and Stephen Danos in Austria. Jack Jensen of Toronto, Canada, produced a goldmine of out-of-print books, as did that ever-helpful institution, The London Library. Thanks also to the curators and staff of military museums in Lisbon, Busaco, Coimbra, Madrid, to the Light Infantry Museum in Winchester and the National Army Museum in London. Lastly, and as ever, to Estelle Huxley, for typing numerous drafts and for her patience in holding the fort while I was away walking battlefields and enjoying myself.

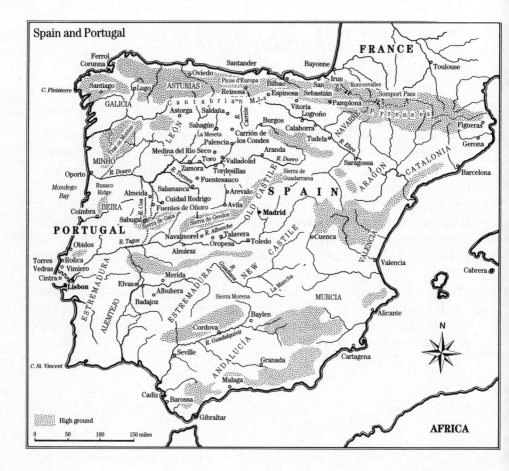

Spain and Portugal

FRANCE

Ferrol
Corunna
C. Finisterre
Santiago
Lugo
GALICIA
ASTURIAS
Oviedo
Santander
Bayonne
Toulouse
Picos d'Europa
Bilbao
San
Sebastián
Irun
Roncesvalles
Espinosa
Reinosa
Cantabrian Mts
Vitoria
Pamplona
Somport Pass
Pyrenees
Figueras
Astorga
Saldaña
Logroño
NAVARRE
Gerona
LEÓN
Sahagún
R. Carrión
Burgos
Calahorra
Tudela
Barcelona
La Meseta
Palencia
Carrión de
los Condes
Aranda
Saragossa
ARAGON
CATALONIA
Tras os Mons
Medina del Rio Seco
MINHO
Zamora
Toro
Valladolid
R. Duero
Sierra de
Guadarrama
Oporto
R. Douro
Tordesillas
R. Tormes
Fuentesauco
OLD CASTILE
SPAIN
Mondego
Bay
Busaco
Ridge
Almeida
Salamanca
Cuidad Rodrigo
Fuentes de Oñoro
Arevalo
Avila
Madrid
Cuenca
VALENCIA
Coimbra
BEIRA
R. Coa
Sierra de Gata
Sierra de Gredos
Sabugal
Navalmorel
R. Alberche
Talavera
PORTUGAL
R. Tagus
Oropesa
Toledo
NEW
CASTILE
Valencia
Cabrera
Obidos
Almáraz
Torres
Vedras
Rolica
Vimiero
Cintra
Lisbon
ESTREMADURA
Merida
Guadiana
La Mancha
Elvas
Albuhera
MURCIA
ALEMTEJO
Badajoz
Baylen
Alicante
ESTREMADURA
Sierra Morena
Cordova
ANDALUCÍA
R. Guadalquivir
C. St. Vincent
Seville
Granada
Cartagena
Malaga
N
Cadiz
Barossa
Gibraltar
AFRICA

High ground

0   50   100   150 miles

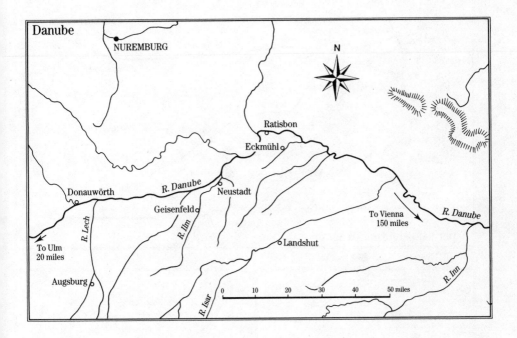

Danube

NUREMBURG

Ratisbon

Eckmühl

R. Danube

Donauwörth

Neustadt

Geisenfeld

R. Lech

R. Ilm

To Ulm
20 miles

To Vienna
150 miles

R. Danube

Landshut

Augsburg

R. Isar

N

R. Inn

0   10   20   30   40   50 miles

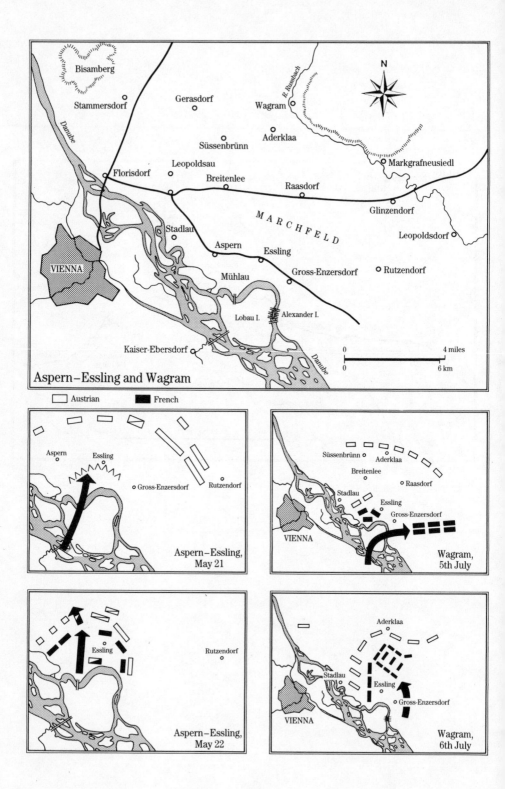

Aspern–Essling and Wagram

Austrian ☐   French ■

Aspern–Essling, May 21

Wagram, 5th July

Aspern–Essling, May 22

Wagram, 6th July

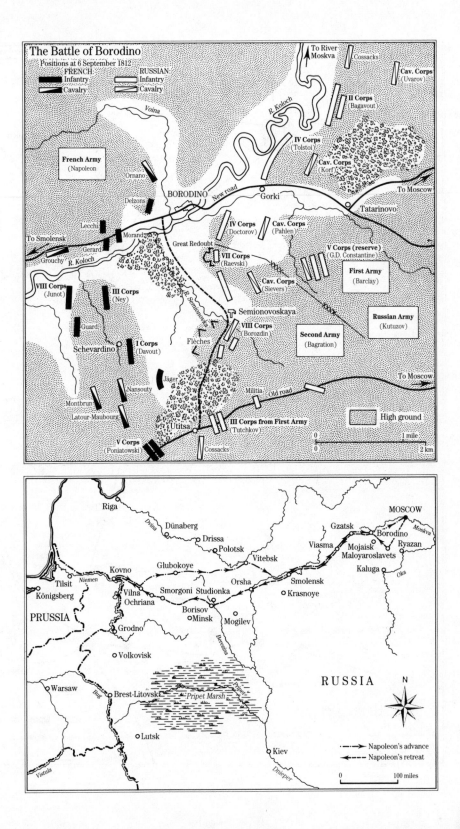

The Battle of Borodino

Positions at 6 September 1812

FRENCH:
Infantry
Cavalry

RUSSIAN:
Infantry
Cavalry

To River Moskva

Cossacks

Cav. Corps
(Uvarov)

R. Koloch

II Corps
(Bagavout)

IV Corps
(Tolstoi)

Voina

Cav. Corps
(Korf)

To Moscow

French Army
(Napoleon)

Ornano

Delzons

BORODINO

New road

Gorki

Tatarinovo

Lecchi

Morand

Great Redoubt

IV Corps
(Doctorov)

Cav. Corps
(Pahlen)

To Smolensk

Gerard

Grouchy

R. Koloch

VII Corps
(Raevski)

V Corps (reserve)
(G.D. Constantine)

VIII Corps
(Junot)

III Corps
(Ney)

Cav. Corps
(Sievers)

First Army
(Barclay)

Guard

Semionovskaya

Russian Army
(Kutuzov)

Schevardino

I Corps
(Davout)

R. Semionovka

VIII Corps
(Borozdin)

Flèches

Second Army
(Bagration)

To Moscow

Nansouty

Jäger

Militia

Old road

Montbrun

Latour-Maubourg

Utitsa

III Corps from First Army
(Tutchkov)

High ground

V Corps
(Poniatowski)

Cossacks

0   1 mile
0   2 km

Riga

Drina

Dünaberg

Drissa

Polotsk

Vitebsk

Gzatsk

MOSCOW

Moskva

Borodino

Viasma

Mojaisk

Ryazan

Maloyaroslavets

Glubokoye

Kovno

Kaluga

Oka

Niemen

Tilsit

Königsberg

Vilna

Ochriana

Smorgoni Studionka

Orsha

Smolensk

Krasnoye

PRUSSIA

Grodno

Borisov

Minsk

Mogilev

Berezina

Volkovisk

RUSSIA

N

Warsaw

Bug

Brest-Litovsk

Pripet Marsh

Pripet

Lutsk

Kiev

Napoleon's advance
Napoleon's retreat

Vistula

Dnieper

0   100 miles

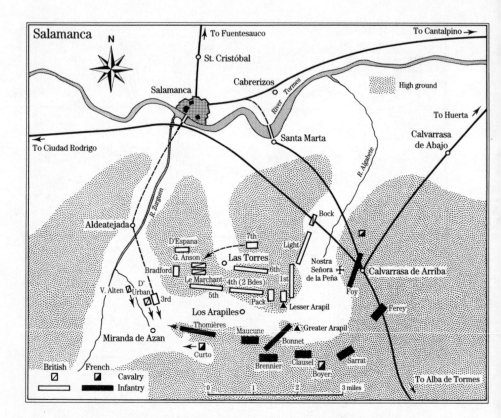

Salamanca

To Fuentesauco
To Cantalpino →

St. Cristóbal

Cabrerizos

High ground

River Tormes

Salamanca

To Huerta ↗

Santa Marta

Calvarrasa
de Abajo

R. Algabete

To Ciudad Rodrigo

R. Zurguen

Aldeatejada

Bock

D'Espana
7th
Light
Calvarrasa de Arriba

G. Anson

Las Torres

Nostra Señora
de la Peña

Bradford
6th
Foy

V. Alten
D'
Urban
Le Marchant
4th (2 Bdes)
1st

5th
Pack
Ferey

3rd
Lesser Arapil

Los Arapiles

Thomières
Greater Arapil

Miranda de Azan
Maucune

Bonnet

Curto
Brennier
Clausel
Sarrat

Boyer

To Alba de Tormes

British French Cavalry
Infantry

0   1   2   3 miles

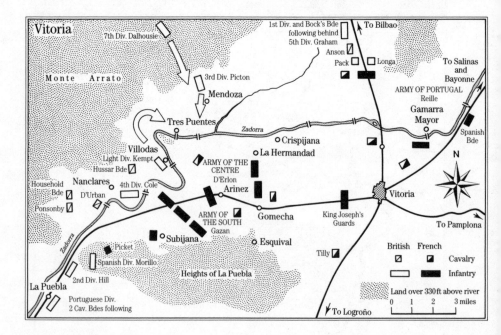

Vitoria

7th Div. Dalhousie

1st Div. and Bock's Bde
following behind
5th Div. Graham

To Bilbao

Anson
Pack   Longa
To Salinas
and
Bayonne

M o n t e   A r r a t o

3rd Div. Picton

Mendoza

ARMY OF PORTUGAL
Reille

Tres Puentes

Zadorra

Crispijana

Gamarra
Mayor

Villodas

La Hermandad

Spanish
Bde

Light Div. Kempt
Hussar Bde

ARMY OF THE
CENTRE
D'Erlon

Household
Bde
Nanclares
4th Div. Cole

Arinez

Vitoria

D'Urban
Ponsonby
ARMY OF
THE SOUTH
Gazan

Gomecha

King Joseph's
Guards

To Pamplona

Subijana

Esquival

Picket
Spanish Div. Morillo
Tilly

British French

Cavalry
Infantry

La Puebla
Heights of La Puebla

2nd Div. Hill

Land over 330ft above river

Portuguese Div.
2 Cav. Bdes following

0   1   2   3 miles

To Logroño

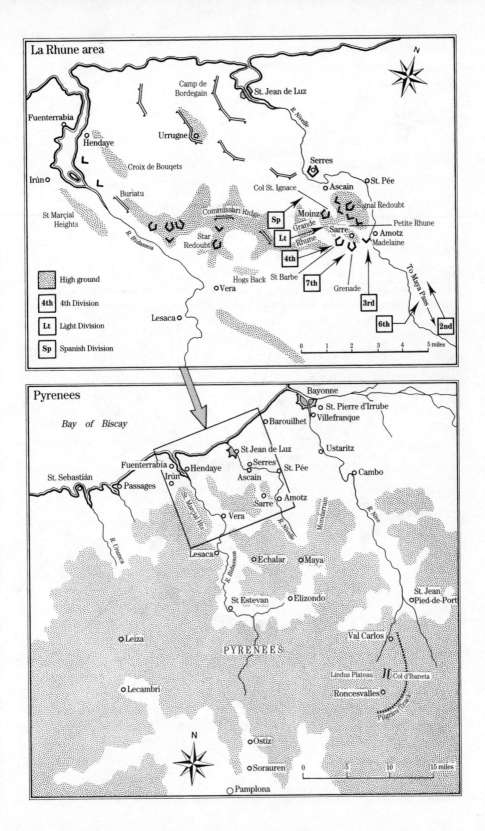

La Rhune area

Camp de Bordegain
St. Jean de Luz
R. Nivelle
Fuenterrabia
Hendaye
Urrugne
Croix de Bouqets
Serres
Irún
St. Pée
Ascain
St Marçial Heights
Buriatu
Col St. Ignace
Commissari Ridge
Signal Redoubt
Sp
Moinz
Petite Rhune
R. Bidassoa
Star Redoubt
Lt
Grande
Sarre
Amotz
Rhune
Madelaine
4th
Hogs Back
St Barbe
To Maya Pass
7th
Grenade
Vera
3rd
Lesaca
6th
2nd

High ground	
4th	4th Division
Lt	Light Division
Sp	Spanish Division

0   1   2   3   4   5 miles

Pyrenees

Bayonne
St. Pierre d'Irrube
Bay of Biscay
Barouilhet
Villefranque
St Jean de Luz
Ustaritz
Fuenterrabía
Serres
Hendaye
Irún
St. Pée
Cambo
St. Sebastián
Ascain
Passages
St. Marçial Hts.
Sarre
Amotz
Mondarrain
Vera
R. Ururea
R. Nivelle
R. Nive
Lesaca
Echalar
Maya
R. Bidassoa
St Estevan
Elizondo
St. Jean Pied-de-Port
Leiza
Val Carlos
PYRENEES
Lindus Plateau
Col d'Ibaneta
Lecambri
Roncesvalles
Pilgrim Track
N
Ostiz
Sorauren
0   5   10   15 miles
Pamplona

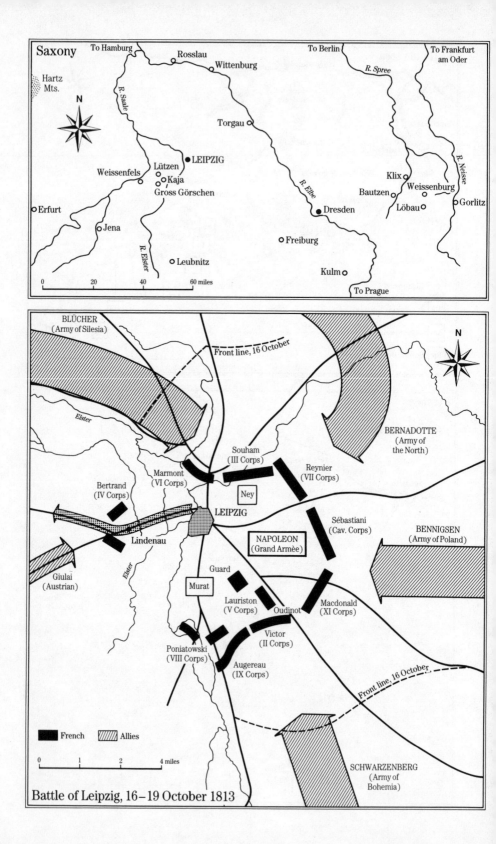

Saxony

To Hamburg
Rosslau
Wittenburg
To Berlin
To Frankfurt
am Oder
R. Spree
Hartz
Mts.
N
R. Saale
Torgau
LEIPZIG
Klix
Weissenfels
Lützen
Kaja
Gross Görschen
Bautzen
Weissenburg
Löbau
Gorlitz
R. Neisse
Erfurt
R. Elbe
Dresden
Jena
Freiburg
R. Elster
Leubnitz
Kulm
To Prague

0   20   40   60 miles

BLÜCHER
(Army of Silesia)
Front line, 16 October
N
BERNADOTTE
(Army of
the North)
Elster
Souham
(III Corps)
Reynier
(VII Corps)
Marmont
(VI Corps)
Bertrand
(IV Corps)
Ney
LEIPZIG
Sébastiani
(Cav. Corps)
BENNIGSEN
(Army of Poland)
Lindenau
NAPOLEON
(Grand Armèe)
Guard
Giulai
(Austrian)
Elster
Murat
Macdonald
(XI Corps)
Lauriston
(V Corps)
Oudinot
Victor
(II Corps)
Poniatowski
(VIII Corps)
Augereau
(IX Corps)
Front line, 16 October

French   Allies

0   1   2   4 miles

SCHWARZENBERG
(Army of
Bohemia)

Battle of Leipzig, 16–19 October 1813

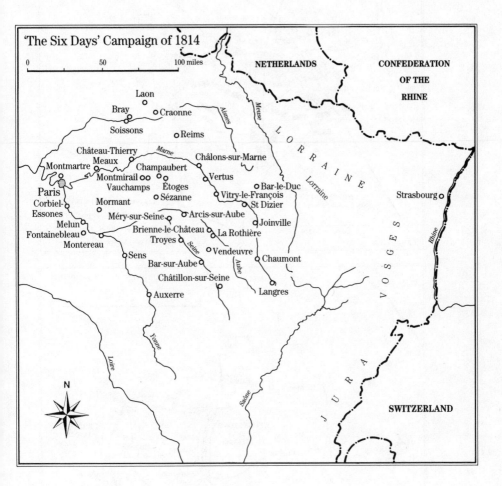

'The Six Days' Campaign of 1814

0   50   100 miles

NETHERLANDS

CONFEDERATION
OF THE
RHINE

Laon
Bray   Craonne
Soissons   Reims

L O R R A I N E

Château-Thierry   Marne
Montmartre Meaux   Châlons-sur-Marne
Paris   Montmirail   Champaubert
Vauchamps   Étoges   Vertus
Corbiel-   Mormant   Sézanne   Bar-le-Duc   Lorraine   Strasbourg
Essones   Vitry-le-François
Melun   Méry-sur-Seine   Arcis-sur-Aube   St Dizier
Fontainebleau   Brienne-le-Château La Rothière   Joinville
Montereau   Troyes   Vendeuvre
Sens   Chaumont
Bar-sur-Aube
Châtillon-sur-Seine
Auxerre   Langres

Seine
Aube

V O S G E S

Rhine

Loire

Yonne

Saône

N

J U R A

SWITZERLAND

Aisne   Meuse

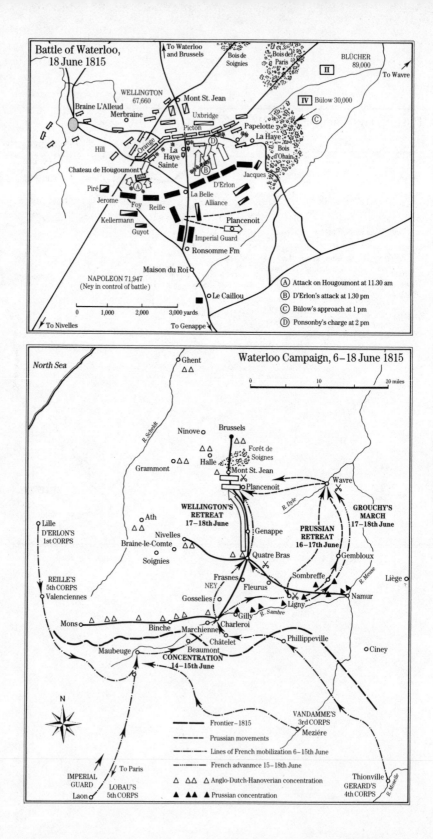

Battle of Waterloo, 18 June 1815

To Waterloo and Brussels

Bois de Soignies

Bois de Paris

BLÜCHER 89,000

II

To Wavre

IV Bülow 30,000

C

WELLINGTON 67,660

Braine L'Alleud

Merbraine

Mont St. Jean

Uxbridge

Picton

Papelotte

La Haye

Orange

Hill

La Haye Sainte

D

Bois d'Ohain

Chateau de Hougoumont

A

B

Jacques

Piré

Jerome

Foy

Reille

D'Erlon

La Belle Alliance

Kellermann

Guyot

Plancenoit

Imperial Guard

Ronsomme Fm

Maison du Roi

NAPOLEON 71,947
(Ney in control of battle)

Le Caillou

Ⓐ Attack on Hougoumont at 11.30 am

Ⓑ D'Erlon's attack at 1.30 pm

Ⓒ Bülow's approach at 1 pm

Ⓓ Ponsonby's charge at 2 pm

0   1,000   2,000   3,000 yards

To Nivelles

To Genappe

Waterloo Campaign, 6–18 June 1815

North Sea

Ghent

0   10   20 miles

R. Scheldt

Ninove

Brussels

Forêt de Soignes

Halle

Grammont

Mont St. Jean

Plancenoit

Wavre

R. Dyle

WELLINGTON'S RETREAT 17–18th June

GROUCHY'S MARCH 17–18th June

Lille

D'ERLON'S 1st CORPS

Ath

Nivelles

Braine-le-Comte

Genappe

PRUSSIAN RETREAT 16–17th June

Gembloux

R. Meuse

Liège

REILLE'S 5th CORPS

Soignies

Quatre Bras

Sombreffe

Namur

Valenciennes

Frasnes

NEY

Fleurus

Ligny

Gosselies

R. Sambre

Mons

Binche

Marchienne

Gilly

Charleroi

Phillippeville

Ciney

Châtelet

Beaumont

Maubeuge

CONCENTRATION 14–15th June

N

VANDAMME'S 3rd CORPS

Meziére

To Paris

IMPERIAL GUARD

LOBAU'S 5th CORPS

Laon

Thionville

GERARD'S 4th CORPS

R. Moselle

Frontier–1815

Prussian movements

Lines of French mobilization 6–15th June

French advanmce 15–18th June

△ △△ △ Anglo-Dutch-Hanoverian concentration

▲ ▲▲ ▲ Prussian concentration

Introduction

Leabharlanna Dhún Laoghaire · Ráth an Dúin

> My destiny is not yet accomplished. The picture as yet exists
> only in outline. There must be one code, one court of
> appeal, one coinage, for all Europe. The States of Europe
> must be melted into one nation, and Paris will be its capital.
>
> Napoleon Bonaparte: 1812

THE DETERMINATION OF Napoleon Bonaparte, Emperor of the
French, to impose his will on Europe and the determination of the other
Powers – but especially Great Britain – to resist him, created a dramatic
story which has kept historians busy for nearly two centuries.

An estimated 50,000 books have been written on Napoleon himself,
and when all the others – on his battles, his love affairs, his politics
and philosophy, his campaigns, his opponents, and his allies – have
been added to the pile, the total must run into six figures. No year
goes by without additions to the existing canon, and the shelves of any
decent library groan under the weight of works on the Napoleonic
Wars. Why, then, add another?

The first reason is personal: to learn more of that turbulent period
in European history, by researching and writing about it. The complexities of the Napoleonic period have been clarified over the last
few decades by the work of such historians as Corelli Barnett, John
Naylor, Christopher Hibbert, Georges Lefebvre, Lawrence James,
Elizabeth Longford, the late David Howarth, and my good friend
David Chandler, until recently Head of the Department of War
Studies at the Royal Military Academy, Sandhurst. All these have
written about the period in an informed and entertaining manner, but
the fact remains that for even an outline of the times, it is necessary

to read a good many books. It therefore occurred to me that there might be room to capture in one volume the developing struggle between Napoleon and the most persistent and successful opponent of his aims, the Duke of Wellington – culminating in their final clash at Waterloo. Those who seek greater detail are directed to the bibliography. My second reason is the belief that history is important because it teaches, as no other subject can, the brutal fact that actions have consequences – a fact nowhere more clearly illustrated than in the last eight years of the Napoleonic era, from the Emperor's triumph at Tilsit in 1807 to his final defeat at Waterloo in 1815. Napoleon Bonaparte was in decline during these eight years, despite his successes on the battlefield and at the conference table, and the reason for that decline may be summed up in one word – Spain.

The British reader may care to add another – Wellington – but in the context of Europe at the time, Wellington was less important than many British history books imply. The Royal Navy, Austria, Prussia and, most notably, Russia, all played a more decisive role in the defeat of Napoleon and the disintegration of his Empire.

No one man played a more decisive part in the struggle than General Sir Arthur Wellesley, later Duke of Wellington. His clear-sighted strategy during the Peninsular War and his tactical successes on the battlefield enabled him to demonstrate time and again that the armies of France could be defeated. Again and again, his victories revived the spirits and the fortunes of the other Allied Powers and slowly chipped away at the legend of Napoleonic invincibility. Wellington could not have achieved all he did without the help of the British Fleet and the Spanish guerrillas. Against such a combination, Napoleon and his marshals struggled in vain.

Napoleon Bonaparte remains a great general. For that we have the word of his most doughty opponent. Field Marshal Wellington, who when asked for his opinion on this point, replied, 'In this age, in past ages, in any age, Napoleon.' From a man who, as one of his soldiers remarked, '. . . did not know how to lose a battle', that opinion deserves consideration.

Napoleon Bonaparte had to be more than a great general. He had to be an Emperor, the ruler of Europe, a reformer, a creator of nations. His aim was to reduce all Europe to his will, and in this he overreached himself. In the end he fell like Lucifer, a victim of his own ambition.

The part played by the Spanish people and the Peninsular Army consisted largely of demonstrating that Napoleon could be defied. The Emperor was defeated by other nations, by Austria, Russia and

Prussia – but the final element contributing to his downfall was the Emperor himself. By going too far, by refusing to recognize that enough was enough, the Emperor continued to wage war until his armies were lost and his reputation in tatters.

The last eight years of the Napoleonic Empire saw the Hon. Arthur Wesley rise from being the most junior general on the Army List to Commander-in-Chief of the Armies of Portugal and Spain, Commander of the Peninsular Army, Field Marshal, Ambassador and, finally, Victor. This is the story of Napoleon and Wellington as it developed over those years, from the moment when their destinies became linked in the Peninsula to their sole encounter at Waterloo, seven years later.

PROLOGUE

The Plains of Maida:

1806

The British infantry are the finest infantry in Europe;
fortunately there are not many of them.
Thomas Bugeaud,
Marshal of France: 1809

SHORTLY AFTER NINE o'clock on the morning of 4 July 1806,
General Sir John Stuart's leading companies finally pushed their way
through the undergrowth cloaking the banks of the River Lamato
and emerged onto the dusty plain of Maida. Before them was a sight
that had already struck fear into half the armies of Continental
Europe. Their musket barrels glinting in the sun, French soldiers were
coming onto the attack, thick columns of infantry screened by sharpshooters, veteran troops driven onward by the sound of drums.

General Stuart's infantry had already been on the march for several
hours, first along the stony beach where they had come ashore three
days before, then through the marshes and scrub on either side of the
shallow Lamato. Splashing across the river in columns of battalions,
the three brigades that made up Stuart's small force struggled onto
open ground and deployed into line. Then, in echelon of brigades and
led by Colonel Kempt's Light Infantry, they began to advance upon
the oncoming French.

The action at Maida on that hot morning hardly ranks among the
great battles of history. The forces deployed were small – just 5,400
British and some 6,500 French, little more than two strong brigades on either side – while the landing itself, on the rugged coast
of Calabria, made no significant contribution to the outcome of the
Napoleonic Wars. The Emperor of the French, Napoleon Bonaparte,

had met, and would meet, other and greater reversals; Maida was a straw in the wind, nothing more. Even so, what happened was significant, to the Wars, and to the way they were fought.

The question asked and answered here was simple: could the column, those furious clumps of disciplined, enthusiastic, valorous French infantry, famed for their *élan* in attack, prevail against two ranks of muskets held by infantrymen known throughout Europe for their stubbornness in defence? Since Valmy, fifteen years earlier, the French columns had carried all before them, scattering the armies of the Continental Powers one after another, spreading the French Empire across half Europe. Here, for the first time, they met British infantry, in roughly equal numbers and in terrain that gave no advantage to either side. The tactical issue of column versus line was about to be tested to destruction.

Stuart's infantry was deployed in three brigades plus an advanced corps of Light Infantry under Colonel James Kempt, made up of the 'Light' companies of the 20th, 27th, 35th, 58th, 61st and 81st Foot, plus a battalion of Swiss infantry from Watteville's Regiment and two companies of sharpshooters from a body known as the Corsican Rangers.

The French had nine battalions of infantry, with 300 cavalry and a battery of horse artillery. Of the infantry battalions, two were Polish and one Swiss – a sign not only that the armies of France were no longer as homogeneous as in the early days of the Revolution and the Empire, but also that, in the war now sweeping Europe, men from the same nation might be found fighting on opposing sides. The French commander, General Jean Louis Reynier, who had fought the British in Egypt and was to fight them again in Spain, was a Swiss from Lausanne.

These two small armies, now within sight of each other, had already formed up in their chosen array. General Reynier's men were in three brigade columns. On the left, Compère's brigade of two French battalions, the 42nd Infantry of the Line and the 1st Light Infantry, mustering a total of 2,800 bayonets, was advancing in column of companies, fifty men wide, directly towards the ranks of Colonel Kempt's Light Infantry, already deployed into two ranks, each 350 men wide. Four hundred yards to the rear of Kempt's force and echeloned to the left came Acland's brigade, 1,300 infantry from the 78th and 81st Foot, covering Compère's 42nd on his right and the three battalions of Poles and Swiss of Peyri's central brigade column, itself mustering some 1,500 bayonets. The last of the French brigades, Digonet's, lay to the right of Colonel Peyri, on a collision course with the two British brigades commanded by Colonel Cole and Colonel Oswald. The latter formed the British reserve, with the support of three pieces of field artillery.

All four British brigades were echeloned, or stepped back, to their left, so the first exchange of fire would come on the British right where Kempt's infantry had halted, waiting for the two battalions of the 1st Light – which Colonel Compère was leading personally – to come within range.

The 1st Light was advancing in the traditional solid column, two battalions wide, urged on by their regimental drums beating the *pas de charge*. With Compère curvetting ahead on his charger, waving his men on with his sword, the cheering infantry had closed to within 150 yards of that silent, implacable British line when the redcoats presented their muskets and opened fire.

The first volley smashed into Compère's ranks with telling and terrible effect. Scores of French infantry went down together, whole files reeling back dead or wounded. The drums beat, the musket smoke cleared and the French column came on again, shouting defiance and eager to charge home with the bayonet. The British infantry, still silent, went through their drill, reloading and presenting their muskets, taking aim. The range was down to eighty yards when that red wall again erupted into flame. Most infantry would have broken, but these were French soldiers and not easily dismayed; they halted and wavered, their feet cluttered with the dead, then they came on again. They were within thirty yards of the British line when a third terrible volley tore into their ragged ranks.

No infantry in the world could stand against the fire of 700 muskets at thirty-yard range. The right-hand battalion of the 1st Light broke and fled. The left-hand battalion, led by Colonel Compère, still tried to come on, beaten about by platoon volleys firing into their ranks. Colonel Compère, already twice wounded but calling on his men to use the bayonet, rode into the British ranks before he fell. Some of his men may have crossed bayonets with the British, but in the thick smoke and dust, the panic and confusion, no one had time to notice and, as Compère fell, Colonel Kempt ordered his men to charge.

Carrying all before them with the bayonet, the British infantry swept the remnants of Compère's brigade off the field, stabbing and bayoneting the survivors all the way back to the village of Maida, ' . . . for Englishmen were not afraid of killing a foe in those days'. While the French 1st Light lost 900 men in those brief few minutes of firing and bayoneting, Kempt lost barely 50 men, and the battle of Maida had hardly begun.

On Kempt's left, Colonel Acland's Second Brigade, somewhat exposed on their right by the precipitate charge of Kempt's victorious troops, was now coming under attack from Compère's other battalion, the veterans from the 42nd Infantry of the Line. Acland's companies opened fire too soon, at 300 yards, but the close column of 1,500 men from the 42nd made a large target. After two volleys which felled a third of their number the 42nd broke and fled, with Acland's infantry in close pursuit.

Colonel Acland kept his men well in hand as they advanced, and when they came upon the three foreign battalions of Peyri's brigade, two more crashing volleys sufficed to send the Polish battalions scrambling back. The Swiss infantry stood their ground and returned volley for volley until the French cavalry came thundering up through the thick clouds of musket smoke, forcing Acland's brigade to form square. There they stood, firing at the circling French cavalry and under fire themselves from the cannon of the French horse artillery, while Cole's First Brigade, on the left of the British line, came under attack from Digonet's brigade and the rallied troops from Peyri's Polish battalions.

Cole's First, with the Third Brigade under Colonel Oswald in support, came into action some twenty minutes after Colonel Acland's Second Brigade, and the French forces opposing them were well handled by General Digonet. Declining to attack, he halted his men on rising ground and took up a defensive position, supported by cavalry and horse artillery, ready to repel the advancing British line. The battle here was more evenly matched, the French and British battalions returning volley for volley. The issue was finely balanced, and ammunition growing short, when the 20th Foot, hastening up from the landing beach, swung around behind Cole's brigade and flung themselves on Digonet's left flank. A few more volleys were enough to settle the matter. Covered by his cavalry and horse artillery, General Reynier withdrew the remnants of his force, leaving the field of Maida to the British. Had General Stuart had any cavalry, the gradual retreat of the French might have been turned into a rout.

When the smoke drifted away and the dust settled, the scale of Stuart's victory was apparent. The British had lost one officer and 44 men killed with fewer than 300 wounded, while General Reynier admitted to 1,300 killed, wounded, or taken prisoner. His actual losses probably exceeded 2,000, about a third of his force. Compared with other battles of the Napoleonic Wars this short, sharp fight was little more than a skirmish, but it taught the British a valuable lesson, one which had nothing to do with skilled command or rapid manoeuvre.

The point proved was that, if British soldiers were well handled and positioned where they could not be galled by artillery or overwhelmed by cavalry, their dour courage and discipline would hold them in the line against an advancing French column, while their skill with the musket and rapid reloading, combined with a stubborn refusal to give ground, would result in the destruction of the French column before they could close with the bayonet. The matter of Maida was summed up a century later by J. W. Fortescue:

> From the days of the archers onwards, the British have won their victories by cool and steady marksmanship. The whole secret of Maida, as of Wellington's triumphs in the Peninsula, lay in the fact that British troops, through good training and strict discipline, could disable at a range of 50 or 100 yards an infantry which, however mighty in appearance, was powerless for delivering mischief at a greater range than 36 inches.

This is the story of two men on a collision course. Although Napoleon Bonaparte and the Duke of Wellington met only once in battle and never in person, they represent the opposing pinnacles of that twenty-year period of political confusion and military struggle which history has come to call the Napoleonic Wars. By studying these wars through the lives of the two leaders, from the apogee of Napoleon's success at Tilsit in 1807 and General Wellesley's arrival in Portugal a few months later, it is possible to reduce the great jumbled canvas of the Napoleonic wars to a comprehensible and human dimension.

It is curious to note, for example, that they were the same age. Both were born in 1769 within a few months of each other. Both wre islanders and from islands estranged from the mainland. Napoleon was a Corsican while Wellington was born in Dublin. Both were younger sons who became professional soldiers and politicians. Napoleon's military training, at Brienne and Paris and then in the Revolutionary Armies, was more comprehensive than that of the young Wellington, who first climbed the military ladder by purchase, before making his name with some successful campaigns in India. There is even the fact that on his way home from India in 1807, Wellington stopped at St Helena where the exiled Emperor Napoleon spent the last years of his life. One should not make too much of these facts. They are a point of departure, nothing more.

Although these men blazed a trail of military glory across the history of Europe, it is relevant to begin their story with that encounter at Maida, since battle was the final arbiter of their struggle. Napoleon came to power as a successful general and supreme strategist. Wellington's forces, in Spain and Belgium, were the means by which that power was finally crushed, and in the end Wellington's tactical skill on the battlefield proved decisive. It was, however, the ordinary fighting men who settled the fate of nations, with musket and bayonet, horse and gun, and unlimited quantities of courage. Wellington never forgot this. 'It all depends on that article, whether we do the business or not,' he said before Waterloo, pointing to a British infantry private gawping at the statues in a Brussels park. 'Give me enough of it and I am sure.' Within days, 'that article' had won the battle and driven the French Emperor into exile.

Many nations, contributed to Napoleon's downfall – most notably Austria, who returned to the field again and again; and Russia, who sapped the strength of the Empire in the campaign of 1812. Britain brought to the conflict an inflexible determination to destroy the French Empire, a powerful navy to enforce a strict blockade, and lavish grants of money to the Continental powers, while the skill and resolution displayed by Wellington's Anglo-Portuguese army in the Peninsula kept the 'Spanish ulcer' open on the southern flank of France. Maida demonstrated that a French army could be defeated, but the journey from Maida to Waterloo took another nine years.

In July 1806, when Stuart's triumphant infantry were driving Reynier's men back across the plains of Calabria, the standing of General Sir Arthur Wellesley and Napoleon Bonaparte could hardly have been more different. Napoleon was already the Conqueror of Europe and, since December 1804, Emperor of the French, while Wellesley, in spite of his great successes in India, was seen at the Horse Guards as no more than a 'Sepoy general', victor of some battles against the wilder tribes of India. On coming home he had been left to kick his heels in Ireland, nursing thoughts of leaving the army completely to take up a career in politics. How their fortunes were reversed is the subject of this book.

I

The Road to Tilsit:

1764–1807

The happiest period of my life? Perhaps at Tilsit – there I
was victorious, dictating laws, having Kings and Emperors
pay court to me.

Napoleon on St Helena: 1818

ON 14 JUNE 1807, Napoleon crushed the Russian Army at the battle
of Friedland. By that victory he destroyed the Fourth Coalition of
European Powers put together in an attempt to limit his ambitions,
and Continental Europe lay at his feet. The Prussians had been defeated at Jena-Auerstedt in 1806, and if the Russian Czar could now
be brought to terms, only Britain of all the European nations would
remain in arms against France.

The peace conference took place ten days after Friedland, at Tilsit, a small town on the River Nieman which marked the western
frontier of Russia. Although the war was not yet over, active hostilities had ceased and Napoleon was anxious to impress the Czar
with his magnanimity, and his military power. Alexander would not
set foot on French-occupied territory, and Napoleon did not wish to
intrude on the sacred soil of Holy Russia. Therefore, according to an
account left by General Savary, a brigade commander of the Imperial
Guard:

> The Emperor Napoleon . . . ordered a large raft to be floated in the
> middle of the river, on which was built a well-enclosed and elegant-
> ly decorated apartment with a door on either side giving into an
> ante-chamber. . . . The work could not have been better executed
> in Paris. The roof was crowned with two weathercocks, one for the

eagle of Russia, the other for that of France, while the two outer doors were also surmounted by the national eagles.

The two sovereigns appeared on the opposite banks at the same moment and sailed their craft at the same time, but the Emperor, having a good boat, manned by oarsmen of the Guard, arrived first on the raft which he boarded alone and went through the ante-chambers to the far door which he opened and waited on the edge of the raft for the arrival of the Emperor Alexander, who did not have such skilled oarsmen. The two Emperors met in a most friend-ly way, at least to all appearances. . . .

This first meeting lasted an hour and a half, and is notable for the fact that the unfortunate King of Prussia, encamped nearby, was neither invited nor permitted to attend. Napoleon had waited a long time for this moment and was in no hurry to conclude a peace. He would settle with Prussia only after he had reached a satisfactory agreement with the Czar of All the Russias. For a man who had set out for the wars as a simple lieutenant of artillery, this was a time to savour.

Napoleon Bonaparte, Emperor of the French, was born plain Napo-leone Buonaparte in Ajaccio, Corsica, on 15 August 1769, second son of a minor Corsican nobleman, Carlo Buonaparte, and his wife Letizia.

Young Napoleone was only just a Frenchman. Corsica had be-longed to the Italian state of Genoa until May 1768, when Louis XV purchased it to replace the naval base lost by the British seizure of Minorca. The majority of the Corsican people, proud of their island and already determined to achieve independence from Genoa, had no wish to become French, and at the time of Napoleone's birth had risen in rebellion against their new owners in a struggle led by Pasquale Paoli – who remains a far greater hero to the Corsican people than their more famous son. Napoleone's first language was Italian and his first loyalties were to Corsica, but his father soon accommodated to French rule and formed a useful friendship with the Military Governor of Corsica, General de Marbeuf. The Buonapartes were noble but not rich, and in December 1778, when Napoleone was nine, it was decided that with the Comte de Marbeuf's assistance he should be sent to France and trained for the army.

The young Napoleone left behind a devoted family. Joseph – or Giuseppe – was the eldest brother, then came Napoleone, Lucien, Louis, and then Jerome. Three of these were to rule kingdoms and

play a prominent part in their brother's future. Napoleone's sisters –
Elisa, Pauline and Caroline – also played their part at the Emperor's
court.

In 1779, after a short spell at Autun to improve his still-hesitant
French, Napoleone was enlisted as a Royal, or Free, pupil at the
military academy at Brienne in Champagne. His father's slight aristocratic connections provided the four quarterings on his patent of
nobility necessary to gain his son a place at the academy, but were
not enough to excite the enmity of the Revolutionary *sans-culottes*
when France fell apart ten years later.

Napoleone was a no more than average student at Brienne. He
excelled at mathematics and enjoyed history and geography, but showed
little skill or interest in more social matters. In October 1784 he
earned his entry to the École Militaire in Paris, where the life of an
officer cadet was much more to his taste, though his time there was
marred by the death of his father in February 1785. In August 1785,
aged sixteen, he was commissioned into the La Fère Artillery Regiment, then stationed at Valence in the Rhône valley. After six months
in the ranks, then customary for officers in the Royal Army, his rank
of *sous-lieutenant* was confirmed in January 1786.

Lieutenant Buonaparte, a slight, intense youth, just five feet three
inches tall, gave himself over to his chosen arm, the artillery, and such
enjoyment of life as he could afford on a small salary in a French
provincial town. He maintained an allegiance to his Corsican origins
and continued to sign himself Napoleone di Buonaparte for the next
ten years. Napoleone became French only by degrees.

In June 1788 Buonaparte was transferred to the Artillery School at
Auxonne commanded by the Baron du Teil, a great consumer of
women and a thinking soldier. Du Teil took a fancy to the thin young
lieutenant, detecting in him signs of that penetrating intelligence
which is the mark of a great soldier. Du Teil encouraged Napoleone
to broaden his field of study, suggesting books not only on tactics and
military lore, but also on politics, history and philosophy. Napoleone,
always a voracious reader, spent much of his meagre pay on books,
and du Teil supplemented this study with tactical exercises in the
field, where theoretical problems were related to the terrain and the
handling of troops.

When the French Revolution broke out in May 1789, Napoleone
was still at Auxonne, where he had become commander of the Artillery Demonstration Company. Despite his cloistered life as an officer
in a provincial town, Napoleone was well aware that the French state,
nearing collapse, would founder unless reforms were introduced at

every level of society. It is not apparent, however, that he saw such reforms being achieved by revolution. His reading on the origins of the English Civil War and the legal and Parliamentary constraints on the power of the British monarch led him to prefer a constitutional monarchy, but the state of affairs in France did not permit such a comfortable solution.

The disorders in Paris soon touched the army at Auxonne. The Baron du Teil's house was burned, his regiment mutinied, and the men stole the regimental funds. As the Revolution spread and passions rose, the Royal Army began to disintegrate. More than half the officers, particularly those of aristocratic lineage, thought it wise to flee abroad, but Lieutenant Buonaparte chose to join the party of the Revolution. He condemned the Royal family's flight to Varennes in 1791, and swore an oath of loyalty to the new Constitution without a qualm. Twenty-one, and a fervent Revolutionary, his rise was now rapid. In October 1791 he took leave from his regiment and returned to Corsica, and by early 1792 had become Lieutenant-Colonel of the Ajaccio Volunteers, a force in the French National Guard.

The sovereigns of Europe, alarmed by the fate of Louis XVI, had taken up arms against Revolutionary France, and in August 1792 the Austrians and Prussians invaded, with the declared aim of restoring Louis to his throne. Although they were repulsed by Kellermann at Valmy in September, the military situation remained critical. It had been decreed that regular officers absent from their parent units must return to their regiments or forfeit their commission and in August 1792 Napoleone, hurrying to Paris, arrived there in time to witness the attack on the Tuileries and the massacre of the Swiss Guard, two incidents which engendered in him a lifelong dislike of the mob. A successful petition to the Revolutionary Committee confirmed his rank of Lieutenant-Colonel of Volunteers, and he was made up to Captain in the Regular Army. Returning to Corsica at the end of 1792, Napoleone spent the next nine months leading his troops against the resurgent Corsican nationalists under their old hero, Paoli. In June 1793, accused of treachery to Corsica and fearing for their safety, Napoleone and his family left the island, for ever; henceforth, he was all French.

Louis XVI was executed on 21 January 1793, and in the summer of that year a counter-revolutionary rising broke out in the Midi. In August the citizens of Toulon closed their gates against the Revolution and opened their port to an Anglo-Spanish fleet commanded by Admiral Lord Hood. France was now run by Revolutionary Committees, but the Committee conducting the siege of Toulon had no

idea what to do. The siege was heading towards failure when in mid
September Buonaparte was sent to take charge of the artillery. His
bravery under fire impressed both his men and his superiors, while
his skilful use of artillery soon forced the British fleet to evacuate
the port. When Toulon fell in December 1793 – to be followed by a
massacre of its defenders – Captain Buonaparte received a glowing
commendation from the commander of the besieging forces, General
Dugommier, which resulted in his promotion, aged twenty-three, to
the rank of Brigadier-General in the Revolutionary Armies.

Such promotion was not without peril and danger to a rising officer
lay not only in the foreign armies now encircling France. Since 1789,
more than six hundred general officers had been dismissed from their
appointments, half to be later shot or guillotined for some supposed
inefficiency or lack of zeal. Brigadier-General Buonaparte wisely decided
to avoid the political quicksands of Paris. In May 1794 he obtained
the command of the artillery in the Army of Italy, then engaged in a
campaign against Piedmont, one of many independent states in the
Italian peninsula. General Buonaparte did well in his first Italian
war. His abilities were noted by Lazare Carnot, Minister of War
and architect of the Revolutionary Armies, and by the all-powerful
Committee of Public Safety.

Napoleone was with the Army of Italy in July 1794 when the *coup
d'état* of Thermidor swept Robespierre to the guillotine and brought
an end to the Terror. It did not, however, improve the fortunes of
the young general. In May 1795 the Committee of Public Safety decided that the army had too many artillery brigadiers and transferred
a number, including Buonaparte, to command the second-rank infantry divisions then engaged in suppressing the Catholic Royalist
revolt in Brittany and the Vendée. When the time came for him to
take up his appointment, Napoleone flatly refused to go. This act of
defiance brought him to the close attention of the Committee of
Public Safety. The Committee, ignoring his good service at Toulon
and in Italy, promptly decreed that 'Brigadier-General Buonaparte
shall be struck off the list of General Officers for refusing to take up
the post assigned to him'. Brigadier-General Buonaparte was now
dangerously exposed to charges of disloyalty, when fate intervened.
The Austrians launched a new attack in July and defeated General
Kellermann, the victor of Valmy. Calling all its soldiers back to the
colours, the Committee appointed Napoleone to the Ministry of War
in Paris with the rank of General. He was still there when the next
crisis arose.

The Convention which replaced the Committee of Public Safety published a decree placing power in the hands of a newly-established Directory of Five, and the Directors proceeded to draft and publish a new Constitution. This Constitution infuriated both sides of the Paris mob. The old *sans-culottes* saw it as a retreat from Revolutionary principles, and those who hoped for a return of the Bourbon King Louis XVIII saw it as a check to their ambitions. At the threat of revolt in Paris, the Directory ordered Paul Barras, leader of the Constitutionalists and recently appointed Commander of the Army of the Interior, to take charge in Paris and suppress any riot.

Barras was no soldier. Casting about for a resolute general – and someone to blame if it all went wrong – his choice fell upon that friendless artillery officer, General Buonaparte, who was ordered to take whatever steps were necessary to subdue the Paris mob. Remembering those bloody scenes at the Tuileries in 1792, Napoleone needed no encouragement. His first act was to send a cavalry officer, Captain Joachim Murat, galloping to the artillery park at Sablons with a squadron of hussars. Murat returned with forty cannon, which Buonaparte set up in the streets leading to the Tuileries. He then surrounded the palace with 5,000 troops and awaited the arrival of the mob. On the afternoon of 5 October 1795 he opened fire on the citzens of Paris, and with his 'whiff of grapeshot' snuffed out the Paris revolt and made himself notorious. About two hundred civilians were killed and twice as many wounded, but Napoleone's name was on everyone's lips. Barras and his fellow politicians were duly grateful to their saviour, and on 16 October 1795 Buonaparte was promoted to the rank of General of Division. Ten days later he replaced Barras as Commander-in-Chief of the Army of the Interior. He was now twenty-seven.

In March 1796, signing himself Napolean Bonaparte for the first time, he married a lady from Martinique, Joséphine de Beauharnais, the widow of a general guillotined by the Committee of Public Safety and former mistress of Barras. Her son, Eugène de Beauharnais, became a loyal supporter of his step-father and a noted general in the coming wars.

Bonaparte's star continued to rise. In March 1796 he was appointed Commander-in-Chief of the Army of Italy and sent to fight a fresh coalition of Britain, the Austrian Empire and the city states of Milan and Naples. The Army of Italy, unpaid, unfed and poorly armed, was in a desperate state when he took command. He lost no time in imposing his will and his character, not least on his divisional commanders, Generals Augereau, Sérurier, Berthier and a colleague from his first campaign in Italy, André Masséna. These men soon learned that their young commander was no ordinary man, though the generals of the Army of Italy were themselves remarkable soldiers, having risen by ability alone from often humble origins. Augereau had led a varied life as a duellist, salesman and dancing master before entering the Royal Army as a private soldier in 1774; Berthier was an engineer who, though a disaster as a field commander, became an unrivalled Chief-of-Staff; Sérurier had first entered the Royal Army in 1755 as a militia volunteer. All eventually rose to the rank of Marshal.

Other officers in the Army of Italy included that impetuous cavalry officer of Paris days, Major Joachim Murat, his colleague Major Andoche Junot, Major Auguste Marmont and the Commanding General's brother, Lucien Bonaparte. These men could lead the army, if the army could be led. Within a few hours of taking command Bonaparte had issued his first inspiring order:

> Soldiers . . . you are naked, hungry, and the Government, which owes you much, can give you nothing. The patience and courage you have displayed buys you nothing. No glimmer of Glory falls upon you. I will lead you into the most fertile plains on earth. Rich provinces, opulent towns, all shall be at your disposal. There you will find honour, glory, riches. . . . Soldiers of the Army of Italy, will you be lacking in courage or endurance?

There could be only one response to such a question. Within hours the Army of Italy was on the march to victory.

The Army of Italy crushed the Army of Piedmont in ten days. On 10 May 1796 Napoleon demonstrated his personal courage by leading his troops in a charge against musketry and cannon fire across the bridge at Lodi. Courage was expected in a General of the Revolution, and courage was all that Napoleon could offer his soldiers – but it was enough. A month after entering Italy his army marched into Milan and began to enjoy the fruits of victory which he had promised.

The Directors in Paris then determined that command of the Army of Italy should be divided between the young General Bonaparte and the celebrated victor of Valmy, General Kellermann. Once again, Napoleon flatly refused to obey the orders of his political masters and offered to resign his command. 'One bad general is better than two good ones,' he declared. The Directors backed down, withdrew their proposal, and agreed to leave Napoleon in sole command.

Inspired by their general, the Army of Italy now carried all before it. Napoleon laid siege to Mantua, and after defeating the Austrians at Castiglione in August 1796 he repeated his success at Arcola in

November. In January 1797 came the decisive battle of Rivoli, where General Masséna saved the day for his future Emperor. Mantua fell, and the campaign in Italy was concluded in October 1797 by the Treaty of Campo Formio. Napoleon, now twenty-eight, displayed alarming signs of independence. The terms of the Treaty of Campo Formio were dictated to the Austrians without any reference to his political masters in Paris.

Napoleon's military successes in Italy were overshadowed by yet another political crisis in France, where politicians of a Royalist persuasion were conspiring against the Directory. Napoleon sent Augereau to Paris with orders to support the Jacobin deputies, if necessary using his sword to expel any Royalist members from both the governing Council of Five Hundred and the National Assembly.

The Treaty of Campo Formio marked the collapse of Pitt's First Coalition and the setting up of a French protectorate in Italy, the Cisalpine Republic. When he returned to Paris in December 1797 Bonaparte found himself a hero, at least with the common people. Politicians and members of the Directory, remembering Augereau's intervention, saw him as a menace. Determined to separate him from his power base in Italy and from the centre of affairs in Paris, in January 1798 they sent him to command the army now mustering on the Channel coast for an invasion of England.

Napoleon soon realized that it was impossible to invade England without a powerful fleet. He put forward another plan: to seize Egypt as the base for an advance on India, striking at Britain via her rich possessions there. Since this would remove their turbulent hero further from the centre of affairs the Directory agreed. In July 1798 Napoleon landed in Egypt, and defeated the Mamelukes at the Battle of the Pyramids. Trapped by Nelson's victory at the Battle of the Nile in August 1798, he remained in Egypt until October 1799, when he abandoned his command to General Kléber and returned to Paris.

Here, fortune again took a hand. The Directory was on the point of collapse, undermined by economic catastrophe and faced by Pitt's Second Coalition, consisting of Austria, Russia and the Swiss cantons. The Coalition nations failed to act in concert and Masséna shattered General Korsakov's Russians at the second Battle of Zürich in September 1799. Recriminations soon led to the disintegration of the Coalition, but the French had lost most of the Italian territory gained by Bonaparte in 1796-7, and the Directory was very unpopular.

Paris was anyway ripe for a change. There was widespread unemployment, brigandage was rife in the provinces, and there was no money to pay for government services. The architect of revolt this time was one of the founders of the original Revolution of 1789, the Abbé Sieyès. Like Barras in 1795 Sieyès, needing the sword of a successful general, allied himself with General Bonaparte.

The coup took place on 18 Brumaire, 9 and 10 November 1799, when troops loyal to Napoleon and led by his brother Lucien purged the Five Hundred (the 'Lower Chamber') and drove the Directors from power. Sieyès' 'Constitution of the Revolutionary Year VIII' had called for the setting up of a Consular Triumvirate but to his considerable chagrin, he was not included. Napoleon was named, with Charles Lebrun, a financier from Normandy and Cambacérès, a lawyer from Montpellier. These former Directors were political ciphers, chosen at Bonaparte's instigation. In February 1800 Bonaparte was appointed First Consul of the French Republic and became the effective ruler of France. He was just thirty.

With his appointment as First Consul, Napoleon entered the political arena, to combine the role of Commanding General with that of Head of State. Military and political successes never blinded Bonaparte to the fact that his first task must be to please and satisfy the needs of the French nation. To that end all other interests were subjugated, and what the French wanted now was peace. France had been at war with the rest of Europe for ten long years. The economy was in tatters and peace was more than just a desire – it was a necessity. When Napoleon assumed power the State Treasury was impoverished while accumulated debts were enormous. Civil servants had not been paid for nearly a year and, as Napoleon and his troops knew only too well, the Army was neither fed nor clothed nor paid. Napoleon was successful in raising short-term loans for his immediate needs, but to secure the future peace was necessary. Austria and Great Britain were still in arms against him and one or other must be brought to heel before peace could be achieved. As Britain was safe behind her Channel moat, the First Consul elected to fall upon Austria.

In 1800 Napoleon led his army over the Alpine passes, arriving in the Aosta valley on 24 May. There the French ' . . . fell on the Austrian army like a thunderbolt', shattering it at the battle of Marengo on 14 June, after which Austria withdrew from Italy and came to terms at the Peace of Lunéville in February 1801. Pitt resigned from office in the same month and Britain came to terms with France at the Peace of Amiens, signed on 27 March 1802. Napoleon had given the French the peace they craved and in gratitude, on 2 August 1802, they appointed him 'Consul for Life'.

The Peace of Amiens did not last. The British suspected, rightly, that Napoleon was but contriving time to revive his economy and rebuild his fleet. The French believed, rightly, that the British did not intend to hand back the territories they had gained in the West Indies and the Mediterranean between 1793 and 1799, including the island fortress of Malta, captured by Napoleon from the Knights of St John in 1798, which had subsequently fallen to the British. Napoleon also detected the hand of Britain, or at least of French Royalists under British protection, in several attempts on his life.

In May 1803 the Peace of Amiens came to an end and as the British fleet renewed its blockade of the Continent, Napoleon began to assemble an invasion army on the cliffs near Boulogne. Nor had he forgotten the attempts on his life. In March 1804 he sent a cavalry regiment across the Rhine into the neutral state of Baden to seize the Duc d'Enghien, a Prince of the House of Condé. The young d'Enghien, carried back to Vincennes and accused of conspiracy against Napoleon's life, was given a travesty of a trial (his grave had already been dug) and then shot by a firing squad in the castle moat. While this act horrified the Courts of Europe, it did not damage Napoleon's standing with the French. In 1804, three million voted in favour of offering him the throne and only three thousand against. Napoleon Bonaparte was crowned Emperor of the French on 2 December 1804.

Any successful invasion of Britain depended on the defeat of the Royal Navy. This was never likely, and any hopes of a successful invasion were destroyed with the defeat of the combined fleets of France and Spain by Admiral Lord Nelson off Cape Trafalgar in October 1805. Pitt had returned to power in April 1804 and formed a Third Coalition, between Britain, Austria and Russia. Relinquishing all thoughts of invasion, Napoleon left a small force on the Channel coast and marched his army east.

Trafalgar did nothing to damage the reputation of France on the battlefield. Fresh triumphs came for French arms, first at Ulm in October 1805 when the Austrian General Mack surrendered with his entire army, and again at Austerlitz on 2 December 1805 when, after a two-week campaign, the Russian–Austrian Army was crushed. This was Austria's third defeat at Napoleon's hands and by the Treaty of Pressburg, three weeks later, France acquired most of Austria's remaining German and Italian possessions. Venice was then added to the Cisalpine Republic to create the Kingdom of Italy and, having created the Kingdom, Napoleon then crowned himself King.

During 1806 Napoleon created the Confederation of the Rhine, the forerunner of the modern Germany, from a score of petty German states on the east bank of the Rhine, to the alarm of Frederick-Wilhelm III of

Prussia, who saw this as a clear challenge to Prussia's dominance of the fragmented German States. It was now the turn of Prussia to feel the full weight of the Napoleonic war machine, for Frederick-Wilhelm had secretly agreed with the Coalition to attack Napoleon once the Emperor's armies were fully engaged with the Austrians and Russians. Napoleon, aware of this proposed stab in the back, now required Prussia to sign a Treaty of Alliance against Britain, and the French army, flushed with its victories over Austria, hovered on the Prussian frontier while the King considered. To sweeten his threats, Napoleon offered Prussia the state of Hanover, one of the larger German Electorates and a fief of the British Crown. In return the Emperor demanded that Prussia should close her ports and markets to all British· goods.

This was a gamble. Prussia, now allied with Saxony, had a powerful army, heirs of the mighty soldiers who had served Frederick the Great, and Napoleon was not anxious to begin a fresh campaign so soon after Austerlitz. Nevertheless, when Prussia rejected his demands and joined Britain, Russia, Saxony and Sweden in the Fourth Coalition, the *Grande Armée* began a march on Berlin. On 14 October 1806 the Emperor crushed the Prussians and their allies at the battle of Jena-Auerstedt; the destruction of the Prussian army took just over a month. Frederick-Wilhelm and his wife fled east, and Napoleon followed them, to attack the last of the Continental Powers still in arms against him – Russia.

The old, half-mad Czar of All the Russias, Paul, had been murdered in 1801. His son Alexander was now Czar and Napoleon had no particular wish to fight him, but Alexander saw himself as the natural leader of the European monarchs in the fight against the egalitarian ideas of the French people and their 'Emperor'. While the young Alexander was maintaining hostilities in the East and remained allied with Great Britain, Napoleon would always be faced with the possibility of a war on two fronts, so Alexander must be detached from this Alliance. The only way to bring that about was another victory, and the French army began to march east in November 1806.

While the *Grande Armée* mustered on the frontiers of Poland and advanced on Warsaw, Napoleon took up residence in Berlin. From there he issued the Berlin Decree, ordering all European nations, friendly, neutral or hostile, to close their ports to British shipping on pain of his displeasure. This decree, reinforced in November 1807 by the Milan Decree, marked the introduction of Napoleon's 'Continental System', aimed at destroying Britain's ability to wage war by strangling her trade and economy. In the face of Britain's powerful fleet and her access to other markets the Continental System was bound to fail, and although it seemed a workable idea in 1807, it caused continual rifts and disputes between the Emperor and his allies. There remained the matter of Russia.

Making due allowance for the constraints of horse transport and poor roads, all Napoleon's campaigns between 1797 and 1807 have the aspect of what a later conqueror called *blitzkrieg*, or 'lightning war'. Napoleon's basic strategy never varied. His aim was to seek out the enemy's field army, and to pin it in position with one of his self-contained army corps while the other corps concentrated. Then, with a superiority of force and having cut the enemy's communications and means of escape, the Emperor's *Grande Armée* would move to destroy its opponents with all the power at its disposal. While this plan did not always work out in detail, as a strategy it succeeded for many years.

Having applied this strategy to his present campaign, Napoleon struck the Russian Army at Eylau on 8 February 1870, and got the fright of his military career.

The Russian conscripts, poorly led and badly organized, put up a tremendous fight against Napoleon's veteran troops. The corps of the veteran Augereau, now a Marshal of France, was completely shattered and the Russian troops were seen beating the French infantry at close-quarter fighting, drawing more French troops into a bitter battle, until only Murat's cavalry corps and the Imperial Guard were left in reserve.

The battle at Eylau was at best a draw. The Russian General Bennigsen avoided encirclement and was able to withdraw his troops, and for the ever-victorious Napoleon a draw was little better than a defeat. About a third of his army were casualties, and however hard his official bulletins and the pages of the *Moniteur* strove to conceal the fact, the Emperor Napoleon had received his first check. The conquered and occupied nations of Europe were quick to notice this, and the cries of *'Vive la Paix'* instead of *'Vive l'Empereur'*, heard from the ranks of the French Army after the battle, did not go unnoticed either.

This time, it was not the French but the Russians who returned to offer battle in the field. After Eylau Napoleon hastened to reinforce his depleted divisions and turned them upon Danzig, which the Russians were obliged to defend. The French and Russian armies met again at the battle of Friedland, on 14 June 1807, where General Bennigsen allowed himself to be caught with his back to the River

Alle and his army was overwhelmed. The battle lasted from dawn until well after dark before the Russians finally retreated, having lost 20,000 men to 8,000 French. This slaughter proved too much for the young Czar, and four days after Friedland Alexander requested an armistice.

On 24 June 1807 the Czar stepped onto the raft at Tilsit and grasped Napoleon's hands.

'I hate the English as much as you do,' he declared.

'If that is the case,' replied Napoleon, 'then peace is already made.'

The Czar's capitulation was total. He agreed to declare war on Britain and to impose the Continental System on his ports and merchants. He agreed to provide a corps for the French army, under the Emperor's command. More than this, he fell under Napoleon's spell. He declared himself the Emperor's ally, and swore to give no further assistance to his former colleagues in the Coalition. Napoleon finally had his peace on the Eastern front, but a general peace was not to be had, even after eleven years of war.

Napoleon had risen from artillery lieutenant to Emperor. He had crushed and humiliated all the Continental Powers. He had seen the sovereigns of great nations bow to his wishes; but out of reach, beyond the Narrow Seas, Great Britain remained in arms, and the Continental System he sought to impose on Europe was drawing the Emperor towards a new and fatal battleground in Portugal and Spain.

If a man's character can be judged by his actions, Napoleon can be seen as a man of vision, a superb leader of men, a considerable politician. He was loyal to his friends and family, ruthless to his enemies, relentless in extracting the last ounce of profit from his victories. While there is some truth in the assertion that most of his wars were not of his making but forced upon him by the Continental Powers, usually inspired by Britain, he has also been described as a 'great, bad, man'. No ordinary man could have achieved all he did, and much of his success was due to his energy, his ambition, and his aptitude for war, but within his undoubted genius there lurked a flaw. For all his skills and ability, the Emperor did not know when to stop.

2

Spain and Portugal:
1807–1808

We must recollect what it is we have at stake, what it is we
contend for. It is for our property. It is for our liberty. It is
for our very existence as a nation.
William Pitt, Prime Minister
London: 1803

The cause of the struggle between the Emperor of the French and the
other crowned heads of Europe was partly ideological. The Napoleonic Empire was an autocracy, but the ideas which motivated the
Emperor were born of the Revolution and were, in the main, democratic. It is for this reason that so many Napoleonic institutions, most
notably his Civil Code, have survived to the present day in parts of
the Continent. It is therefore curious that the Emperor's most implacable foe was Great Britain, a country where constitutional government, though of a strictly limited kind, had been in existence since
the end of the Civil War. At the end of the eighteenth century few of
the other European nations, and especially Prussia and Russia, had
democratic institutions of any kind.

One can make too much of the Emperor's liberal intentions. The
Emperor's philosophy may have been broadly democratic but many of
his actions were those of an autocrat. He conscripted unwilling recruits
into his armies from France and his allies. He suppressed free speech,
banned newspapers, burned books. He had those who dissented too
openly against his rule exiled, imprisoned or shot. He might create his
own nobility, put crowns on the heads of his brothers and appoint his
marshals Dukes and Princes of the Empire, but none of this impressed his
enemies. At heart Napoleon Bonaparte remained a revolutionary.

Britain had apparently less to fear than other nations from the spread of democratic and Revolutionary ideas, but even those British politicians who had welcomed the French Revolution in 1789 soon came to regard its expansion and philosophy with suspicion. 'It is not the enmity but the friendship of France that is truly terrible,' wrote Edmund Burke. 'Her intercourse, her example, the spread of her ideas, are the most dreadful of her arms.' In other words, the sovereigns of Europe had less to fear from the Napoleonic armies than from the three dread hounds, Liberty, Equality and Fraternity, trotting at their heels. For the royal rulers of continental Europe, resisting Napoleon was a matter of self-preservation.

There were other reasons. The British were not prepared to permit any one nation to hold the balance of power in Europe. Britain's burgeoning economy enabled her to maintain the struggle against Napoleon, most notably by supplying his enemies with arms and money, and the Continental System was Napoleon's way of attacking the basis of British resistance.

To reduce the complexities of the time to manageable proportions, it may be noted that the 'Great Powers' of Europe in 1807 were France, which stood head and shoulders above the rest, Austria, Russia and Great Britain. In the second rank came Prussia, Bavaria, perhaps Spain. Then the lesser Powers: Portugal, Holland, Saxony and the Kingdom of Naples – all pawns in this game of Titans – followed by a host of petty states, Electorates and independent dukedoms.

Tilsit saw Napoleon at the summit of his powers, a fact he certainly realized later. He had achieved all he could ever have hoped for: why then did he take that fatal step further which led from Tilsit through Spain and Russia to the battlefield of Waterloo? Historians and philosophers have produced a score of reasons or theories. Perhaps the best answer is that for a conqueror there is always another conquest to be made; for a politician, always another problem to overcome. When he ceases to advance, a conqueror is already in retreat, and such retreats are usually fatal; and while historians see Tilsit as the summit of his achievements, for Napoleon there remained one relentless and implacable enemy – Great Britain. It was to attack Britain that Napoleon turned his attention to Portugal a few weeks after his success at Tilsit.

Until 1807, Britain's major contribution to the struggle against Napoleon was at sea, where 'Those weather beaten ships of the Royal Navy stood between Napoleon Bonaparte and the mastery of the world.'

Now and again, as at Maida and later with much less success at Walcheren in 1809, the British did put a military force ashore on the Continent, but these expeditions were little more than pin-pricks. Britain mainly fought Napoleon with money, munitions and political encouragement for his enemies. Pitt put together the early anti-French Coalitions; Britain put muskets into the hands of hostile armies and wielded her trade and her money to thwart the Emperor's advance at every turn.

At Trafalgar the Royal Navy had demonstrated that Napoleon could not hope to gain control of the Channel for long enough to ship an army to the coast of Kent. If he was ever to bring the British to heel, he must do so economically – hence the Continental System, but for this to succeed it must be imposed on every state in Europe. Every loop-hole must be stopped, every port closed. Not only would this affect the profits from trade which were financing his enemies, but the Royal Navy, the bulwark of the British nation, had a great need of Scandinavian timber, Russian hemp and Stockholm tar. If the supply of these vital materials were to be cut off, the Royal Navy's effectiveness might well decline.

Unfortunately, all the nations of Europe, including France, had a great need of British manufactured goods. The soldiers of the *Grande Armée* wore greatcoats woven from British wool and boots made of British leather. Napoleon's customs officials and gendarmes could not hope to police a coastline 2,000 miles long where every merchant and fisherman was either conniving to evade restrictions or openly smuggling British goods. The Continental System simply added to the growing list of grievances against the Emperor's rule, while bringing him few advantages in return. Wherever it was introduced, smuggling thrived and licences were granted to cover a lengthening list of exemptions. Napoleon's own brother Louis, King of Holland, lifted the ban on British goods when his Dutch subjects claimed to be facing ruin. For similar reasons and despite the agreement struck at Tilsit, Russia applied the System only when and where it suited her. The Papal States, and others, refused to apply it at all. To all such reluctance Napoleon had but one reply – force.

Portugal had been England's ally since the Middle Ages. Britain was her largest trading partner so for economic reasons Portugal refused to apply the Continental System and felt secure in doing so. To the west lay the wide Atlantic, open to British ships carrying men, arms and supplies, while to the east was the rampart of Spain and the Pyrenees. British goods and Portuguese wines continued to keep the docks of Lisbon and Oporto busy. If it should prove necessary to bring Portugal to heel by military means Napoleon, lacking supremacy at sea, would have to cross Spain – but Portugal's Spanish bastion was crumbling.

In 1807 Bourbon Spain was an ally of France. A corps of Spanish troops, 15,000 strong under the Marquis de La Romana served with the *Grande Armée* in Germany, and Spain's Chief Minister, the sycophantic Manuel Godoy (known in Spain as 'The Prince of Peace'), was deep in Napoleon's pocket, adored by King Charles IV and his Queen, but otherwise detested. Spain was a turbulent country, impoverished, corrupt and decadent, still dominated by the Church and the Inquisition, the refuge of the last of the Bourbons. While the King, his Queen and Godoy continued to strive for Napoleon's friendship, the Emperor saw no problem in overawing Spain and so securing the passage of his armies to Lisbon, should it prove necessary. Soon after Tilsit he began to exert pressure on Portugal by means of a series of open threats to the Portuguese Ambassador in Paris, demanding that the ports of Portugal and Brazil be closed to British ships by September 1807. The French Ambassador in Madrid was instructed to enlist Godoy's help towards this end, and Godoy agreed to a Joint Convention with France to force the closure. The terms of this Convention were that if Prince John, the Regent of Portugal, declined to accede to Napoleon's demands, Spain and France would declare war on Portugal. To add muscle to this threat, in August 1807 a French corps under General Andoche Junot marched to Bayonne, close to the Spanish frontier.

This pressure increased. On 9 August 1807 Portuguese shipping was embargoed at all French ports, and Junot's corps at Bayonne was elevated to a full 'Army of Observation'. On 17 September 1807 it was admitted to Spain, and on 23 September Napoleon harangued the Portuguese Ambassador at a diplomatic reception in Paris:

> If Portugal does not do as I wish, the House of Braganza will not be ruling in Europe in two months' time. I will not tolerate a single English envoy in Europe; I will declare war with any power that defies me. I have 300,000 Russians at my back and with such an ally I can do anything. The English say they will not respect neutrals at sea; I will not recognize them on land.

Those who regard Napoleon as the voice of reason and moderation should consider this outburst – a naked threat against a neutral nation, its only justification the French force now hovering inside the frontiers of Spain.

If Spain were to combine with France while Russia remained quiescent in the east, Portugal would be totally exposed. Prince John therefore agreed to close Portuguese ports to British shipping and to declare war on Britain. He also agreed to seize all Britons resident in Portugal, but refused to hand over their property to France. That single *caveat* gave Napoleon his excuse – and he had already decided that Spain, like Portugal, must be made subject to his rule.

Prince John had privately assured the British Ambassador in Lisbon that while he must give ground before the power of France, he would send the Portuguese fleet to Brazil or Madeira, out of Napoleon's reach. He would also cede the island of Madeira to Britain to compensate the Royal Navy for the loss of the Portuguese ports. While these arrangements were being made, Junot's army marched. The French entered the Spanish city of Salamanca on 12 November 1807 and were in Lisbon by 30 November. They should have learned from this march that warfare in the Peninsula would not be easy. The roads were terrible, heat and thirst tortured the soldiers, horses died by the hundred. It took Junot much longer than he had expected to reach Lisbon, and fewer than 2,000 of his veterans were still with the colours when he entered the capital, too late to achieve his main purpose. The Portuguese fleet had already sailed with the Princes of Braganza for Brazil. Thwarted but not dismayed, Junot's army settled down to loot Lisbon of every treasure it possessed.

Spain did not simply let the French pass. Godoy and Napoleon had struck a deal and in return for permitting French troops to march through Spain, the King – or to be exact, Godoy – had been promised that all Portugal south of the Tagus would become Godoy's personal principality. France would retain the port of Lisbon, while the mountains north of Portugal would be given to the Italian House of Etruria to compensate them for the loss of Tuscany, which the Emperor had given to his sister Elisa. This carve-up of an ancient kingdom was proposed without shame. The House of Braganza would disappear, while the recalcitrant states of Europe would receive another example of the length and power of the Emperor's arm. This bargain between the Emperor and Godoy was sealed by the Treaty of Fontainebleau on 27 October, some weeks before Junot began his march.

Napoleon's armies always lived off the countryside, and where possible ran their campaigns at the enemy's cost. While Junot's soldiers looted Lisbon, the Emperor demanded 100 million francs from the Portuguese Government to pay for the costs of his invasion, and ordered the agreed division of Portugal and the imposition of the Continental System in Spain and Portugal.

There remained two other prizes. To the south lay the British enclave of Gibraltar. If Napoleon could seize Gibraltar, he could close the Mediterranean to the British fleet, enabling him to retake Malta and, in alliance with Russia, march on Turkey, India and the East. Everything seemed possible in the early months of 1808, but first there was the matter of Spain. Flushed with his political and military successes, Napoleon did not see Spain as a problem. King Charles IV was little better than an imbecile, his Queen was Godoy's mistress, Crown Prince Ferdinand was cautious but craven, and the Spanish government was profoundly corrupt. It seemed to the Emperor that one good push would be sufficient to bring down this rotten edifice, and that the Spanish people would both welcome and benefit from French rule.

Napoleon had already arranged for the marriage of Prince Ferdinand to his niece Louise, the daughter of his brother Lucien. In January 1808, with Portugal now secured and with more French regiments spilling into Spain, Napoleon suddenly accused Charles IV of conspiring to prevent this marriage. Napoleon then informed King Charles that his son, Prince Ferdinand, was planning to depose him. Charles promptly had his son arrested and imprisoned for treason. Having set the Spanish Government in turmoil and the Bourbon family at each other's throats, the Emperor decided to strike.

On 16 February 1808, all the French garrisons in towns along the southern edge of the Pyrenees, from Pamplona in the west to Figueras in Catalonia, left their camps and occupied the Spanish cities. With the exits from the passes secure, strong French reinforcements commanded by Marshal Murat then came flooding over the Pyrenees into Spain. By mid- March 1808 the French had three full army corps in Spain, a total of nearly 180,000 men, and the Spanish people suddenly woke up to the knowledge that their country had been invaded and virtually overrun.

The Spanish court was plunged into alarm by news of the seizure of Pamplona and Barcelona. Godoy advised flight, without any attempt at resistance, but on 17 March a mob marched from Madrid to the summer palace at Aranjuez, a few miles south of the capital, and laid the King and Godoy under siege. Rioting then spread to Madrid, providing Marshal Murat with an excuse to enter the city, ostensibly 'to restore public order'. The arrival of his army on 23 March 1808 was greeted by cheering crowds of citizens who had not yet realized that the French intended to stay, supposing only that their allies were on their way south to seize Gibraltar.

King Charles had been persuaded to abdicate in favour of his son, Prince Ferdinand, but once Murat had quelled the mob in Madrid and the immediate danger was averted, the King changed his mind. Murat, however, continued to recognize Prince Ferdinand as the new King of Spain.

Napoleon had now arrived at Bayonne and on 20 April 1808 he summoned Godoy, King Charles, his Queen, and Prince Ferdinand to a meeting at which he proposed to arbitrate in their dispute. After a week of alternating threats and blandishments, Prince Ferdinand agreed to restore the throne to his father. Napoleon then turned on Charles and pressed him to abdicate, and Charles gave way on 7 May. The King, his Queen and their beloved Godoy were exiled to Compiègne, while Prince Ferdinand was sent under strong guard to Talleyrand's château at Valençay. Napoleon's choice as the next King of Spain was his elder brother, Joseph, currently King of Naples. Naples would be given to the Emperor's loyal Marshal and brother-in-law, Joachim Murat. With reluctance, for he enjoyed Naples, Joseph ordered his carriages for Spain.

The daring and arrogance of Napoleon's actions in Spain are breathtaking. The Emperor had made and unmade kings before, but this time it was going to be different. Five days prior to their King's abdication in Bayonne, the Spanish people had risen in revolt against the French army in Madrid.

Napoleon had omitted two elements from his calculations: the Spanish people, and the Catholic Church. He had nothing but contempt for the Spanish Royal family, for Manuel Godoy, and for what passed for the Spanish government. He was sure that the benefits to be derived from his removal of these undesirable elements and their replacement by efficient French rule would be obvious to and welcomed by the Spanish people. In this he was quite wrong.

Much as they detested Manuel Godoy, the Spanish people detested heretical foreigners far more, as their British allies were later to discover. The French, who had occupied their country and were seeking to impose strange customs and an alien rule, were enemies as well as heretics. The Spanish Catholic Church exerted an immense influence over the people and shared the Pope's detestation of the secularity of the French Revolution. Napoleon should have known this, for his spies were everywhere and his advisers well-informed. There had been widespread rumblings of discontent in Spain as French troops entered the country during the winter of 1807–8, but the first major explosion came in Madrid on 2 May – *el dos de Mayo* – 1808.

Early on the morning of 2 May General Grouchy, the Military Governor of Madrid, issued a warrant for the arrest of Don Francisco de Bourbon, a Prince of the Royal House. The detachment of troops sent to escort the Prince was attacked by a mob in the central square of the city, the Puerta del Sol. This was no passing incident but a concerted uprising, and within minutes French troops were being bludgeoned, shot and stabbed all over the city.

That night Marshal Murat rode in with his Mameluke Guard. Rioters and 'revolutionaries' were rounded up, given a short trial or no trial at all, and shot against walls in different parts of the city; these are the scenes depicted in Goya's *Dos de Mayo* and *Tres de Mayo*. Such executions did nothing to quell the spirit of the Spanish people; within weeks, the revolt of the *dos de Mayo* had spread to every corner of Spain. French governors in cities as far apart as Badajoz and Cadiz were murdered. In the countryside, French couriers were ambushed and small French patrols massacred to the last man. Within days the French could move nowhere except fully armed and in company strength. As revolt met with reprisal, the level of violence and terror rose. The French burned and looted, raped and hanged and shot men down by the hundred. Whole villages were wiped out. The Spaniards struck by night and from ambush, and those who died in their attacks were the lucky ones. French wounded and prisoners were mutilated, buried alive, drowned, boiled, nailed to trees, crucified. Terror stalked Spain, from the passes of the Pyrenees to the Mediterranean shore.

In the absence of any central government, provincial governments – Juntas – were set up in all the provinces of Spain, raising troops, seizing arsenals, issuing arms to any Spanish citizen willing to fight. Every hilltop became an observation post, every village a nest of resistance. The Juntas applied to the British garrison at Gibraltar for munitions and muskets, where their requests met with an immediate and favourable response, the old Anglo-Spanish hostility forgotten in the face of the common enemy.

The British government realized, long before Napoleon, that this rising in Spain was quite different from the resistance the Emperor had encountered elsewhere. In Austria, in Italy, in Prussia and in Russia, he had met only the armies of the rulers. When these had been defeated, their rulers capitulated, prevaricated or gave Napoleon what he wanted, and the soldiers went home. In Spain it was not like that. Their King had left them, their government was useless, their armies had yet to assemble, but the whole nation was in arms. In small towns and villages, on the hilltops where ragged bands of peasants, *guerrilleros*, were to give their name to a new style of fighting, the Spanish people prepared to give the French army and the French Emperor all the war they could handle.

British muskets went at once to anyone who asked for one and knew how to use it. The Spanish Corps serving in North Germany under General La Romana slipped aboard a Royal Naval convoy at Gothenberg and was conveyed back to Spain. The Juntas made formal peace with Britain and proposed an alliance, and in June 1808 the British government decided to send an expedition to the Peninsula. This would not be a small-scale landing force, but a fully-equipped professional army. The victor of Assaye, the conqueror of the Mahrattas, Lieutenant-General Sir Arthur Wellesley, set sail from Cork with 9,000 fighting men.

3

Arthur Wellesley:
1769–1808

His Majesty has determined to direct a corps of troops to be
prepared for service under your orders in affording the
Spanish and Portuguese people every aid in throwing off the
yoke of France. The aim of your expedition shall be the
final and absolute evacuation of the Peninsula by French
troops.

> Lord Castlereagh,
> Secretary of State for War to
> Lieutenant-General Sir Arthur Wellesley –
> 30 June 1808

ARTHUR WELLESLEY, THIRD son of the first Earl of Mornington,
was born at No. 6 Merrion Street, Dublin on 1 May 1769. The
Wellesley family belonged to that section of local society known as the
Anglo-Irish Ascendancy, and had a long connection with the country.
The Wellesleys had been in Ireland since the first half of the thir-
teenth century, a Wellesley had been Seneschal of the royal castle of
Kildare in the fourteenth century, and by the next century the family
were considerable landowners in Meath. This steady advance in
wealth and status was halted in the middle of the seventeenth century,
by which time the family had become the 'Wesleys', the Irish version
of their name, and taken to Catholicism.

By the time of the Restoration of Charles II in 1660, the Wesley
family had retreated from this error of judgement and were comfort-
ably settled in the town of Trim in County Meath. It should not be
thought from all this that Arthur Wesley ever thought of himself as
an Irishman. As he himself remarked, 'The fact that a man is born in
a stable does not make him a horse', and unlike his Corsican contem-
porary, young Wesley was no passionate nationalist, though the fam-

ily had done well out of Ireland. The future Duke of Wellington's grandfather, Richard Wesley, was born in 1690 and in 1746, as a reward for a lifetime of public service and good works, became the first Lord Mornington.

When Richard Wesley died in 1758, the barony went to his son Garret. Garret became the Earl of Mornington in 1760, in which year his first son, Richard, was born. The birth of Richard wa followed by that of William in 1763, Anne in 1768, and the third son, Arthur Wesley, in 1769. There were two other sons, Gerald born in 1770, and Henry in 1773.

By all accounts, Arthur Wesley was an unremarkable child. He was dreamy, feckless, fond of music and horses, but in no way outstanding. He began his schooling at Trim, and at the age of twelve was sent to Eton. There is no evidence of the Duke ever attributing his success at Waterloo to lessons learned on those hallowed playing fields. He left at fifteen, his years there apparently having made little impression on either side. It was decided that Arthur must follow the path of other none-too-bright younger sons of the aristocracy and enter the army.

The Wesleys were by no means wealthy. When the Earl died in 1781 the Countess of Mornington decided she could live more cheaply in Brussels, and Arthur stayed some time with her there in 1785. He spent 1786 at the Royal Academy of Equitation at Angers on the Loire, where he shot up in height and filled out, and his latent talents finally began to emerge. He rode well though with more courage and dash than elegance, and was recognized as a bold and competent horseman. He also learned fluent and colloquial French and became at ease with foreigners and strangers. When he returned to England at the end of 1786 his mother, who had previously declared that 'My awkward son Arthur is food for powder and nothing more', hardly recognized him. 'He really is a charming young man . . . never did I see such a change for the better.' His elder brother Richard, now the second Earl of Mornington, purchased him a commission. On 17 March 1787, Arthur Wesley, nearly eighteen, was gazetted Ensign or 2nd Lieutenant in the 73rd Highland Regiment. A year later he was appointed aide-de-camp to the new Viceroy of Ireland, the Marquess of Buckingham, and at Christmas 1787 he became a full Lieutenant in the 76th Foot. The 76th, however, were destined for service in the East Indies, so Arthur exchanged into the 41st Foot. In February 1788 he arrived at Dublin Castle, to flit about the Viceroy's Court, untroubled by military duties. He was a courtier, a messenger and a placeman, and so he remained while the French Revolution cast its long shadow over Europe.

In 1790 Arthur Wesley became MP for the family seat of Trim, sitting in the Irish Parliament in Dublin. During this time he met and began to court the Honourable Kitty Pakenham, who later became his wife. He had transferred to the 12th Light Dragoons in 1789, became a Captain in the 58th Foot in 1791, and exchanged into the 18th Light Dragoons in 1792. He borrowed £125 from his brother Mornington, and in 1793 purchased first his Majority and then a Lieutenant-Colonelcy in the 33rd Foot, later the Duke of Wellington's Regiment. His prospects remained far from bright, however, and his offer to Miss Pakenham was rejected. Perhaps from disappointment, perhaps because of events in France (1793 was the year of the Terror), he now began to apply himself seriously to his military career. In March he had asked to be attached to the force being gathered for an expedition in support of the Dutch, then engaged against the Revolutionary Armies of France. This scheme came to nothing, and it was not until June 1794 that Lieutenant-Colonel Wesley sailed out of Cork with the 33rd Foot to reinforce the Duke of York's doomed expedition in Flanders. The fiasco of this expedition later became the subject of a popular nursery rhyme, but as Wellington himself remarked years later, 'Well, at least I learned what one ought not to do, and that is always something.'

Wesley was given command of a brigade comprising the 33rd, the 41st, some light dragoons and a battery of artillery and immediately had to take them round by sea from Ostend to Artwerp. Antwerp proved perilous, and the British, swiftly hustled north by the French, withdrew into Holland. Wesley came under fire for the first time at Boxtel in the Netherlands on 15 September 1794, when his battalion was attacked by a French column. Bringing his men into line, he opened fire on the advancing French at close range and blew the French formation to pieces.

By November the 33rd Foot were freezing and starving in water-logged trenches along the River Waal. Undaunted by the weather the French stormed north across the frozen rivers and canals and forced the famished and disillusioned British army to march eastwards, into George III's Continental domain, the Electorate of Hanover. The Duke of York was recalled to England in December 1794, but Arthur stayed in the field until early March 1795, when he and the much-depleted 33rd Foot came home again.

In December 1795 the regiment was ordered to the West Indies, but a winter gale forced the transports to scatter and return to Poole. In April 1796 the 33rd Foot received orders for India. India was to be the making of the young Lieutenant-Colonel. He returned in 1805 as a Major-General, his reputation as a soldier firmly established and with a great deal of practical experience under his belt.

Wesley joined his regiment at Calcutta in February 1797. Life was pleasant for an officer in India, where military duties allowed ample time for shooting, socializing and drinking, in which activities Arthur took a full part. The popular image of Wellington as a sober, reserved and severe figure does not quite tally with the facts of this period: Colonel Wesley of the 33rd may have been serious about his profession, but he also believed in having fun.

India was then the fief of the East India Company. The bulk of Indian territory was still in the hands of native rulers, Nawabs, Maharajahs and various Princes, who paid nominal allegiance to the Company but generally did exactly as they pleased. French influence in India had been checked rather than destroyed by Robert Clive's victory at Plassey fifty years earlier and many of the Indian princes saw in Britain's growing conflict with France an opportunity of regaining power and lands lost or ceded to the Company.

British Army regiments in India were on loan to the East India Company, who paid their costs, to aid the Company in the slow imposition of order on the subcontinent. War was endemic in India, and in these wars Wesley was to learn the elements of his profession, how to command armies, how to combine the various arms into a powerful whole, and the vital importance of supply.

First, however, came a change of name, and a fortunate appointment. In 1798 the Wesley family reverted to the old Anglo-Norman spelling of Wellesley. Then, in May 1798, Arthur's eldest brother Richard, Earl of Mornington, arrived as Governor-General of India. Mornington had helped to advance his brother's career before; he was unlikely to be less helpful now. When the time came to take the field against the current enemy of British rule, Tippoo Sahib, the Sultan of Mysore, a stout ally of the French, Richard made sure that Arthur was given command.

Tippoo Sahib, 'The Tiger of Mysore', had long been a thorn in the side of the Raj. General Cornwallis had stormed and captured his capital, Seringapatam, in 1793, and the Sultan was again conspiring against British interests. An army was raised incorporating troops from the Nizam of Hyderabad and when the officer for whom the command was intended died in a duel, the Commander-in-Chief appointed Colonel Wellesley. This army was nothing if net exotic. Wellesley had 10,000 infantry, Indian and European, including his own 33rd; 6,000 assorted cavalry, a large number of elephants and a supply train pulled by 120,000 bullocks. Surrounding his effective fighting force of 16,000 men were 150,000 camp followers.

Tippoo's army had been trained by the Revolutionary French, and fought in the French fashion. On 26 March a full brigade of his infantry attacked the 33rd, who swiftly deployed into line and cut their attackers down with steady volley fire. On 5 April Wellesley's army arrived at Seringapatam and settled down for a siege which continued until the morning of 4 May, when after artillery had battered a breach in the walls the city was carried by storm. Wellesley commanded the reserve, and the assault troops were led by his second-in-command, Major-General David Baird, who had a score to settle. Baird (twelve years Wellesley's senior) had been captured by Tippoo Sahib's father during Cornwallis's expedition and spent nearly four years chained in a dungeon at Seringapatam. Baird's temper was notorious, and there is a story that when news of his capture was brought to his mother, her only comment was, 'Heaven help the poor soul chained to my Davie.'

The city was duly carried, Tippoo Sahib was killed, and Colonel Wellesley was appointed Governor of Mysore. Baird was as furious about this as about Wellesley's original appointment to command the expedition. Wellesley also received the useful sum of £4,000 in prize money, paid from the treasury of the dead Sultan.

During Wellesley's Mysore command he was kept busy fending off attacks from yet another dissident Indian, Daundia Wagh, a Mahratha prince who had escaped from Tippoo's dungeons when the British stormed Seringapatam. Daundia was finally hunted down and killed in September 1800, and in an age when personal courage was an attribute of command, it is noteworthy that the cavalry charge which overran the Mahratha position was led by Colonel Wellesley, sabre in hand. Wellesley had enhanced his reputation, but by Baird (and others) his preferments and profitable appointments were attributed to his brother's influence rather than to his own ability.

The Wellesleys were aware of this. In a letter to Arthur in 1800, Richard wrote: 'Great jealousy will arise among the general officers as a consequence of my employing you; but I employ you because I rely on your good sense, discretion, activity and spirit, and I cannot find these qualities united in any other officer in India.' In April 1802 Wellesley was appointed Major-General and given the task of finally suppressing the turbulent and warlike Mahrathas who were constantly raiding into British India.

Like those of Tippoo Sahib, the Mahratha armies were French-trained, and not infrequently French-led. Diplomatic maneouvres having failed, the Mahratha war began in August 1803, with the British laying siege to their hill-fortress of Ahmadnagar. This fell within two days, to the great amazement of a Mahratha chieftain who remarked: 'These English are a strange people. They came here in the morning, surveyed the wall, walked over it, killed the garrison and returned for breakfast.'

The next event of the Maharatha war was a major encounter between Company forces and the Maharatha army at Assaye on 23 September 1803. The Maharathas were skilled artillerymen, with more than a hundred cannon to Wellesley's twenty-two, and 40,000 men to his 7,000. They had taken up a strong defensive position behind the Kaitna river at Assaye and greeted Wellesley's advance with an intensive bombardment, followed with grape and chain shot at closer range. Nevertheless, the British advance continued, crushing the enemy centre and overrunning many of their guns. The fighting was bloody, even by the standards of the day; Wellesley lost a third of his force, 1,600 men killed or wounded to the enemy's 6,000, and the memory of the success and bloodshed of this day remained with him throughout his life. Years later, when asking Wellington what was the 'best thing' he had ever done in war, his questioner expected to hear of Talavera, Salamanca or Waterloo, but the old Duke replied briefly, 'Assaye'.

On 29 November 1803 Wellesley fought the Mahrathas at Argaun, killing and capturing thousands for the loss of less than 600 men. He moved on to lay siege to the fortress of Gawilgarh, which fell by assault on 15 December 1803, the entire garrison of 8,000 men being put to the sword. This defeat shattered the confidence of the Maharatha Confederation, whose members now hastened to make peace and sign alliances with the Company.

With these successes came rewards. Wellesley was presented with a sword and a golden vase worth more than £2,000. He was made a Knight of the Bath in August 1804 – the announcement reached him in February 1805 – and his personal fortune, after eight years in India, stood at the very substantial sum of £42,000. It was enough. He sailed from Calcutta in early March 1805, and after a month on St Helena in the South Atlantic (where, unlike Napoleon later, he found the climate 'most healthy') arrived in England in September.

The nine years of his absence had transformed Arthur Wellesley from a Colonel of Infantry to a Major-General with a knighthood. He had learned the business of command at all levels, from single battalion to full army; he had also learned the vital importance of morale, how to handle the difficulties of supply, and how to work with diffi-

cult, factious and often uncomprehending allies – all experience
which would prove useful in the Peninsula.

Britain's morale was raised by the victory at Trafalgar in October,
a triumph dimmed by the death of Lord Nelson, whom Wellesley had
met briefly in Downing Street before Nelson left to join HMS *Victory*.
Elation faded with news of Napoleon's overwhelming success at Austerlitz, shortly followed by the death of William Pitt and the collapse
of the Third Coalition in January 1806.

Matters were also going awry for the Wellesley family. Lord Mornington (now Marquess Wellesley) had been recalled from India to face
charges of irresponsibility and dishonesty, but Pitt had been sympath-
etic and other friends remained loyal. The Wellesleys survived, and
Marquess Wellesley in time regained Cabinet office.

In October 1805 Sir Arthur Wellesley proposed to Kitty Pakenham,
whom he had not set eyes on for eleven years; on 10 April 1806 they
were married in Dublin. He took extended leave from the army and
in January 1806 became MP for Rye. Ambition and what soon proved
an unsatisfactory marriage inclined Wellesley to seek a foreign command but few were available and he determined to concentrate instead on his political career, supporting the Coalition Government
(ironically nicknamed the 'Ministry of All the Talents') formed after
the death of Pitt. This ministry collapsed in March 1807 and was
replaced by the Tories. The Duke of Richmond was appointed Lord
Lieutenant of Ireland and took Arthur to Dublin as Irish Secretary.

Wellesley was in Ireland at the end of May 1807 when he heard of
the proposed expedition to Copenhagen. Denmark had joined the
Continental System at the behest of her pro-French Crown Prince,
and the Cabinet decided upon action to prevent the Danish fleet
falling into French hands. The Royal Navy set sail for Copenhagen
with an expeditionary force led by General Lord Cathcart, with
General Sir Harry Burrard as his second-in-command. Wellesley's
reluctant subordinate from Mysore days, General Baird, commanded
a division, Wellesley only an infantry brigade. His successful Indian
campaigns and conquests cut little ice at the Horse Guards.

Wellesley's brigade was put ashore near Copenhagen on 16 August
1807, secured their position, and fought the only battle of the campaign at Kiöge, taking 1,500 prisoners. The garrison of Copenhagen
asked for terms on 8 September, and Wellesley was one of the three
Commissioners appointed to negotiate the surrender. By 30 September he was back in England, where he received the thanks of Parliament for his 'zeal, valour and exertions'. In England, too, he was now
seen as a coming man.

Matters on the Continent were coming to a crisis. On 20 October 1807 Napoleon declared war on Portugal and General Junot began his march on Lisbon. In April 1808, a few weeks before the Madrid massacres of the *dos de Mayo*, Wellesley was raised to the rank of Lieutenant-General and in June 1808 he accepted command of an expedition of 9,000 men intended for an attack on the Spanish colonies in South America. This expedition never sailed.

In June 1808 representatives of the Juntas of the Asturias, Galicia and Andalucía arrived in London to request British cash and arms, and General Wellesley's force at Cork, waiting to sail for Buenos Aires, now received fresh instructions. Wellesley was to sail for Portugal and rendezrous with a force of 5,000 troops from Gibraltar. Taking command of this small army of 14,000 men, he was to land in Portugal or on the coast of Spain and wage sharp war upon the French. Wellesley's transports left Cork on 12 July 1808 and while the British were at sea, the French General Loison, in reprisal for an attack on his couriers, massacred the entire population of the ancient city of Evora, east of Lisbon. Following this atrocity, the Portuguese population rose in arms.

Wellesley had by now acquired the experience on which his later successes were founded. He knew about command from the ground up, about the importance of logistics, about campaigning in a hostile environment. He knew his way around the Court, and as a Member of Parliament was on familiar terms with government ministers. He enjoyed political influence, and realized the need to maintain support at home. Above all, he had gained a clear idea of how, by setting attainable objectives and relying on his own force and abilities to carry out his intentions, a campaign could be fought and won.

4

Arms and the Men:

1808–1815

Our business, like every other, is to be learned only by
constant practice and experience; and our experience is to
be had in war, not at reviews.
Lieutenant-General Sir John Moore: 1809

IT WAS NOW 1808. With the Emperor Napoleon Bonaparte and
Lieutenant-General Sir Arthur Wellesley both in the field, the time
has come to examine the soldiers and the equipment they had to work
with, for the armies of the day, their weapons and numbers, and the
way the regiments were employed, all form part of this story.

At the time of the Napoleonic Wars, every European state of any
size had an army. All used similar weapons and every campaign was
governed by the constraints imposed on any army making war with
muzzle-loading weapons in an age of horse transport. The armies of
France and Great Britain offer the most striking differences, while
sharing certain similarities, and the most significant difference lay in
their size. Britain's armies were far smaller than those of France,
because French armies were raised by conscription. British armies
were entirely volunteer, though the Peninsular Army also contained
large conscript contingents from Portugal, Hanover and Spain. When
Wellesley took up his command in Portugal in 1808 at Mondego Bay,
west of Coimbra, he had just 13,000 infantry. When Napoleon went
to Russia in 1812, he took with him more than 600,000 men. That is
the scale of the difference.

Wellington's 'Army' – actually little more than a division (though
the division as a formation was only introduced to the British Army,
by Wellesley, later in the Peninsular Campaign) – was initially too

weak, particularly in cavalry and transport, to be truly effective in the field, while Napoleon's army in Russia was too large for any general to control. It was impossible to provision or command and began to disintegrate from the moment it crossed the Russian frontier. Accounts and histories seem to indicate that the most effective armies during the Napoleonic Wars numbered between 50,000 and 250,000 men. These armies were divided into sub-units, the French favouring the 'corps', which might consist of anywhere between 20,000 and 50,000 men, and the British the 'division' of 10,000 or 15,000.

Shortage of men was a constant problem to the British Government, which did not dare to introduce conscription. An army saying has it that 'One volunteer is worth three pressed men', and this volunteer army came to make up in skill and professionalism what it lacked in manpower. Unfortunately, at the outset it was matched against Napoleon's veterans, already highly professional and well able to look after themselves on campaign or in battle. Furthermore, the soldiers of the Peninsular Army – a very high proportion of them from Scotland and Ireland – were often in the ranks more from necessity than from any overwhelming desire to fight the Corsican Tyrant.

Wellesley frequently deplored the behaviour of his soldiers and, scarcely less frequently, the lamentable capabilities of his officers. In 1811 he wrote to the Horse Guards concerning some of his commanders:

I have received the letter announcing the appointment of Sir William Erskine, General Lumley and General Hay to this Army. The first I understand to be a madman. I believe you agree that the second is not very wise. The third may be useful. Colonel Saunders, who I sent away last year for incapacity, is sent out again. I have to appoint him Colonel on the Staff because he is senior to the others and I wish to prevent him spoiling a good regiment. Then there is General Lightburne, whose conduct is scandalous . . . I only hope that when the enemy reads the list of their names he trembles as I do.

Wellesley was no less scathing about his soldiers, often with good reason. Much as he praised their conduct in battle he knew that, off the battlefield or in retreat, they were much given to drink and looting. Order was kept with frequent use of the lash and occasional resort to the hangman's rope. Public hangings for desertion and looting were not uncommon during the Peninsular War, and floggings were a daily affair. As there was no corporal punishment in their army, such proceedings appalled the French, where good leadership and the rewards of medals, badges and decorations kept the soldiers obedient, though cowards and deserters were given brief trials and shot by their comrades. French soldiers were equally addicted to looting but with more excuse. Since they were not provisioned they had no option but to live off the countryside. The conduct of the French armies in Spain and Portugal, was to play a major part in rousing the peasantry against them.

Another significant difference lay in the officers of the French and British armies. British officers came mainly from the gentry and although many were men of outstanding ability, many more had joined the army because they were incapable of making a career at anything else. Commissions were bought, and promotion was by purchase, rather than by seniority or outstanding leadership and ability. Nevertheless, men such as Picton, Kempt, Graham, Colbourne, Paget, Packenham and Hill would have won renown in any army, at any time. Wellesley, in many ways conservative in military matters, was a great devotee of the purchase system. This, he felt, enabled the army to be officered by gentlemen who had acquired the habit of command from birth.

He was less impressed with their devotion to duty. Apart from an occasional day's hunting, Wellesley took no home leave between 1808 and 1814. His officers, on the other hand, were forever pressing for leave in England, or at least in Lisbon. Wellington usually felt unable to refuse, though he did stipulate that leave in Lisbon should not last longer than 48 hours, '. . . because two days is quite long enough for any man to spend in bed with a woman'. Some of his officers' failings were Wellington's own fault. Though a great general, he had little inclination to delegate, preferring to keep the reins in his own hands and believing, often all too correctly, that when he relaxed his grip on a campaign, matters quickly went wrong.

In the French army, men rose by ability. Military life really was 'a career open to talents'; in Napoleon's own words, 'Every soldier carries in his knapsack the baton of a Marshal of France', and his soldiers knew this to be true. Many of his marshals had begun at the very bottom, and some even rose higher than the baton: Murat, who became King of Naples, began as a cavalry trooper; André Masséna, Duke of Rivoli and Prince of Essling, enlisted as a private soldier; Michel Ney, who joined as a trooper, became Prince of the Moskowa and even Commander-in-Chief of the French armies under Louis XVIII; Bernadotte, a common soldier, become Charles XIV of Sweden.

The French officer corps provided superb front-line leadership to the troops. Valour was expected, and never in short supply, and those who were brave and conducted themselves well under the Emperor's eye could look forward to riches and rewards, whatever their origins. Such leadership was essential in the command of large conscript armies but the British Army, though small, was an efficient and effective force in 1808. Entirely professional, it owed much of this efficiency to the training methods tested and then adopted by General Sir John Moore, 'The Father of the British Infantry'. Moore applied humanity and common sense to the little-known science of man-management, advocating and demonstrating the worth of a new and caring attitude by the officers towards their men. He also developed individual initiative among the soldiers. He expected the officers and NCOs to encourage such initiative by example and control their men with wisdom and kindness, rather than by reliance on blind obedience and the lash. In Moore's Light Infantry regiments, the 95th, 52nd and 43rd, rewards and praise became more important than punishment and rebuke. The army as a whole soon benefited from this enlightened and successful form of leadership, and the later successes of the Peninsular Army owe much to Moore's encouragement and example.

The British had learned the importance of skirmishing and marksmanship the hard way, fighting Indians and American woodsmen in Canada and New England during the Seven Years' War and the War of Independence, but Moore's ideas combined and extended these two elements in a quite revolutionary way. Fortunately he had the support of the Commander-in-Chief, the Duke of York, who ordered the formation of an Experimental Rifle Corps under Moore's command at Shorncliffe in 1803.

Moore believed in the trained, alert soldier. He believed that a soldier, having been told what to do, and why, should then be trusted to do it. He believed that officers had to earn their men's respect and that the most useful form of discipline was self-discipline. This philosophy combined with extensive training in drill, marksmanship and skirmishing tactics produced remarkable results. Battalions which had passed through Shornecliffe were some of the most efficient, successful and highly-regarded in the army.

Above all, the men were happy. Desertion was almost unheard of and punishment rare. The officers cared for their men, and the men did their best for their officers. This example spread. The British Army which went to war in the Peninsula in 1808 was superior to the Continental armies in training, discipline, marksmanship and tactical ability.

Credit must also be given to the traditional stubbornness of the British infantry soldier, and to the regimental system. Prowess in defence dated back to Agincourt and the Battle of Hastings: put the British soldier in a position, order him to defend it, and he will not be easily dislodged. The regimental system evolved during the latter half of the eighteenth century, regiments having been before 1790 virtually the private property of their colonels. Gradually the regiment developed into something akin to a family, and its members, from commanding officer to private soldier, were fiercely loyal to the regiment and to each other – as they are today.

Again and again throughout the Napoleonic Wars, and through all the wars since, the infantry battalions of the British Army have stood and fought and died, not for the cause or for their country, but because they would not and could not let their regiment and their comrades down. Hard battles are won by soldiers who feel like that.

The armies of the French Revolution and the Napoleonic Empire may have been raised by conscription, but here too national pride and regimental honour played a part, inspiring the soldiers and reinforcing that natural *élan* which was the French counterpoint to the stubborn stolidity of the British infantry. At the age of seventeen all Frenchmen were drafted into annual 'Classes' and reported to depots. Here they were given basic training in drill and weapon-handling; they were then despatched to their regiments, where training continued under experienced officers and senior NCOs. Since these men were going to fight together, there was a vested interest in instilling the highest standards of skill and discipline in the recruits. The absence of corporal punishment has already been noted: the floggings common in the British army were held to prove that British soldiers would not fight without such coercion.

To reduce his huge armies to manageable units, Napoleon perfected the 'corps' system which had originally been introduced into the Royal Army by Marshal Broglie. Under this system, self-supporting corps made up of three or more divisions, mustering perhaps 30,000 men of all arms – artillery, cavalry and engineers, as well as infantry – became the main unit of manoeuvre. Napoleon set out the advantages of this formation:

A Corps of 25,000 to 30,000 men can be left on its own. Well handled, it can fight or avoid action as it chooses, according to circumstances and without any harm coming to it, because an opponent cannot force a Corps to accept an engagement – though if it chooses to do so it can fight for a long time.

Like Wellesley, Napoleon found it difficult to delegate, and like Wellesley he suffered for it. Most of Napoleon's twenty-six marshals had made their names as corps commanders, and under his eye they did well. Only when he left them in charge of entire campaigns, as in Spain, did things go wrong. Like Wellesley, Napoleon was well aware of the benefits of encouraging regimental loyalties. He gave his men Colours to carry and Eagles to guard, medals and decorations to wear with pride. Napoleon also possessed the useful gift of remembering names and faces, and would wander about the camp ground in the evening or pause during a review to pick out old soldiers from the ranks and chat to them about the dangers they had shared together. All this enhanced the effect of his personality on his men. Wellesley noticed this, commenting: 'His presence on the battlefield is worth 40,000 men.' These qualities of leadership, as much as his military abilities, made Napoleon Bonaparte a formidable general, and his men would have done anything for him.

Some of Wellesley's men felt the same way about their general. Captain John Kincaid of the 95th observed, at the battle of Fuentes de Oñero: 'We anxiously longed for [his] return . . . as we would rather see his long nose in the fight than a reinforcement of ten thousand men'; but on the whole, he was regarded with more respect than affection. His men trusted him, because he knew his job, and felt safe – or, at least, safer – when he was with them. 'Where's our Arthur?' asked one Fusilier as his battalion advanced into the fray at Albuera. 'I don't know,' replied his companion, 'but I wish he were here.'

The fighting forces of the Napoleonic Wars were divided into three main arms – infantry, cavalry, artillery – and a general's success largely depended on how he used them in combination. Whether French or British, their weapons were similar: musket or rifle for the infantry, sword or lance for the cavalry, cannon of various calibres for the artillery. The weapons themselves imposed distinct limitations.

Infantrymen carried a flintlock musket tipped with a twenty-one-inch bayonet, known as the 'Brown Bess', which had come into use in European armies at the end of the seventeenth century, had scarcely changed since Marlborough's day, and was retained until the Crimean War. It took training and discipline to handle a musket well, especially in battle. To load, prime and fire the infantryman had first to flick open the 'priming pan'; then, having torn open a paper cartridge with his teeth, he would tip a little gunpowder into the pan and flick it shut. Rain or wind made this simple action very difficult.

The rest of the gunpowder, and the musket ball, were dropped into the barrel; a wadded cartridge was then packed in on top and rammed home with two strokes of the ramrod, which was otherwise kept clipped onto the barrel. The musket was then cocked, presented, aimed and fired, a spark from the flint igniting the powder in the pan, which flashed through a vent into the barrel to fire the main charge. A well-trained infantryman could fire 2 or 3 shots a minute, but the musket was notoriously inaccurate and largely ineffective at much more than 200 yards. Gunpowder, the only propellant then in use, produced great clouds of white smoke which swiftly covered the battlefield and obscured the target. The best infantry held their fire until the last possible moment, which took much training, firm discipline, and a steady nerve.

Rifles were sometimes used by the skirmishers who went ahead of the main battalions and by some but by no means all of the 'rifle' regiments. The British used the Baker rifle, a muzzle-loaded weapon with a groove in the barrel to spin the ball in flight. This improved accuracy but increased fouling, and rifles were slower to load and more prone to misfire.

French infantry regiments fell into two categories, light infantry, and infantry of the line. Light infantry were used in a more mobile role, though their equipment was identical to that of the line infantry, and all line battalions contained 'élite' companies of *voltigeurs*, fit, trained men who could skirmish ahead of the advancing column and keep up with any supporting cavalry. In the battalions of the Imperial Guard such skirmishers were known as *tirailleurs*.

The limitations of the musket dictated the formations adopted by the infantry. The musket could not be loaded lying down – the men had to stand in order to drop in the bullet and wield the ramrod. Since the musket was inaccurate, individual fire was largely useless so large formations firing volleys on command at close range were needed to produce an effective weight of fire. The British had discovered that a two-rank formation of infantry was more effective than the three-rank formation common in the Continental armies, and increased the weight of fire by one-third. French armies preferred to attack in column and did their best work with the bayonet, which the British also wielded effectively. Two or three volleys followed by a bayonet charge was the common battlefield tactic.

Infantry formations were vulnerable to artillery, which could play havoc with close-packed ranks, and also to cavalry, which could ride down scattered troops or charge through a thin line. Under attack by cavalry the infantry would 'form square', presenting a hedge of bayonets which the horses would not approach – so a competent opposing general would bring up cannon to weaken the square and make gaps for the cavalry to charge through.

Cavalry was the most expensive arm, and also the most difficult to raise, train and control. It might be 'light' or 'heavy', and lancers – originally Polish, though French and Dutch regiments were later equipped with this weapon – featured in the French armies. Light cavalry units – hussars – were vital for skirmishing and reconnaissance, but the bulk of French cavalry was made up of dragoons or 'heavy' cavalry who carried a short musket and could fight on foot as well as on horseback. The British cavalry was made up of hussars and dragoons, who were, at least in theory, accompanied into action by troops of horse artillery, for use against infantry squares. Despite the increasing effectiveness and range of missile weapons – cannon, rifle and musket – cavalry remained an essential arm, vital for reconnaissance and the pursuit of a defeated foe, deadly against infantry in open order.

The French cavalry outnumbered the British, and was better trained and more efficient. The British cavalry, though relentlessly gallant, was prone to over-excitement in the charge and a subsequent failure, at crucial moments, to turn and reform to support the rest of the army. Accounts of Peninsular battles are full of accounts of British cavalry vanishing off the field after a whirlwind charge and becoming a spent force for the rest of the engagement.

The deadliest arm, the one most feared by the infantry, was artillery. Napoleon was a gunner, a great believer in the use of artillery, the *ultimo ratio regis* – the last argument of kings. All his battles began with a fearsome cannonade of the enemy formations, to weaken them before he committed his infantry and cavalry, and the usual tactics of Continental commanders in drawing up their infantry fully exposed to cannon fire only served to increase this destruction. One of Wellesley's simplest but shrewdest moves was to place his troops on the 'reverse slopes' of hills or ridges, where they were relatively safe from artillery fire and where their position and numbers were difficult for the French to estimate. In other armies the infantry stood fully exposed to cannon fire, and suffered terribly in consequence.

Both sides employed three types of artillery: horse artillery to serve with the cavalry, field artillery to support the infantry, and siege artillery to reduce the walls of fortresses. Apart from solid 'round-shot', cannon also fired 'grape', 'case' or 'canister' shot, all basically a tin shell or linen bag filled with musket balls which spewed out of the container and were lethal to infantry or cavalry, especially at close

range. The infantry hated and feared cannon fire: the effect of even
one cannon ball on a battalion of infantry could be terrible. Whole
files of men might be swept away, legs and heads carved off . . . one
account records seventeen men struck down before the force of a
cannon ball had been expended. An added horror was that the infantry could frequently see the cannon ball coming and observe it in
flight until it crashed into their ranks. Two British inventions, not
used by the French, were shrapnel, a shell packed with explosive and
musket balls which was timed to explode over the heads of advancing
enemy formations, and the rockets devised by Sir William Congreve;
Wellesley had a poor opinion of rockets, as they were notoriously
inaccurate and unpredictable, though they were occasionally used in
siege warfare, and could be useful against cavalry.

Recoil mechanisms did not exist, so all cannon had to be manhandled back into position and aimed afresh after every shot. This
called for speed and teamwork from the gun crew, often obliged to
work in the open, fully exposed to counter-battery fire, sharpshooters
and cavalry assaults. Wellesley had less regard for the artillery arm
than Napoleon, preferring to rely on his infantry, but he was well
served by his gunners, especially the horse artillery, who often stood
to their guns to support the infantry in the face of much heavier
French fire and onslaughts by French cavalry.

Apart from the 'teeth', the infantry, cavalry and artillery, there
were engineers, doctors, support and supply echelons. Some of these
elements, notably the engineers, were highly regarded. The exploits
of French engineers in throwing and maintaining bridges across the
Danube before and during the battles of Aspern-Essling and Wagram
were remarkable, while their actions in bridging the freezing Berezina
river during the retreat from Moscow in 1812 are beyond all praise.
British sappers were equally efficient and courageous, and were highly
commended during the various Peninsular sieges, though there never
seemed to be enough of them and their equipment was often totally
inadequate for the tasks they were asked to perform.

Logistics, by means of which armies are maintained in the field,
were hardly considered. Most armies foraged. The supply element,
such as it was, varied from adequate on the British side to appalling
on the French. As a matter of policy, Napoleon expected his armies
to live off the country and his enemies to pay for his wars. Every
peace treaty he enforced required the defeated nation to pay an
indemnity to cover the cost of the campaign by which it had been
defeated and every occupying French army was paid by means of
contributions levied locally – which did nothing to endear the army

to the defeated people. It reduced the burden of taxation on the people of France, which was the main idea, but wages alone were just part of the cost: armies had to be fed and clothed, supplied with boots and ammunition, saddles and fodder. Much of the equipment came from depots in France, but food was usually obtained by foraging parties, and where they foraged, the local population starved.

Wellesley was quick to appreciate the part played by French for-aging in rousing the people of Spain and Portugal against the French. He was under no illusion that matters would be much different if his troops behaved in the same way and forbade his men to forage, flogging or hanging those who disobeyed. His men's food was con-veyed from Britain in transports protected by the Royal Navy. What had to be acquired locally he paid for, although getting enough gold coin from the British government to finance his campaigns was an-other of his problems. Despite all his efforts, his men were frequently on short commons.

Medical services were even less well organized and sickness took a steady toll of all the armies of the day. Any seriously wounded solider could expect to die of gangrene or septicaemia if he did not die immediately from the pain, shock and loss of blood caused by his wound. Anaesthetics did not exist. Most amputations were carried out soon after the battle, while the wounded were still in shock. It is surprising that so many survived, enduring the trauma of amputation without complaint and submitting to the probing and sewing-up of wounds with only alcohol to dull the pain – and the combination of drink and shock was frequently fatal. Both French and British made great efforts to look after their wounded and it is pleasant to record that each side was happy to leave their wounded in the other's hands if necessary, knowing they would be well treated. Every army was accompanied by a vast train of camp followers – wives, sweethearts, mistresses, servants, sutlers – people who followed the army through choice or necessity, sharing the fortunes of the soldiers and a great many of the risks.

Napoleon had made a close study of strategy, and had decided views on the art of war, evolving a method of warfare that hardly changed between the fight at Lodi in 1796 and the battle of Waterloo in 1815. He often claimed that he did not have 'a strategy' – '*Je n'ai jamais eu un plan d'opération*' – but meant by this that he aimed to adapt his strategy or battlefield tactics according to the particular circum-stances of the day. This may be true, but he also had a number of precepts which served him well for many years and which might be described as a 'Napoleonic Strategy'.

His first precept was speed in the advance. Within the limits imposed by foot and horse, Napoleon's armies moved fast: they were frequently upon the enemy before he knew it, and this gave them a great psychological advantage.

The second Napoleonic precept was concentration of force. Having found the enemy's main body and pinned it down by sending forward a corps or two to probe for a weakness and force it to engage, he would employ the *manoeuvre sur les derrières* to threaten the enemy's communications and line of retreat. When the enemy lines began to waver, he would attack with everything he had, aiming especially for encirclement. This manoeuvre was first employed at the battle of Lodi in 1796 and frequently thereafter; when successful, it forced a panic or a rapid retreat. Just to hold the field of battle at the end of the day was not enough for Napoleon Bonaparte: the enemy must be crushed, annihilated, scattered, destroyed. Having achieved that, he could enforce a peace on his own terms.

Although every battle will depend on terrain, objectives, and the numbers and composition of the armies involved, Napoleon's did follow a certain pattern, and if that pattern is understood, the complicated details of particular battles will become clear. A fearsome cannonade at the outset of battle was intended to knock out enemy artillery and reduce the strength and resolve of their infantry or cavalry formations. While this was in progress, Napoleon would be moving his infantry divisions forward, keeping in contact to hold the enemy in position, always probing for the flank and rear of the opposing force. The object was to get the enemy off-balance before the crux of the battle; once he was shaken by cannon fire, infantry and cavalry assaults, the French would move *en masse* to the attack from the flank and rear as well as the front. Then, as the enemy fell back, the large French cavalry arm would come surging forward to turn the retreat into a rout.

Napoleon's method of combining speed, overwhelming force and relentless pursuit was not widely seen again until the twentieth century, and he made other innovations. He put a high value on security, concealing his intentions from all but the necessary few and making his advances behind a thick screen of cavalry; tight security matched with speed often gave him the advantage of surprise, and on many occasions his battles were half won before the first shot was fired.

There were certain limitations to any early nineteenth-century battle. The most difficult, recurring problem was that of command. The only method of communication was by courier and sending messages by horseback was neither quick nor certain, especially in the pall of white smoke produced by musketry, which also rendered observation of events difficult. Napoleon briefed his marshals and generals most carefully before a battle, telling them exactly what he expected. Even so, once the battle began, matters were far less certain. The Emperor's arrangements frequently went awry even when his orders were precisely followed, not least because his opponents did not always react as he anticipated they would.

Napoleon succeeded so well for so long – he fought sixty battles and won most of them – because he had an enthusastic and hard-fighting army, because he always laid out a sound but simple plan beforehand, and because his marshals were superb soldiers who would act on their own initiative if they saw a problem arising or a situation developing that they could turn to advantage. All his officers led from the front and although this meant they suffered appalling casualties, at least they were on the spot to see what was going on and take the appropriate action.

The basic strategy of envelopment, the *manoeuvres sur les derrières*, was employed in at least half those sixty battles. Napoleon had little use for the line-against-line, full-frontal battles typical of the middle years of the eighteenth century, preferring to use all the elements of his army – infantry, cavalry and artillery – in expert combination. Furthermore, the combination of these elements on a corps basis more than once proved his salvation when his plans were foiled by the enemy or something went wrong – as at Jena-Auerstedt where, with the additional help of Davout's special genius, one corps alone was able to fight the bulk of the Prussian army for most of the day. Napoleon's problem in fighting the British army was in the matter of tactics, not strategy.

The armies of Royalist and Imperial Europe involved in the Napoleonic Wars – those of Austria, Russia, Prussia and their satellites – were 'traditional' armies, relics of another age, glorious to look upon but ponderous, unwieldy, poorly officered, and filled with reluctant conscripts. They fell easy prey to French armies full of zealous, hardy, well-trained troops, led by officers who knew their duty and commanded by a general of genius. On the battlefield, French *élan* and a skilful combination of all arms culminated in the battering-ram of the attack in column.

The early successes of the Revolutionary Armies resulted from the fearsome effect of those columns on the 'traditional' armies of the continental Powers. A column might be anything from fifty men to a full battalion wide. Preceded by sharpshooting skirmishers it bore down on an enemy line exhausted and cannon-wracked after a fearsome artillery bombardment from the French guns to which their commanders usually left them quite exposed. The mass of French infantry came forward at the *pas de charge*, to the accompaniment of a stirring, rolling beat sounded on the regimental drums, while the sharpshooters picked off the enemy officers, NCOs and colour-bearers in the waiting line.

These sharpshooters acted with the artillery to weaken the enemy lines before the columns came up. The French column itself made little use of fire power but was a battering ram of bayonets, a solid mass of men aiming to punch a hole straight through the enemy line. The tactic worked for many years, in many encounters, but there was a flaw in this formation. The column attack relied on the sharp-shooters and bayonets carrying the day and on the opposing line crumbling. If fire-power was employed against the column and the opposing line refused to budge, the formation was a death trap. Strategy is well enough, but for a battle to be won, the right battle-field tactics are crucial.

Wellesley's first step towards countering the French superiority of numbers and their use of artillery was to opt for a defensive battle, fought on ground where that artillery would have less effect. On the battlefield he kept his men out of sight, on the reverse slope, or lying down. Only when the French were almost upon his line did his stolid, implacable infantry rise to meet them, as this account by the French Marshal Bugeaud clearly reveals:

The English generally occupied well chosen defensive positions having a certain command, and they showed only a portion of their forces. The usual artillery action first took place and soon, in great haste, without studying the position, without taking time to examine if there were means to make a flank attack, we marched straight on, taking the bull by the horns. About 1,000 yards from the English line the men became excited, spoke to one another and hurried their march; the column began to be a little confused. The English remained quite silent with ordered arms, and from their steadiness appeared to be a long red wall. This steadiness invariably produced an effect on the young soldiers. Very soon we got nearer, shouting, '*Vive l'Empereur! En avant . . . à la baionnette!*' Shakos were raised on the muzzles of the muskets; the column began to double, the ranks got into confusion, the agitation produced a tumult; shots were fired as we advanced. The English line remained silent, still and immovable, with ordered arms, even when we were only 300 yards distant, and it appeared to ignore the storm about to break. The contrast was striking; in our inmost thoughts each felt that the enemy was a long time in firing, and that this fire, reserved for so long, would be very unpleasant when it did come. Our ardour cooled. The moral power of steadiness, which nothing shakes (even if it be only appearance), over disorder which stupefies itself with noise, overcame our minds. At this moment of intense excitement, the English wall shouldered arms; an indescribable feeling rooted many of our men to the spot; they began to fire. The enemy's steady concentrated volleys swept our ranks; decimated, we turned round seeking to recover our equilibrium; then three deafening cheers broke the silence of our opponents; at the third they were on us, pushing our disorganized flight.

The confrontation between the French and British armies that began in 1808 with the French invasion of Portugal became, effectively, a contest between two sets of principles governing the management of armies. The French, toughened by years of campaigning and with the confidence that came from years of victory, could still carry all before them against the armies of Continental Europe. Even here, as Napoleon discovered at Eylau in 1807, victory became increasingly difficult of attainment as the Continental armies grew more proficient and the quality of the French armies steadily declined, weakened by years of war, the loss of veterans, and the introduction of foreign, often reluctant troops from Napoleon's satellite, subjugated states.

Nevertheless, the French armies in Spain should have been able to make short work of Wellesley's army, which lacked experience, cavalry and artillery and was, to begin with, much smaller. They failed to do so in the face of constant harassment at the hands of the Spanish and Portuguese guerrillas, Wellesley's outstanding tactical sense, and the solid resistance of the British infantry when battle was finally joined. Wellesley was far too cagey and agile to permit the execution of any *manoeuvre sur les derrières*, or to let the French pin him in any position where he could be overwhelmed by their superior numbers. He fought only when he wanted, how he wanted and where he wanted. Unlike Napoleon, and as the following pages will reveal, he rarely fought the same way twice. Wellesley was a highly intelligent and versatile general and had the advantage that, thanks to the steady supply of captured French documents and information brought into his lines by the Portuguese and Spanish, he always knew what the enemy was up to. The French, by contrast, hated by the local inhabitants, were often woefully short of such useful intelligence.

It is fair to say that the French marshals did not know what to make

5

War in the Peninsula:

Spain and Portugal, 1808

In a Civil War every important point must be occupied. It is
not enough to march in all directions.

Napoleon Bonaparte
Bayonne: 1808

THE RISING OF *dos de Mayo* took Napoleon completely by surprise.
He could see no reason for popular resistance. He had relieved the
Spaniards of an incompetent king, a corrupt government and the
Inquisition-tainted shambles of the Catholic Church, all that to be
replaced with an enlightened and democratic rule based on the
proven benefits of his Civil Code. He had even provided the Spaniards with a new king, his respected elder brother, Joseph . . . and
now this.

However, if certain ungrateful elements of the Spanish population
were unhappy about the imposition of Imperial rule, there was apparently little they could do about it in the face of the large French forces
in the country. By the spring of 1808 the French were able to deploy
170,000 men in Spain and Portugal. The main French army of 80,000
under Ney and Moncey held the Pyrenees and had bases as far south
as Toledo. Further south still, on the Sierra Morena between New
Castile and Andalucía, lay the 24,000-strong army of General Dupont. To the north of the *meseta*, the great plain north of Madrid and
the Guadarrama mountains, Marshal Bessières had a division of
13,000 troops in Old Castile and another 12,000 in Aragon. To this
could be added Junot's Army of Portugal in Lisbon, mustering 25,000
men, and General Duhesme's 13,000 troops in Barcelona.

Against this the Spanish Royal Army could muster perhaps 100,000 men, half-trained and poorly led, most deployed in isolated garrisons. These now began to concentrate into larger formations and within a few weeks of the *dos de Mayo* there were some 30,000 men under the Spanish-Irish General Joachim Blake and General Cuesta in Galicia, and a further 30,000 in Andalucía under General Castaños. Napoleon regarded Blake's army in the north as most likely to cause trouble, either by cutting French communications to the Pyrenees or by taking the ports of Santander and Ferrol, through which the Spanish might be supplied with arms by the British fleet then hovering off the coast.

Marshal Bessières was ordered to seize these ports and to reinforce French garrisons along the routes from Madrid and Burgos to the Pyrenees. In the south, General Dupont was ordered to cross the Sierra Morena, take Córdoba and march from there down the Guadalquiver valley to seize Seville and Cadiz. The rest of the French army was to make its presence felt in the towns and the countryside and suppress any sign of resistance from local bandits. The troops were not up to the task. The veterans were with the *Grande Armée* in France, Germany or Portugal, and the new recruits who made up the Army of Spain were unable to cope with the guerrilla warfare developing all about them.

To this activity the arid and mountainous terrain of Spain was ideally suited. Roads were few, the population relentlessly hostile, the scope for ambush unlimited. French sentries were found at their posts with their throats cut, cavalry patrols vanished, or the troopers were found later, their bodies hideously mutilated. Muskets cracked from hillsides to topple riders from their saddles, and small detachments would be overwhelmed by sudden stabbing rushes of *guerrilleros* from a nearby *arroyo*. The strength of the French army was sapped by these attacks and by the need to supply escorts for convoys and couriers and to maintain garrisons in every village along the routes to France.

General Dupont crossed the Sierra Morena into the soft orange-blossom-covered countryside of Andalucía, but failed to take Seville, or to hold Córdoba, though he looted the churches and abbeys. Plagued by guerrillas who cut his communications he fell back on Andújar at the southern foot of the Sierra. Matters were little better elsewhere. Marshal Moncey failed to take Valencia, and Bessières was too occupied by risings in every town of Old Castile to send men across the Picos de Europa to seize Santander. Two Spanish officers, the Palafox brothers, seized Saragossa, killed those soldiers of the garrison who failed to flee, then dug in to hold the city against the 8,000-strong division of General Verdier. Saragossa lay on the only viable route from Madrid to Barcelona and it was essential that it be retaken, but General Savary, who now commanded all French forces in Spain, could spare no men to reinforce Verdier. Napoleon seemed to have no option but to cross the Pyrenees and take personal charge.

This marked the real beginning of all his problems, for he could not be everywhere. His power base was Paris, the centre of his Empire, but he had to dominate the Prussians, Austrians and Russians in the East and keep an eye on the northern provinces of Belgium and Holland. With Spain added to these demands, a crisis somewhere was inevitable, and the rest of his reign saw Napoleon moving frantically about his Empire in the attempt to suppress trouble and win battles on one front after another.

He began by commanding his brother Joseph, now enthroned in Madrid, to hold the city at all costs. Joseph's second task was to support and reinforce General Dupont in Andalucía. Dupont was now dangerously exposed, with only one guerrilla-infested road over the Sierra Morena to keep him in touch with the main French army at Toledo, and very few of the couriers who set out in either direction down this road reached their destination. The French then had a little luck. On 14 July the 24,000-strong Spanish Army of Galicia chose to stand and fight a small French force on a hilltop near Medina del Rio Seco, just north of Valladolid. This was a mistake. The 12,000 sorely-tried French soldiers, itching to get to grips with a Spanish force, stormed the hill in short order, driving the Spanish away in full retreat and taking swift and satisfying revenge on any stragglers who fell into their hands.

Hardly had this achievement been celebrated in Madrid than dire news arrived from Andalucía. The troops at Andújar under General Dupont, an experienced officer who had fought at Austerlitz and Friedland, had been reinforced by the arrival of another division, under General Vedel. But Castaños's Army of Andalucía, now mustering some 30,000 men, increased daily in numbers as every Spaniard with a sword or a musket hastened to take the field. Dupont was on the horns of a dilemma. His orders were to advance on Seville and Cadiz, while common sense and long experience told him to retire at all speed across the Sierra Morena. Fatally, he prevaricated, and while he did so Spanish forces, both regular and guerrilla, moved in to surround him. Eventually, but far too late, Dupont decided to withdraw.

This proved difficult. His army was burdened with 500 carts containing the loot of Córdoba, and more than a thousand sick or wounded men who could not be left behind. He ordered General

Vedel to clear the road ahead over the Sierra Morena, but the Spaniards simply fell back to let Vedel's force march past and then, in the absence of strong pickets to keep it clear, promptly closed in on the road again. A gap of some thirty miles opened up between Vedel's advance division of 10,000 men and the 13,000 men in Dupont's main army. Into this gap surged Castaños's Army of Andalucía and a great mob of armed peasants, who seized the town of Bailén and kept the two parts of Dupont's army well apart. Exhausted, surrounded by a resolute enemy in hostile country, where heat and lack of water soon added to their miseries, the French troops began to despair.

Dupont was a man not easily dismayed. He attacked the Spanish at Bailén five times on 18 July, but failed to force his way through to the north, and the morale of his force was further shaken when a brigade of Swiss infantry deserted to the Spaniards. On 19 July Dupont asked for an armistice, hoping to be able to withdraw and protect his evergrowing number of wounded. That night General Vedel rejoined Dupont, instead of marching his men off to Toledo and saving something from the débâcle. Negotiations continued during the 20th and on 21 July 1808 Dupont agreed to surrender his entire force to the Spaniards. Two days later, under the 'Convention of Bailén', 20,000 fully armed French soldiers surrendered to the ragged Spanish Army of Andalucía.

French armies had been checked before but they had never known anything like this. A French army – or at least, a French army corps – had laid down its arms, and to the Spanish. All over Europe, in Prussia and Austria, in Sweden and in the petty principalities of Germany and Italy, nationalists and patriots began to take heart. The image of French invincibility was cracked and the British army was not yet in the field.

Napoleon was furious with Dupont – not because he had been defeated, for defeat can happen to anyone, but for his surrender. 'A soldier's duty is to fight,' he said. 'Study the situation, map in hand, and there will never be a better example of an action so stupid, foolish or cowardly.' Nor did his opinion on that point alter. When Dupont and Vedel were paroled and returned to France, both were promptly court-martialled and imprisoned, Dupont for years. More junior officers were also marked by this defeat. Six months after Bailén Dupont's Chief-of-Staff General Legendre, who had played no part in the surrender, was humiliated by Napoleon in front of the entire French army during a review at Valladolid. Even so, the generals were lucky: imprisoned by the Spanish in offshore hulks or on the barren island of Cabrera, most of Dupont's 20,000 men died of neglect, brutality or simple starvation.

The news of the French defeat at Bailén prompted Joseph to evacuate Madrid, just eleven days after occupying his throne. Napoleon's instructions were that Joseph and his Chief-of-Staff, General Savary, should make a stand on the Duero at Valladolid, but Joseph ignored this command and elected to pull back another hundred miles to Burgos and the Ebro. In this he was probably wise, for bad news was pouring in from every quarter. The siege of Saragossa had had to be abandoned, while in Catalonia General Duhesme's army had been driven from the countryside, checked outside Gerona and cooped up in Barcelona with Spanish guerrillas prowling about the city walls and occupying the suburbs.

There then came news, at the end of August 1808, that an English army under General Wellesley had landed in Portugal and dealt a swift thrashing to General Junot. Like Dupont, Junot had been obliged to ask for an armistice, and his troops were even now being evacuated from Portugal. Clearly, matters were getting out of control – and all this within three months of the *dos de Mayo*.

Arthur Wellesley's first foray in the Peninsula was of short duration. He was appointed to command the expedition on 15 June 1808, received his orders on 30 June, and his army landed at Mondego Bay, west of Coimbra, on 1 August. By 4 October he was home again to face a public enquiry and a possible court martial. It was not an auspicious beginning.

However, none of the calamities surrounding this venture were General Wellesley's fault. Indeed, he notched up three useful victories, for his army, if small, was extremely pugnacious. Two weeks fter the landing the 95th Rifles tore into the French pickets at Obidos, and on 17 August 1808 Wellesley attacked General Delaborde's division at Roliça. Delaborde should have avoided battle until reinforcements under General Loison had come up from Evora but, not having fought the British before, he decided to stand and fight, although he had only 5,000 men to Wellesley's 13,000.

Wellesley deployed his men before the French centre, while sending two brigades around to Delaborde's flank. Delaborde was able to withdraw, but when the 29th Foot (later the Worcestershire Regiment) attacked his columns from the flank, French discipline failed and after a brief engagement Delaborde's army fell back in full retreat. Roliça was a confused affair, and Wellesley had no cavalry with which to pursue the French, but they lost 700 men to 487 British and Wellesley might claim a victory.

Wellesley then received further reinforcements, 4,000 men under Major-General Spencer, which increased his force to 17,000. Less welcome were the two British generals arriving in Spain, both senior to Wellesley and eager to take command of a force which hardly amounted to more than a strong division. As the most junior Lieutenant-General on the Army List Wellesley had known that he would be superceded on the arrival of Sir John Moore from the Baltic. Wellesley had no objection to this. He admired General Moore, but Moore was detested by the Government, who therefore approached two other, even more senior generals to comand the Army in Portugal, thinking that Moore would then decline to serve. In this they were mistaken, for Moore had far too strong a sense of duty to decline any chance of employment. Wellesley therefore was about to be superceded by not one but three senior officers, only one of whom was competent.

The two senior generals *en- route* for the Peninsula were Sir Hew Dalrymple of the Guards, currently the Governor of Gibraltar, and his second-in-command, another Guardee, Sir Harry Burrard, Sir Harry arrived off the Portuguese coast on 20 August and he was still on board HMS *Brazen* when General Junot's 30,000 men attacked Wellesley's force of 17,000 men at Vimeiro. Happily, the British forces already occupied an admirable position on a series of ridges and hills around Vimeiro with the élite battalions, including the 43rd and 52nd Light Infantry, on the flat top of Vimeiro Hill, just south of the village.

Junot attacked with four infantry columns, led by Delaborde and Loison, each column fronted by a swarm of sharp-shooters. Wellesley kept the bulk of his troops out of sight behind the ridges, swiftly containing the French skirmishers with the rifles of the 95th. Only when the French columns reached the crest of the ridge did the British infantry come forward in line, fire one destructive volley and then, wrapping themselves around the sides of the French columns, began to deliver a series of rolling platoon volleys, pouring a hail of fire into the close-packed French ranks. The British then swept in with the bayonet and drove the French down the hill in disorder.

Junot's men remustered and came on again and yet again, only to be driven back in the same fashion with great loss. Attracted ashore by the firing, Sir Harry Burrand arrived on the battlefield during the third French attack when, after two hours of fighting, the French were in full retreat, having lost more than 2,000 men in the battle. Wellesley urged Burrand to order an advance and cut off Junot's retreat to Lisbon.

'Sir Harry,' he said, pointing south, 'now is the time to advance . . . the enemy are completely beaten . . . in three days we shall be in Lisbon.'

Sir Harry said, 'No!'

Sir Harry continued to say 'No' for several days and *his* superior, Sir Hew Dalrymple, who arrived to take command on 22 August, agreed with him. Both generals remained deaf to Wellesley's urgings, and were equally deaf to Sir John Moore on his arrival. Wellesley wrote of this to his brother William:

The General [Dalrymple] has no plan or any idea of a plan, nor do I believe he knows the meaning of the word plan. He has not uttered one word to me upon the subject . . . Moore was simply ignored . . . [Dalrymple] told him last night that he [Moore] might land his Corps or not, as he saw fit.

What happened next was disgraceful. On 22 August General Kellermann, son of the victor of Valmy, rode into the British camp under a flag of truce with a request for an armistice, and a proposal. The proposal was for a convention under which the beleaguered French Army of Portugal, faced with a British Army and surrounded by outraged Portuguese, should be evacuated back to France. Not only this, but it should also be evacuated in British ships and allowed to take with it all its arms and all its loot. With hardly a second's hesitation, Dalrymple and Burrard agreed.

The French and British duly drew up an agreement, the Convention of Cintra, and the French army sailed away to France. The news of the Convention reached London on 3 September 1808, four days after the news of Vimeiro had been celebrated, and the Government and people were first appalled and then furious. Dalrymple, Burrard and Wellington were execrated, only Moore escaping the general condemnation, and the three of them were swiftly relieved of all command in the Peninsula and ordered home to face a Court of Inquiry.

The Court sat at the Chelsea Hospital on 14 November 1808, and after hearing the evidence duly whitewashed all three defendants, which was the result desired by the Horse Guards. Burrard and Dalrymple were allowed to slip into obscurity and were never employed again. Fortunately, in the case of General Wellesley, the unravelling of the facts surrounding the armistice and the Convention of Cintra restored him to popularity. He had only signed the armistice when required to do so by his superiors, and he had not signed the Convention or endorsed its humiliating terms. Duly exonerated, he was restored to duty, taking up a fresh post in Ireland.

The defeats of Bailén and Vimeiro convinced Napoleon that he must take a personal hand in the Peninsula. He ordered three veteran corps of the *Grande Armée*, more than 100,000 men under the command of the redoubtable marshals Ney, Victor and Mortier, to leave their positions on the Elbe and march for Spain. There Napoleon would join them when he had secured his eastern flank against the possibility of attack from Austria.

To do this, Napoleon must impose his will yet again on the young Czar Alexander, whose passion for his friendship and ideals had cooled during the twelve months since Tilsit. Napoleon invited the Czar to a conference at Erfurt in Germany on 27 September 1808. He hoped to impress Alexander with the strength of the *Grande Armée*, and to secure his support against any attack from Austria or Prussia by means of a few territorial concessions. To add to his lustre Napoleon ordered the attendance of various princes from the Confederation of the Rhine, for hard bargaining and veiled threats were to be backed by pageantry, balls, and army reviews. None of this pomp had much effect on the Czar.

Alexander was not an experienced politician, but he was no fool. Since Tilsit he had come to see that the divergence between French and Russian interests was all but irreconcilable. The French reversals in Spain, now widely known in Europe, weakened Napoleon's position and Alexander was able to exact concessions. He obliged Napoleon to confirm his acceptance of Russia's occupation of Finland, and to concur with further Russian advances in the Balkans. Napoleon also agreed to reduce Prussia's war indemnity (following Tilsit) by 20 million francs, although with new campaigns looming in Spain he was short of funds. He further agreed not to interfere in any conflict between Russia and Turkey and accepted a Russian offer of 'mediation' between France and Great Britain.

All the Emperor received in return for these concessions was a vague promise of a Russian 'denouncement' if Austria, now rapidly re-arming, should attack France while Napoleon was engaged in Spain. He came away from Erfurt feeling that he had been out-manoeuvred, but there was little he could do about it. His divisions were already marching on Spain, and he hurried south to join them on the Ebro.

In 1808, some three hundred years after its unification under Ferdinand and Isabella – *los Reyes Catolicos* – Spain was still scarcely a nation. The peoples of its ancient kingdoms and provinces – Catalonia, Castile, Aragon, Andalucía, Valencia – were all very different, and the provincial Juntas which came into being after the abdication of Prince Ferdinand were reluctant to cede their local authority to any national executive. Such disunity promised Napoleon every opportunity of conquering Spain piecemeal, playing off one province against another.

The Central Junta of 35 members which met at Madrid in September 1808 was no more than an assembly of factions, without any agenda or rules of procedure, or any authority to enforce whatever decisions it might arrive at. Orders, often conflicting, went out from Madrid directing the movements of the various provincial armies now marching about the Peninsula, but the vital appointment of a commander-in-chief was not even discussed and, indeed, the Spanish generals were not noted for their competence. The best, General Castaños, the victor of Bailén, was very unpopular with the guerrillas and the provincial militias, whom he in turn openly despised. The newly-promoted General Blake was an experienced officer, but the defeat at Medina del Rio Seco in July had dimmed both his reputation and that of the aged General Cuesta. The latter refused to accept his dismissal by the Central Junta and stayed in command of his army. None of the provincial armies was fed, paid, supplied or supported.

The Central Junta could call on three main armies. In the northwest of the country near Reiñosa to the north of León, General Blake commanded the Army of Galicia with 30,000 men; away to the east and south, somewhere around Logroño, lay the Army of the Centre under General Castaños numbering about 35,000 men; and in the east lay General Joseph Palafox's Army of Aragon, with about 25,000 men in the field plus another 4,000 pinning down General Duhesme in Barcelona. Other forces included the Army of Estremadura, some 14,000 men under General Galluzzo, which was roaming the *meseta* near Burgos, and General La Romana's 10,000-strong division, rescued from Sweden and recently shipped back to Santander by the Royal Navy. To this total of about 125,000 can be added tens of thousands of guerrillas in small roving bands.

The only other efficient and significant force in the Peninsula when Napoleon arrived was the 20,000-strong British Army of Portugal, now commanded by General Sir John Moore. As General Moore was probably the finest soldier in Europe, it would have been sensible for the Central Junta to place all the armies of Spain and Portugal under his command, but – given the general Spanish antipathy towards foreigners – there was no likelihood of this. Sir John Moore left Portugal in October, suffering great delays and difficulties but hoping to effect a junction with one or more of the Spanish armies. He was not impressed by the plan eventually conceived by the Central Junta, describing it on first sight as 'A sort of gibberish'. The proposal was to involve the northern Spanish armies in a double envelopment of the French forces now concentrated around Burgos and in Navarre. Blake's Army of Galicia was to march east to join Moore, coming north from Lisbon, while Castaños and Palafox were to attack Marshal Moncey at Pamplona. The rest (effectively, Galluzzo's 12,000-strong Army of Estremadura) would hold Ney and Bessières around Burgos and along the Ebro.

This plan stood no chance of success and suited the French perfectly. Like all armies plagued by guerrillas, the French longed to fight against a regular Spanish army, sure in the knowledge that there was none which could stand against them in open battle. The French also had a clear superiority of numbers and the advantage of interior lines. Blake's army in the east was separated by the French army and 200 miles of arid country from the army of Palafox and Castaños in Aragon, while the idea that any division-size Spanish army under Galluzzo could stop French veterans commanded by the mighty Ney and Bessières doing exactly what they wanted, is almost laughable. Ney and Bessières opened the campaign by lashing out at Castaños and swiftly occupied Logroño. This gave the Spanish generals pause and while Castaños hesitated and then withdrew towards Saragossa, Napoleon arrived in Spain.

The Emperor was soon well aware of Spanish positions and intentions, and these suited him very well: the more they attempted to envelop his forces along the Ebro, the deeper they would march into a trap of their own making. Napoleon's plan was that Ney and Moncey should thrash Castaños and Palafox in the east, while Victor and Lefebvre enveloped and destroyed Blake in the north. Meanwhile the Emperor, with the rest of the army plus two reserve corps, including the one commanded by Junot and recently repatriated from Portugal following the Convention of Cintra, would cross the *meseta* and the Sierra de Guadarrama and retake Madrid.

This fine and simple plan failed to take into account the British army under Sir John Moore which was somewhere to the west. Moore does not appear anywhere in Napoleon's calculations, which is surprising, since Junot was now on hand with details of Vimeiro and what British infantry could do when they put their minds to it. Napoleon, having laid his plans, seemed content to pause while the Spanish armies advanced within striking distance.

On 31 October 1808 Marshal Lefebvre's corps attacked Blake's army as it straggled across the Picos de Europa mountains between Reiñosa and Bilbao. Lefebvre's intention was to prevent Blake reaching the coast and making contact with the Royal Navy, but his rewards were slight; the attack alerted Blake to his peril, and he retreated swiftly to the west. Napoleon ordered Lefebvre to harry Blake with Victor's corps in support. The Emperor's own part of the campaign opened on 7 November but his armies had scarcely left their bivouacs when news arrived of another reversal.

While pursuing Blake to the west, Lefebvre and Victor had allowed their divisions to become scattered on the mountain roads north-west of Burgos and Blake was unexpectedly reinforced by the arrival of General La Romana's 10,000-strong Spanish Corps. General La Romana was a fighter, and the Spaniards turned and fell on the French vanguard under General Vilatte. In the ensuing stiff fight Vilatte's division, unsupported by the rest of the corps, lost a number of men killed and many more taken prisoner. That check delivered, Blake and La Romana led their men away into Galicia.

Lefebvre was admonished, Victor was placed in command of the western wing of the French army and the pursuit continued. On 10 November 1808 Victor caught up with Blake near the town of Espinosa, where after two days of fighting the Army of Galicia was broken and Blake's men fled, but it was not an easy victory. The Spanish had held their ground and fought Victor's men to a standstill. The rest of Napoleon's plan was going even less well. Marshal Bessières had failed to take Burgos, so on 9 November he too was removed from command and replaced by Marshal Soult, under whom the IInd Corps promptly and easily overwhelmed the 10,000-strong Army of Estremadura. Napoleon occupied Burgos on 10 November to put the French campaign back on schedule, and the Spanish front began to unravel.

On 11 November Soult was sent north to take up the pursuit of Blake's Army of Galicia, now fleeing west across the mountains, while Ney's corps went south to clear the way towards Aranda de Duero. At the cost of abandoning his baggage train, Blake managed to elude Soult's thrust, and got away across the mountains to join General Moore. Unaware of Moore's presence, Soult, Victor and Lefebvre abandoned the pursuit of Blake and marched south onto the flat *campo* of Castile to Saldaña and Carrión de los Condes, ready to follow Napoleon to Madrid. From Aranda, Ney was to hook east and north to encircle Castaños and the Spanish Army of the Centre, so opening the road to the Guadarrama mountains. Napoleon now had a firm grasp on the campaign, but clear-cut success continued to elude him – not least because, thanks to the vigilant Spanish guerrillas watching every road, communications were difficult and his orders to the widely separated marshals frequently failed to arrive.

In Aragon and Catalonia, Moncey and Ney with 27,000 men were preparing to envelop the 45,000-strong armies of the squabbling Castaños and Palafox, uselessly engaged in a bitter and distracting dispute over who was actually in command. Not until 21 November, when news arrived that French formations were approaching Calahorra and Tudela, did the Spanish generals realize that a trap was about to be sprung. Marshal Lannes had now replaced Marshal Moncey, and on 23 November he attacked and defeated Castaños's army at Tudela, the Spanish losing more than 4,000 men and a large quantity of artillery. Marshal Ney, however, failed to get his VIth Corps in Castaños's rear. The two days allowed for his infantry to cover the 120 miles from Aranda de Duero to Tudela were not enough, even for Michel Ney. Napoleon was displeased by this failure, for once again his hope of total victory slipped away as Castaños and his battered army retreated towards Cuenca.

Despite such setbacks, the French position in Spain had improved remarkably since Napoleon's arrival. All the Spanish armies had been mauled or scattered, and the roads to Madrid, even to Lisbon, appeared to be open. The Emperor ordered his men south across the *meseta* towards the distant Guadarrama mountains, with only guerrilla activity and the usual supply problems to cause him any concern. The barren plains of Castile offered poor foraging to French armies accustomed to live off the country, the towns and villages had already been stripped of supplies, and the problem was exacerbated by the guerrilas. Hunger began to stalk the ranks of the French army.

It is impossible to overstate the effect of the Spanish *guerrilleros*: they cost the French army men, reduced French confidence, and denied the French the means of controlling events. No one was safe, by day or night, from their watchful attentions. Many of Napoleon's personal aides and staff officers disappeared without trace while attempting to deliver his orders, and strong detachments had to be left along the roads as the French marched south to Aranda de Duero. They arrived there on 23 November, and received their first news of the British army. General Moore had emerged from the mountains of Portugal and was said to be approaching Salamanca.

Napoleon decided to ignore this potential threat. His *Armée d'Espagne* had received further reinforcements which included the Imperial Guard, and with Castaños defeated it was clearly time for the next phase of the campaign: the advance on Madrid.

In Madrid, the Central Junta reacted to events by dismissing Castaños and Blake, their two best generals, and no decision was taken on who should replace them. The Junta then directed Sir John Moore to march on the Duero, gathering up Blake's army on the way, and so threaten Napoleon's communications – a task already being more than capably performed by the *guerrilleros*. The defence of Madrid was left to 21,000 assorted troops under General Eguia, the commander of the Reserve Army, who set off to guard the two passes over the Guadarrama to the north of Madrid.

The French advance over the 6,000-foot-high Guadarrama mountains began on 30 November 1808. Despite the onset of winter, Napoleon's army easily brushed aside Eguia's forces, and French cavalry patrols entered Madrid on 2 December. After a heavy bombardment of the Retiro on 4 December, the city surrendered on the 5th. French infantry filed into the city, hot on the heels of the Junta fleeing to the fortress of Badajoz on the Portuguese frontier. It had taken Napoleon just a month to recapture all the Spanish territory lost since the *dos de Mayo*; his brother Joseph could now return to his capital. Napoleon was now able to turn his full attention to the task of defeating Sir John Moore and his army.

6

The Retreat to Corunna:

1808–1809

> The position of the Spanish armies I cannot understand.
> They are separated, the one in Biscay, the other in Aragon,
> on the two flanks of the French, leaving the whole of Spain
> exposed to French incursions, and leaving the British Army
> to be attacked before it is united.
>   Lieutenant-General Sir John Moore, November 1808

WHILE NAPOLEON WAS re-establishing French domination in Spain, a British army of 20,000 men under General Sir John Moore had been making its painful way north from Lisbon, aiming to link up with the Spanish armies operating in Old Castile. Moore, appointed to the command of the British army in Portugal in October 1808 while the conduct of its previous commanders was under scrutiny in England, had received strict instructions not to hazard his country's only field army unnecessarily. He would require reinforcements from Britain and support from the Spanish forces in the field in order to engage in any useful action.

Moore intended to rendezvous somewhere near Valladolid with 12,000 reinforcements under General Sir David Baird, who were due to land at Corunna in mid October. They were then to combine with the Spanish forces and undertake some decisive blow against the French.

Sir John Moore, now aged 46, was a fine general and a superb leader of men, with long experience of the difficulties and frustrations of war. He had been a professional soldier since he was fifteen, when his father, a Glasgow doctor, purchased him a commission in the 51st Foot. Like Wellesley he was a Member of Parliament, and like Wellesley and most generals of the time, he enjoyed some political influence – he had been a close friend of William Pitt and was much admired by the Commander-in-Chief of the British army, the Duke of York.

Moore had been wounded in action five times in the course of many campaigns, and had fought the French in Egypt and in the Baltic. If anyone could out-fox them it was Moore, and that he failed to do so indicates the difficulties facing any foreign commander attempting to work with or support the curiously-led armies of Spain. That he made the attempt was to his credit, and led to his downfall. It was never intended that the British army should attack the French on its own. Moore's orders, in a letter from Castlereagh dated 25 September 1808, are quite specific on this point:

> His Majesty, having determined to employ a corps of not less than 30,000 infantry and 5,000 cavalry *to cooperate with the Spanish Armies in the expulsion of the French from that Kingdom*, has been greatly pleased to entrust you as the Commander-in-Chief of this force.

Moore's intention had been to move immediately into Spain and attack the French by November, before the onset of winter made campaigning impossible. He was also aware of the political importance of the British being seen to be doing something in support of their Spanish allies. Misled by poor maps and much incorrect advice from his Spanish and Portuguese advisers, he sent his artillery and cavalry into Spain by a more circuitous route than that taken by his infantry. In consequence, having arrived in Salamanca with his infantry on 13 November, Moore was then forced to wait for his cavalry and artillery to come up. Napoleon and the French, meanwhile, were sweeping the Spanish forces from their path away to the east.

Baird's transports had arrived off Corunna on 13 October, which should have allowed him plenty of time for the junction with General Moore, but Spanish bureaucracy got in the way. The Governor of Corunna refused him permission to land. General Baird's famous temper and the resultant argument kept his men afloat for a further two weeks. When they finally streamed ashore, on 26 October 1808, it was discovered that no transport wagons had been provided by the Spanish; nor was there any food. Baird had been sent out without any money, and he was obliged to borrow from the English plenipotentiary in Spain, Mr Frere, in order to provide transport for his equipment and some food for his men; it was not until the end of November 1808 that he was able to leave Corunna. From there he advanced to Astorga, south of the Montes de León, and sent gallopers to Moore for orders. General Baird eventually joined Moore's army on 20 December 1808.

As he marched north-east from Lisbon to Salamanca via the frontier fortress of Almeida, Moore saw that the route followed by his infantry would have been perfectly adequate for his cavalry and light artillery. The delays caused by this unnecessary splitting of his force and Baird's difficulties meant that before Moore was in a position to combine effectively with any Spanish forces, they had been scattered on the *meseta* of Castile and in the Cantabrian *cordillera* by Napoleon and his marshals. The defeat of the Spanish now left Moore dangerously exposed to the full attention of the Emperor and his armies.

Fortunately, Napoleon decided to press on to Madrid and consolidate his gains there, assuming, with some reason, that Moore, finding himself without support, would retreat to Lisbon. In the circumstances this would have been sensible, but Moore's orders had been to co-operate with the Spanish armies, and he would not abandon his task so readily. There was also the political element to consider, for it was felt necessary in London that support be given to the Spanish cause. As Moore noted in his diary at Salamanca, 'We have no business here, but being here it would never do to abandon the Spaniards without a struggle.'

Moore was under particular pressure from Hookham Frere, the British Minister in Spain and a close friend of George Canning, the Foreign Secretary. Frere had little grasp of military affairs and quite failed to appreciate the difficulties Moore was under in attempting to co-operate with the Spanish. A passionate supporter of the Spanish cause, Frere chose to believe that Moore was simply reluctant to fight, though how Moore was to fight 200,000 veteran French troops with an army of 30,000 redcoats and no support from his Spanish allies, Frere was unable to explain.

Napoleon, in Madrid, was so sure that Moore must and would retreat that on 5 December he issued a bulletin to the Spanish people claiming that they had been '. . . abandoned by their British Allies, who had refused to fight and were even now running back to Portugal'. This bulletin encouraged Hookham Frere to send a particularly offensive and unjust letter to General Moore:

After the representations made to you from other quarters, I can hardly hope that a remonstrance from me can have any effect, but this much I must say, that if the British Army had been sent abroad with the express purpose of doing as much harm as possible to the Spanish cause . . . the measures now announced have completely fulfilled that purpose.

General Moore had no intention of retreating to Portugal without a fight but could not fight without support, and on November 28 he heard the news of Blake's defeat at Tudela and it seemed unlikely that he could expect much help from that quarter. However, his cavalry and artillery finally arrived at Salamanca on 3 and 4 December, having followed a wide detour which had taken them within twenty miles of Madrid. The prospect of effecting a junction with Baird's forces also seemed brighter and news received on 5 December of events in Madrid determined him to make a bold stroke.

The news which prompted Moore to action was that the people of Madrid were preparing for a desperate resistance against the French army assembled about the capital. In fact, Madrid had surrendered on 4 December. He resolved therefore to fall on the French flank at Valladolid and harry their communications. He supposed the Emperor to be more anxious to drive the British from Spain than to secure any particular province, and that Napoleon would be likely to concentrate his forces to this end. Such action by the British would demonstrate support for the Spanish cause and give the Spaniards in the south a breathing space in which to recover their courage and organize their defence. Moore was well aware of the risk of an unsupported advance deeper into Spain. As he wrote to Baird at Astorga, 'If Madrid falls, we shall have to run for it.'

News of the surrender of Madrid reached Moore on 9 December, but he decided to press on, hoping to cut the French lines of communication around Valladolid or Burgos. The plan was fraught with risk, since the exact position of the various French corps was not known, and winter was closing in, but perhaps Moore felt that he had changed his plans often enough. He marched north-eastward from Salamanca on 11 December and on 13 December, by a happy accident, a despatch with orders from Marshal Berthier, Napoleon's Chief-of-Staff, to Marshal Soult came into his hands. It contained the first reliable information Moore had received about the size of the French armies in Spain – about 200,000 – an indication of their whereabouts, and of Napoleon's plans. Discovering that Marshal Soult, with 20,000 men, was in an isolated position on the river Carrión north of Valladolid, and that the Emperor was unaware of his own position, Moore swung his army north to Sahagún, aiming to cut Soult's route down the old pilgrim road, the *Camino Frances*, that led to Santiago de Compostela in Galicia.

Baird finally joined Moore on 20 December, but brought the disappointing news that Soult had halted at Saldaña, north of Carrión
de los Condes and some distance north-east of Sahagún, to await
reinforcements from Marshal Ney. On 21 December Moore's cavalry
won a sharp little engagement with a body of French dragoons at
Sahagún, and he established his headquarters there. This morale-
boosting victory was a nasty surprise for Soult, who had had no idea
of the British presence. Soult concentrated his forces at Saldaña and
sent couriers to Madrid, while General La Romana, having succeeded
Blake, was bringing up the remnants of the Army of Galicia to
Moore's aid. Unknown to Soult or to Moore, however, Napoleon was
already on his way from Madrid with all the force at his disposal.

On receiving the news of Moore's advance towards Burgos on 18
December, Napoleon ordered his army back across the snow-filled
Guadarrama, himself leading them through blizzard conditions and
then at breakneck speed across the plains, determined to catch and
thrash this impertinent British army. By 23 December he was just
south of Valladolid and Moore, learning of his swift advance, knew
he had no option but to retreat, abandoning any idea of attacking
Soult – an engagement which would have simply invited Napoleon to
fall on his rear. The British army wheeled west down the Pilgrim
Road towards Astorga, not a moment too soon, marching hard for
the safety of Corunna.

Retreat is never good for morale, and few retreats were as bad as that
on Corunna. Rifleman Harris of the 95th, part of General Craufurd's
Light Brigade, recalled in his memoirs how the 95th were advancing
by night towards Carrión de los Condes, trudging over the frozen
meseta under a full moon, when a dragoon galloped past to hand
Craufurd a letter which he read as he rode along, turning it this way
and that to catch the moonlight. Then he turned in his saddle and
bellowed 'Halt!' The Light Brigade slammed to attention and within
minutes were marching back to Sahagún, their spirits in their boots.

The British army in Spain had been constantly on the march for
three months, but apart from the victory of their cavalry at Sahagún
had apparently achieved very little. The men in the ranks were heart-
ily sick of the Spanish people, the Spanish climate, and the constant
changes of plan. They could not know that by their very presence
in Spain and their unanticipated threat to the flank of the French
communications, they had thrown Napoleon's plans into disarray. It
seemed that they were running away; morale plummeted, and straggling, looting and drunkenness soon began to thin their ranks. Like

all the armies of the day Moore's was accompanied by a great number of non-combatants and civilians, including many soldiers' wives and children, sometimes mere toddlers or babes-in-arms. In that bitter winter retreat, harried by the French, their families' pitiful plight added to the soldiers' misery.

General Moore cannot be blamed for his decision to retreat. If he and his officers can be blamed for anything, it is for failing to explain its necessity to the men, who simply thought it shameful. Moore's situation was as straightforward as it was desperate. The full weight of the French army in Spain, outnumbering his force six to one, was being deployed against him, and it was already clear that to extricate his army would not be easy. Fortunately, the deteriorating winter weather hampered the French advance as much as it did the British retreat, and the cavalry protected the rear with spirit and skill. On 29 December, as the main body fell back on Astorga, Lord Paget's hussars wheeled about and at Benavente cut to pieces the *chasseurs à cheval* of the Imperial Guard, taking prisoner their commander, General Lefebvre-Desnoëttes. The morale of the British cavalry, constantly in action, was high; that of the infantry, underemployed and too often retreating, was not.

Napoleon had been urging on the pursuit in person, but Lefebvre-Desnoëttes' capture and news from Paris prompted him to delegate the harrying of the British to Ney and Soult. Within days Napoleon was back at the Tuileries, and he never returned to the Peninsula.

Moore's retreat from Astorga to Corunna now became a race between his straggling 25,000 men and Soult's 36,000, closely supported by a further 16,000 under Ney. Its story is recounted as one of the epics in the glorious annals of the British army, but survivors' tales and official histories show the dark side. Many of the soldiers were sick and exhausted. Typhus was ravaging the ranks. Clothes were in rags, and boots worn out so that many of the men marched barefoot in the snow. Food was short. Towns and villages were looted and wrecked by drunken soldiers. General Moore took the drastic step of ordering the execution of a soldier taken in the act of plundering, and floggings were a daily occurrence, sometimes with the enemy in plain sight. Only a battle, the scent of victory, the chance to hit back and end this demoralizing retreat, could restore the army to some semblance of order.

Faced with the disintegration of his army, General Moore decided to stand and fight while he still had troops to fight with. On 6 January he offered battle at Lugo, but Soult, aware of what was happening from stragglers and deserters, was cunning enough to wait and unwill-

ing to engage. The retreat began again, and by 11 January three of
Moore's divisions were in Corunna, with Paget's cavalry bickering
with the French four miles further back. At Corunna, Moore's dis-
pirited army received a further blow; there was no sign of the Royal
Navy in the harbour, and Soult was coming up hard on their heels.

A battle now could hardly be avoided and the British soldiers were
glad of it. They took up defensive positions about the town, but there
was then a further delay while Soult paused until Ney's corps came
up. The Royal Navy finally appeared on 14 January and that night
Moore began to evacuate his sick and wounded, those horses worth
saving and some of his guns. He had lost more than 5,000 men in the
retreat, nearly twenty per cent of his army, and was determined to
save what he could of the remainder.

By the afternoon of 15 January only 15,000 infantry and nine guns
were left to hold Soult, who finally attacked on the afternoon of 16
January. At last the infantry had their battle, and Soult could make
no headway against their steady volleys. By evening the British line
had advanced, the French were falling back in confusion, and Sir John
Moore had been mortally wounded. General Hope, upon whom the
command devolved, judged it prudent to continue the embarkation
during the night, and the transports finally sailed on 18 January 1809.

The French lost about 2,000 men at Corunna, some ten per cent
of their force – the British perhaps 800, and Sir John Moore. He was
buried in the citadel at Corunna, and Marshal Soult later erected a
splendid memorial over his grave.

Moore's fellow countrymen were much less appreciative. Hookham
Frere, who had urged Moore to take action while ignoring the difficulties that surrounded him, was among the first to blame him for
the retreat and for the losses suffered by his army. Shock and outrage
were widespread when the transports bearing Moore's exhausted and
typhus-wracked army arrived in England. Wellesley, appointed on 15
April 1809 to command the British army in the Peninsula, stood aloof
from the general condemnation. He had himself suffered interference
from higher authority and realized the difficulties of working with the
Spanish and Portuguese.

The perceptive among those in Britain, at the time and later, valued
Moore's actions in the Peninsula for their effect on Napoleon's strategy
for Spain. But for Moore, Napoleon would have been able to
consolidate his gains at Madrid and complete the subjugation of
Spain, perhaps as far south as the Sierra Morena. As it was, he
returned to France and left the war in Spain and Portugal to his
marshals, who failed to cope with either General Wellesley, the Pen-

insular Army, or the Spanish guerrillas. The 'Spanish ulcer' eventually drained the Emperor's strength, and it was Sir John Moore who kept it open during that bitter winter campaign of 1808–9. That apart, General Sir John Moore's most enduring contribution to eventual victory was the effect of his methods on the regiments of the British army.

General Sir John Moore altered the very nature of the army by changing the way the private soldier was regarded, treated, and trained by his superiors. Moore turned the army from a crude and sullen force, brutalized by its officers, into a proud, flexible fighting machine, and achieved this not by diktat but by leadership and example. His belief in what good leadership could achieve eventually spread throughout the British army to give Sir Arthur Wellesley those fine soldiers, and those superb regiments, with which he defeated the French. Sir John's final victory was achieved by Wellington at Waterloo, years after Moore went to his lonely grave on that rainy winter morning in Corunna.

7

Austria and Portugal:

1809

In conformity with a declaration made by the Emperor of
Austria to the Emperor Napoleon, I hereby apprise the
General-in-Chief of the French Army that I have Orders
to advance with my troops and treat as enemies all who
oppose me.

> The Archduke Charles of Austria
> to Marshal Lefebvre: 9 April 1809.

ALL THE VICTORIES of Wellington and his Peninsular Army should
not obscure that fact that for most of the Napoleonic Wars the campaigns in the Peninsula were a sideshow. The Emperor felt able to
leave the war in Spain to his marshals, while he dedicated himself to
more important matters on the Central Front. History may say that
in this the Emperor was mistaken, but that was not how it appeared
at the time.

Napoleon abandoned his personal pursuit of General Moore when
it became apparent that the chance of destroying Britain's field army
was gone, at the same time as he received information that trouble
was brewing in Paris and with Austria. It may be significant that his
only sight of the British *army* prior to Waterloo showed it in headlong
retreat before him. This reinforced his conviction that the British
were indifferent soldiers led by incapable generals, and the subsequent
defeats suffered by his marshals in the Peninsula did not cause him to
think otherwise. The marshals were not Napoleon. In this excess of
confidence lay the seeds of his later defeat. Leaving Spain before he
had conquered it was a fundamental error, ensuring as it did that he
was then committed to war on two widely separated fronts.

Napoleon returned to Paris on 23 January 1809 and rapidly squashed the rumours of his decline put about by Fouché, his Minister of Police, and Talleyrand, his former Foreign Minister. Fouché was motivated by natural craftiness and private ambition, but Talleyrand, for all his duplicity and treachery, sincerely believed that Napoleon would eventually overreach himself and drag France down with him when he fell. Talleyrand detected the first signs of approaching Nemesis after Tilsit with the Emperor's decision to extend the Continental System to Portugal. Making no secret of his doubts over the sincerity of the Franco-Russian accord, Talleyrand resigned as Napoleon's Foreign Minister and entered into discreet communications with the hostile courts of Europe – in particular with Count Metternich, the Austrian Foreign Minister – intimating that the French people were sick of war.

The Emperor could still dismiss political intrigues as irrelevant, but his economic and military problems were far more serious. The war in Spain and the clash that was coming with Austria required soldiers, but the supply of recruits was already beginning to falter. The rising of the *dos de Mayo*, the defeat and capture of an entire French army at Bailén, Wellesley's early victories in Portugal and Moore's foray across Castile, were all events which had shaken the façade of French invincibility.

During the years following their defeat at Austerlitz in 1805 the Austrians had rebuilt and retrained their army, which was now the focus of national hope rather than the tool of military ambition. Determined to wipe out the shame of Austerlitz and regain the territories surrendered to France, the Austrians saw that with Napoleon checked in Spain and his armies divided between the Peninsula and the garrisons of Italy and Prussia, the time had come for war. Archduke Charles, the commander of the Austrian forces, had two prerequisites for an attack on Napoleon: a well-trained army of at least 350,000 men, and allies with forces already in the field. Allies he already had, in Britain, Spain and Portugal, while the Austrian army, better equipped, reorganized into corps in the French fashion, and with a number of regiments beginning to train in the skirmishing tactics of the *voltigeurs*, was a different proposition from that which had crumbled before the French at Ulm and Austerlitz.

The 'wild card' in the impending clash was Russia. At Tilsit, and with greater reluctance at Erfurt, Czar Alexander had agreed to support Napoleon in any war with Austria: 'In the case of Austria declaring war against France, the Emperor of Russia undertakes to denounce Austria and make common cause with France.' However, the precise nature of his 'support' was undefined and the 'common cause' was dependent upon Austria being the aggressor. Ostensibly France and Russia were allies, but it was an alliance open to interpretation; Czar Alexander's was that he should not be openly hostile to French intentions. What he might do on the declaration of war was another matter. From Talleyrand, Count Metternich had received the impression that the French nation was weary of war, and the information from his Russian contacts was that the Czar had no intention of intervening in any fight between France and Austria. If Napoleon was disappointed by the Czar's attitude after the promises of Tilsit and Erfurt, he cannot have been surprised. His confidence in the successful outcome of any war with Austria was based on his own resources – some 200,000 men – plus another 100,000 soldiers to be provided, with varying degrees of enthusiasm, by his allies in the Confederation of the Rhine. Nevertheless, it was becoming increasingly difficult to find sufficient conscripts for Napoleon's various armies. In December 1808 more recruits had been called in from the Classes of 1806 to 1809, plus 80,000 from the Class of 1810, which should not have been summoned for at least eighteen months. The cream of these new recruits was channelled into another élite formation, the 'Young Guard'; a formidable addition to the army, but one which never achieved the status of the Old or Middle Guards. The Old Guard was summoned hurriedly from Spain and such measures brought in another 110,000 men, but the Emperor's resources of manpower were becoming sorely stretched.

The financial resources of France had been so strained by incessant war that the clothing, equipment and provisioning of Napoleon's troops left much to be desired, and in drawing on corps of raw conscripts and recruits, quality was now sacrificed to quantity but the calibre of Napoleon's commanders remained high. The marshals and generals now commanding corps or divisions in the *Grande Armée de l'Allemagne* or in Italy included Masséna, Lefebvre, Oudinot, Marmont, and the formidable Davout. With these, and his excellent Chief-of-Staff, Berthier, a man who could reduce the most complicated plan to a clear set of fighting instructions, Napoleon could regard the coming campaign with some degree of confidence.

He anticipated that the Austrians would attack on two fronts, in Italy and along the Danube valley into Bavaria, their aim to recover their Italian territories and, by defeating the French on the Danube and entering German territory, to cause defections from the Confederation of the Rhine. An Austrian victory might even encourage the Prussians to re-enter the struggle against France.

Prince Eugène de Beauharnais, the Empress Josephine's son, was entrusted with the task of coping with any Austrian insurgence in Italy, leaving Napoleon free to deal with the main threat along the Danube. Napoleon intended to concentrate his forces between Ratisbon, Landshut, Augsburg and Donauwörth, but such a concentration could not reasonably be accomplished before mid-April. The Emperor placed Berthier in command, instructing him that if the Austrians should attack before 15 April the army was to fall back westwards to the Lech. By the end of the first week of April, Davout was north of the Danube with the IIIrd Corps, marching on Ratisbon, but it had become evident that the concentration of the French forces could not be carried out before the Austrians would be in a position to intervene.

The French had about 89,000 men in five groups strung out along a front approximately 112 miles in length, with a further 76,000 men between Donauwörth and Augsburg, when on 10 April Archduke Charles crossed the Bavarian frontier with 176,000 men. The first intimation of the Austrian attack was contained in a polite note sent by Archduke Charles to Marshal Lefebvre on 9 April: 'In conformity with a declaration made by His Majesty the Emperor of Austria to the Emperor Napoleon, I hereby inform the Commander of the French Army that I have orders to advance with my troops and treat as enemies all who oppose me.' Twenty-four hours later the first of the Austrian troops were over the River Inn and pouring into Bavaria.

Napoleon was still in Paris and Berthier, though a superb staff officer, was quite hopeless as a field commander. His attempts to counter the sudden Austrian advance threw the various French corps commanders into confusion. While Berthier sent frantic appeals to Paris for Napoleon to come and take command, the Austrians continued to advance. News of this advance reached Napoleon on the evening of 12 April and he arrived at his Field Headquarters near Donauwörth on 17 April 1809. On the previous day Lefebvre's 30,000-strong Bavarian Corps had been attacked near Landshut by six full corps of the Austrian army under Archduke Charles, and the French army was in danger of being cut in two.

Napoleon's first requirement was a full concentration of the *Grande Armée*. Confused by Berthier, the French forces were now widely scattered on both sides of the Danube. Davout, always superb in a crisis, had sent troops to occupy the vital crossings at Ratisbon, but was now too far forward, his flanks clearly exposed. Napoleon ordered him to fall back south-westwards on Neustadt, while Masséna was to advance on Ingolstadt from Augsburg. Napoleon's information was incorrect; he thought the Austrian thrust towards Ratisbon consisted of a single corps when in fact a full army of six corps was advancing south of the Danube, with a further two corps sweeping towards Ratisbon from the north. Davout's position was potentially disastrous, but his brilliant generalship enabled him to throw back an Austrian attack on the 19th, aided by Archduke Charles's failure to pursue his advantage energetically.

Lefebvre's Bavarian Corps was ordered to contest every foot of the ground as they fell back from the River Isar, to give Davout's troops time to retreat. On the south bank of the Danube, Masséna and Oudinot came forward with their corps to form the left flank of the Emperor's line, and as Davout's men fell back they regrouped on the Emperor's right around Geisenfeld. A garrison of 2,000 men remained in Ratisbon to delay either the Austrian seizure of this important crossing or the junction of the Austrian wings, or to hold the city until Napoleon's army came east once again. Within hours of his arrival, the *Grande Armée* felt the benefits of Napoleon's military genius and firm command.

On 20 April, Davout and Lefebvre having rejoined the *Grande Armée*, Napoleon ordered his forces to advance. On the 21st the Austrian left wing was cut off as it was retiring upon Landshut, and Davout forced the right wing to retreat. The decisive blow against the Austrians was struck on 22 April with the battle of Eckmühl, fifteen miles south-east of Ratisbon.

Napoleon had taken part in the fighting on the 21st and pursued the Austrians as far as Landshut, from where he despatched Masséna to follow their retreat along the Isar, believing at this stage that he had the main body of the Austrian army before him. During the night of the 21st/22nd he seems to have realized his error, and that the main Austrian forces must still be in the north, towards Ratisbon. Issuing orders that Davout, Oudinot and the cavalry should concentrate with all speed at Eckmühl, he rode back from Landshut on the Ratisbon road, arriving as the engagement between the advance forces began.

The Austrians had not the mobility of the French, nor had their troops completely mastered their new training, and Archduke Charles's men were not able to hold out against the French until their reserves came up. The Austrians were driven back in considerable disorder, but were saved from complete disaster by the fatigue of the French troops. Napoleon stopped the pursuit, and Archduke Charles was able to restore order and withdraw towards Ratisbon, which had fallen into Austrian hands on the 20th, the bridge intact. The French reached Ratisbon on the morning of the 23rd, but the Austrians were able to hold out until the last of their stragglers had reached the safety of the north bank of the Danube. It was here that Napoleon was slightly wounded, for the only time in his career. Leaving Davout at Ratisbon to observe the Archduke's retreat, Napoleon rode after Masséna in pursuit of the Austrian left, under General Hiller. Their rearguard, checking Masséna at Ebelsburg, enabled Hiller's men to reach the north bank of the Danube.

Ratisbon had been recaptured, the Austrians had lost 30,000 men, the road to Vienna lay open, and those in Prussia and Russia who had assumed (or hoped) that Napoleon's military prowess was in decline were forced to revise their opinions. Napoleon pushed the whole of his army down the right bank of the Danube and entered Vienna on 12 May.

Archduke Charles was still in the field. Although his army and his confidence had been shaken, he was now regrouping his forces in Bohemia and preparing to renew the struggle. He effected a junction with Hiller in the vicinity of Wagram, picketing the line of the Danube and collecting all the boats. Czar Alexander had failed to come in on Napoleon's side, and further battles on the Danube were inevitable.

Nor was this all. During the brief pause while the Emperor advanced on Vienna, there came disquieting news from Portugal. That persistent British general, Sir Arthur Wellesley, had returned to Lisbon and taken command of the British and Portuguese armies on 20 April, the day of Eckmühl. Three weeks later, on 11 May 1809, he had defeated Soult's army at Oporto.

Wellesley was a man who could learn from mistakes, his own, and other people's. On returning to the Peninsula, he took care to avoid being put in Moore's position, a prey to local feuds, Spanish incompetence and political pressure. He resolved that the British army under his command would only undertake actions within its own capabilities, placing no reliance on the Spanish or anyone else. He was also determined that discipline should be a priority. Although he was to experience many of Moore's troubles, he was at least aware of some of the potential problems.

Wellesley had 18,000 British troops to command in the Peninsula, and was also to raise and command Portuguese battalions to be armed, fed and paid by the British government. With this Anglo-Portuguese Army, which included the Hanoverian troops of the King's German Legion, he was to expel Soult from Oporto and secure Portugal. Soult had 13,000 men at Oporto, little more than a strong division, while a larger force of about 20,000 under Marshal Victor was poised just across the southern frontier, around the town of Merida in Estremadura.

The military situation in Spain and Portugal had not changed dramatically in the four months since winter gripped the Peninsula, putting a stop to serious campaigning, and although the dying went on in a thousand guerrilla skirmishes, there had been no major gains or losses. When the weather eased a little, at the end of March 1809, Soult began his march south from Corunna to Lisbon, across the Portuguese frontier and the northern mountains. He followed a most gruelling route, but by mid-April 1809 his army had arrived at Oporto, the wine town on the River Douro. Soult was now well behind the schedule imposed by the Emperor, but his army was exhausted and in sore need of a rest. He was still at Oporto on 11 May 1809 when his scouts reported British redcoats on the south bank of the river.

During the night of 11–12 May, Wellesley positioned his artillery on the south bank of the river and sent scouts out looking for boats. By midnight his troop had discovered a small rowing boat on the southern shore and three large wine barges tied up on the north bank. A party sculled across in the rowing boat and by dawn the barges had been brought across; within half an hour three companies of the 3rd Foot (the Buffs) had been ferried across the river. There they established themselves in the walled garden of a seminary close to the city walls and were covering the ferrying of more troops when the French discovered their existence.

Soult sent a full brigade against the seminary but musket volleys from the Buffs backed by sweeping artillery fire from Wellesley's batteries on the south bank of the river smashed the advancing French battalions. In the brief lull which followed, citizens of Oporto crossed to the British side in large boats and two more battalions were ferried across to reinforce the Buffs.

Soult pulled back to avoid the British artillery fire but as the French retreated the entire civilian population of Oporto swarmed down to the river and ferried more British troops across, using every kind of craft. Within an hour of first light Wellesley had 6,000 men across the river, storming through the streets of Oporto with the bayonet, driving the French out into the countryside, and by mid morning the battle was won. It was a confused and scrambling affair, but a success for Wellesley and highly gratifying for his men.

Nor was this the end of the affair. Soult's army was now adrift in hostile country. Portuguese forces under Beresford were cutting off his retreat up the Douro into Spain, and he was surrounded by a vengeful population. Any idea of regrouping for a counter-attack had to be dismissed, and Soult was forced to escape by goat-tracks over the hills into Galicia, burning his baggage, destroying his artillery, and abandoning his wounded as he went. Even his treasury fell into British hands. Wellesley regretted being unable to secure a total victory, but was satisfied that he had rendered Soult's corps ineffective. With the Portuguese irregular militia, the *ordenança*, in the hills, Portugal's northern frontier was now secure. General Wellesley returned to Lisbon to prepare for an advance against Marshal Victor's Army of Castile, just across the frontier in Estremadura.

8

Austria:

1809

Battle should only be offered when there is no other turn of
fortune to be hoped for, as from its very nature the fate of a
battle is always dubious.

Napoleon Bonaparte,
Emperor of the French: 1809

IN VIENNA NAPOLEON had decided to inflict upon the Austrians
the sort of crushing defeat which would convince them that war with
France should never be contemplated again. The Archduke Charles
was regrouping his forces on the north bank of the Danube, and to
occupy an enemy's capital while he was still in the field went against
Napoleon's usual strategy. As he himself said: 'To cross a river like
the Danube in the presence of an enemy knowing the ground and
having the sympathies of the inhabitants, is one of the most difficult
military operations conceivable.'

Since any delay might enable Archduke Charles to bring up reinforcements – Archduke John had been recalled from northern Italy,
where he had inflicted defeats on Prince Eugène's army at Sacile and
Caldiero – the attempt had nevertheless to be made, and with all
speed. Reconnaissance of the river indicated a point opposite the
island of Lobau for the crossing, but the Danube is wide at this point
and was in spring spate. Bad weather combined with the Austrians'
diligence in destroying bridges, boats and any useful materials meant
that it took more than a week of the utmost effort for the French
engineers to span the 2,000 yards' width to Lobau. During the night
of 19 May the French began to occupy the island, and by the evening
of 20 May Masséna's corps had crossed to the north bank and were

dislodging the Austrian outposts along the river. At midday on 21 May Napoleon had 25,000 men on the Marchfeld, the large plain on the north bank of the Danube, with his left on the village of Aspern and his right in Essling. They had to advance northwards from the river to make room for the main body to form up. During the day the bridge became increasingly unsafe, owing to the violence of the current, and the passage of French reinforcements was frequently delayed.

Until this point the Austrians, though not unaware of what was happening, had taken no action, their aim being to allow as many French to cross as they felt they could deal with, and then fall on them. Napoleon seems to have underrated his opponents, and to have assessed this risk too lightly.

Archduke Charles moved to the attack with his whole army of 98,000 men in five columns, three under Hiller, Bellegarde and Hohenzollern to converge on Aspern and two under Rosenberg to attack Essling, with the Austrian cavalry in the centre ready to move out against any French cavalry which might attack the heads of columns. Aspern was defended by Molitor's division under Masséna and Hiller took the village in the first rush, but Masséna, fighting tenaciously, recaptured it, and the three Austrian columns could do no more than drive the French to the edge of the village before nightfall.

To create a diversion Napoleon directed his cavalry, in the centre under Bessières, to charge the Austrian artillery, which was deployed in a long line firing into Aspern. The first attack was repulsed. The second over-rode the guns but failed to break Hohenzollern's infantry squares and the cavalry retired to their old position. At Essling the French under Marshal Lannes delayed the Austrian assault by repeated attacks on Rosenberg's flank and held the village as night fell.

Early in the morning of 22 May Masséna finally drove the Austrians from Aspern, while Rosenberg stormed Essling. Lannes resisted desperately, however, and was able to drive him out when reinforcements came up. By 7 a.m. Napoleon had about 70,000 troops across the river and launched a combined attack on the Austrian centre. The Austrian line was broken, between Rosenberg's right and Hohenzollern's left, and French squadrons poured through the gap. At the vital moment Archduke Charles brought up his last reserves and, seizing the banner of the Zach Regiment, led his soldiers into the fray, Lannes was checked and the impetus died out along the French line. The French regiments of horse, having overthrown the Austrian cavalry in a magnificent charge, fell back before the enemy grenadiers.

Meanwhile, Aspern had fallen to a counter-attack by Hiller and

Bellegarde and, most seriously of all, Napoleon heard that the Danube bridges had been cut by heavy barges sent down-river by the
Austrians. He thereupon decided to suspend the attack and retire to
Lobau. Early in the afternoon Essling fell to Rosenberg, and though
the French then drove him out, he directed his efforts on the French
centre as they retired to the bridge. The withdrawal was costly, and
only the steadiness of Lannes and the increasing exhaustion of the
Austrians prevented the French being driven into the Danube.

Napoleon was now in a desperate situation. Essling had fallen except for one central position in a granary and the French centre,
weakened by Lannes' gallant but futile charge onto the Marchfeld,
was visibly crumbling. Only on the left, around Aspern, was the front
secure. A bayonet charge by two battalions of the Young Guard
retook Essling, but they could not hold it and were soon driven out
again. It eventually needed five battalions of the Young Guard to
capture Essling, and they were the last reserve available on the north
bank.

The Emperor finally realized that his bridgehead across the Danube was untenable. He therefore handed over command to Lannes
and withdrew across the newly-repaired bridge to Lobau, where he
began to organize the withdrawal of the French troops from the
bridgehead. This withdrawal had hardly begun when a cannon ball
struck Marshal Lannes, shattering his leg. Lannes was carried from
the field and his leg was amputated. For a day or two he seemed likely
to recover but then gangrene set in and he died of his wounds a few
days later, his death a terrible blow to the Emperor and the entire
French Army. Lannes was the first of the marshals to die in battle, a
portent of things to come.

The battle for Aspern and Essling was lost even before Lannes was
borne to the rear, for the French had been fought out and the Austrians were triumphant. By nightfall the French were back on Lobau
and some time after midnight, covered by the fire of their artillery,
the French sappers dragged their pontoons back from the north bank
onto Lobau island. The firing slowly petered out and by dawn on 23
April the battle of Aspern-Essling was over.

Casualties on both sides were appalling. The French had lost about
20,000 killed and wounded, including the gallant Marshal Lannes,
Austrian losses were just under 24,000, and both armies were totally
exhausted. Archduke Charles made no attempt to follow up his success but this failure to take advantage of the critical situation of the
French does not make Aspern-Essling less than a defeat for Napoleon. He chose to ignore the flooded state of the river, the swiftness

of the current, and the certainty that the Archduke would attempt to sever his only line of communication. It is to the credit of the French army that they held out so long, but this does not constitute a victory.

Not until the 24th did Napoleon begin preparations for the next phase of his campaign, and on 25 May the bridge from Lobau to the south bank was re-opened.

Napoleon is sometimes held to have been indifferent to the sufferings of his men. It was indeed so, but this was not the case after Aspern-Essling. No effort was spared to give the wounded the best medical treatment available, and when some generals complained to the Emperor that the Chief Surgeon, General Larrey, had seized their horses to make soup for the sick, Napoleon promptly created Larrey a Baron of the Empire.

For the next two months there was a pause along the Danube. Two bridges, protected by staked barriers upstream, were built across the river to Lobau, and an armed flotilla was organized to command the waterway. Vienna was ransacked for guns, stores and appliances, and the island of Lobau was turned into a fortress, with 100 guns trained on the Austrian side. Every man, horse and gun at the Emperor's command was called up from Italy and Germany.

Archduke Charles was being tantalized by vague offers of help from Prussia which came to nothing as he replenished his battalions and waited for Archduke John to come up from Pressburg. Following his victories over Prince Eugène, John had retired to Willach on hearing of the Austrian repulse at Eckmühl. Prince Eugène, considerably reinforced, had driven him into Hungary and on 14 June defeated him at Raab. Archduke John retreated from there to Pressburg, from where he was summoned back to the Danube.

The Austrians, in the face of the French batteries on Lobau, had given up the local defence of the river and withdrawn to an arc overlooking the Marchfeld, from the Bissamberg in the west to Markgrafneusiedl on the east, leaving a gap from this point to the Danube below Lobau for Archduke John's forces to fill.

Napoleon, having secured his passage from the Vienna side of the Danube to Lobau, put preparations in hand for three bridges to be thrown across from Lobau to the Aspern-Essling side, and seven more on his right hand between Gross Enzersdorf and the main river. The Emperor continued to convey the impression that he was planning another general assault through Aspern-Essling, though he had no intention of attacking the Austrians there. If he could pull the Archduke's army forward to the north bank of the river, the Archduke might impede any French crossing there, but his position would make it easier for a French crossing elsewhere to cut behind the Austrian mass.

The Austrians observed the French proceedings from their positions but did not interfere, becoming so accustomed to the passage of small detachments of French soldiers that when an advanced guard was put across near Gross Enzersdorf on the afternoon of 4 July, they made nothing of it. Under cover of this detachment Napoleon's pontoniers put the seven bridges in place, and during the night troops began to stream across. By 9 a.m. on 5 July the three front-line corps (under Davout, Oudinot and Masséna) were deployed and moving forward to make way for the second line (Eugène and Bernadotte) and the third (Marmont, Bessières' cavalry and the Imperial Guard). The general advance began at noon, the French fanning out to give themselves room for manoeuvre.

The Austrians held a strong position along the line of the Russbach from Wagram to Markgrafneusiedl on their left, their right held ready to roll up the French attack from left to right at the appropriate moment. The movements of the great French masses on the Marchfeld were slow, however, and while their left under Masséna pushed the Austrians back beyond Leopold and Süssenbrunn, it was not until early evening that the main attack on the line of the Russbach took shape. The various corps did not attack simultaneously, and the Austrians repulsed the French from the heights of Wagram with heavy loss. Early the next morning, Achduke Charles directed four corps upon Masséna, who had bivouacked his troops overnight on the line Leopoldsau–Süssenbrunn–Aderklaa – the latter a strongly-built village providing the equivalent of a bridgehead to the passage of the Russbach at Wagram. Another corps with a strong cavalry unit was directed to pivot around Markgrafneusiedl to attack Davout on his right. Archduke John was expected to arrive on this flank later in the day.

By 11 a.m. Masséna's left division had been driven back almost to Aspern and his right, despite assistance from Bernadotte, had failed to recapture Aderklaa, from which the Austrians had driven his advanced posts earlier in the morning. The struggle for Aderklaa was as bitter and prolonged as that for Aspern two months earlier. The Austrian right pressed forward victoriously by Süssenbrunn and Breitenlee to the Danube. It was a critical moment for the French, who were not fighting with the spirit of former years. Napoleon, a master of the psychology of the battlefield, knew that matters were much the same for the Austrians and gave orders for a great counterstroke.

One hundred guns – the historic 'grand battery' – were ordered up to check the Austrian right. Davout on the French right was to press his attack on Markgrafneusiedl and roll up the Austrian left flank; for the time being Oudinot, next to him, was to do no more than engage the enemy on the heights with artillery fire. The capture of Markgrafneusiedl was to be the signal for the main stroke against the Austrian centre, by Prince Eugène's two corps under Macdonald and Grenier, which were then moving up. Meanwhile Masséna on the French left was to move laterally across the front to aid his isolated division in guarding the left flank.

Macdonald formed his 30,000 men in a gigantic hollow square – two lines, each of four deployed battalions, closed up so that the whole was six ranks deep, while the remainder of the infantry marched behind in column on either flank, and 6,000 horse closed the rear. Austrian cannon balls cut swathes through this dense square, and the trail of dead and dying shook all who saw it; the advance, shrunken from losses and stragglers, finally came to a halt in a sandpit a mile short of Süssenbrunn, but when reinforcements came up Macdonald resumed his advance and reached his objective.

Oudinot was now ordered to cross the Russbach and strike the joint of the Austrian line at Wagram. The Austrian left centre had been weakened by having to send reinforcements to their left, where Davout eventually rolled up Rosenberg's forces at Markgrafneusiedl. Oudinot was able to gain Wagram and thus split the Austrian army; the right wing was being forced back by Masséna at Aspern.

Learning that Archduke John's forces could not arrive from Pressburg to fall upon the French right flank before evening, Archduke Charles ordered a general retreat about 2.30 p.m., his main army westward and the left wing to the north. The Austrians withdrew in good order, beaten but not broken, without leaving a flag or gun in French hands.

Napoleon had his victory, but not of the sort to which his armies had grown accustomed. Victory on the Danube had been purchased at a terrible cost in lives. French losses at Wagram exceeded 32,000 men, those among officers being unusually heavy: some 40 generals and more than 1,300 other officers were killed or wounded. The Austrian losses were equally heavy, at about 35,000 men, and for both sides these were in addition to the losses of Aspern-Essling. Although Austria was defeated, the battle of Wagram remains one of the most brilliant feats of arms in her history.

After some further skirmishing at Znaym on 10 and 11 July, on 12 July an armistice was arranged. The Austrian Emperor, Francis I, at first refused to sanction it, but reluctantly consented to its ratification on 17 July 1809.

The peace negotiations initiated by the armistice made no progress for several months. Serious differences of opinion arose between Archduke Charles and his brother the Emperor Francis, which resulted in the former resigning the supreme command and retiring into private life – an irreparable loss to Austria and her army. Negotiations were in the hands of Count Metternich, and Napoleon at first demanded the abdication of the Emperor Francis – 'I want to deal with a man who has the gratitude to leave me alone for the rest of my life.' To this Francis would not agree, and in the middle of September it looked as though Austria might be preparing to renew the war with Prussian aid. Peace was desperately needed now and the French and the Austrians reached an accommodation at the Peace of Schönbrunn, signed at that palace in Vienna on 14 October 1809. By this Peace the Austrians ceded large tracts of territory to the French and handed over their Polish territories to the Grand Duchy of Warsaw. They also paid a war indemnity of 85 million francs, recognized Joseph Bonaparte as King of Spain, and agreed to comply with the Continental System. The Emperor was once again triumphant, but total peace was still not in his grasp. While he had been locked in bloody battle with the Austrians, his marshals were being roughly handled by the British army in Spain.

9

Spain – Talavera and a Title:

1809–1810

> You will consider the defence of Portugal the first and most
> important object of your attention.
> > Orders to General Sir Arthur Wellesley: 1809

GENERAL SIR ARTHUR Wellesley spent the weeks after the Douro
battle giving his victorious troops a much needed injection of discipline, for his men had celebrated their victory over Soult at Oporto by
breaking into the port warehouses and getting stupendously drunk.
Wellesley had no intention of letting his army disintegrate like
General Moore's and ordered liberal applications of drill and the lash
to restore his men to duty. On the matter of strategy, Wellesley was
attempting to co-ordinate his actions with the Spanish forces and in
particular with the Commander of the Army of Estremadura,
Captain-General Gregorio Cuesta. This proved exceedingly difficult.

General Cuesta was an old man, much set in ways which were
not those of Wellesley, and there is reason to suppose that Cuesta
opposed all Wellesley's suggestions largely because he was reluctant to
do anything proposed by anyone other than himself. It soon became
as clear to General Wellesley as it had to General Moore that the
attitude of the Spanish generals was not the least of the difficulties to
be faced in the Peninsula, yet it was essential to come to terms with
them. On his own, Wellesley did not have the men, the supplies or
the transport to defeat the French, and *had* to augment his troops with
Spanish and Portuguese. Arrangements negotiated during the winter
of 1808/9 had placed the Portuguese army under British control, and
General Beresford had been in Portugal since February effecting its
reorganization. On his own arrival in Portugal Wellesley toughened

his Portuguese infantry by putting one battalion into each of five British brigades, and they eventually became excellent soldiers. The Spanish generals were far less tractable.

The Spanish position is understandable. Britain and Spain had been enemies since the days of Drake, and the British were Protestant heretics. Until recently, Spain had been allied with France, and their combined fleets had been defeated by Nelson at Trafalgar in 1805. In 1807, only a year before the *dos de Mayo*, the British had sent an expedition to the River Plate with the intention of destroying the Spanish Empire in South America. Dire necessity might have forced the Spanish into an alliance with the British; they did not have to like it.

Wellesley left Lisbon on 27 June and crossed the frontier into Spain on 4 July 1809; his headquarters arrived at Plasencia on 8 July, and Wellesley travelled to Almáraz to meet General Cuesta and his army on 10 July. He was not encouraged by this meeting. The Spanish soldiers displayed bravado and a willingness to fight, but their ragged regiments and shambling battalions were cursed with bad officers and a commander who, having once been ridden over by his own cavalry, now proceeded about the countryside in a large coach pulled by nine mules. Thanks to poor maps, terrible roads, and an incompetent guide, Wellesley arrived five hours late for the meeting and had to inspect the Spanish Guard of Honour by torchlight – which did not improve Cuesta's always uncertain temper.

The two commanders then discussed plans for attacking the French, the Spanish Adjutant-General, General Odonoju (or O'Donoghue – he was of Irish descent) acting as interpreter. Cuesta flatly rejected most of Wellesley's suggestions and the conference went on for hours, Wellesley concluding that it was '. . . impossible for me to say what plans General Cuesta entertains'. It took two days for the generals to agree a plan for their forces to combine on 21 July at Oropesa, at the southern foot of the Sierra de Gredos, and from there advance upon Marshal Victor. Meanwhile the Army of La Mancha was to make an attempt to draw off Sebastiani and, if that failed, march cautiously towards Madrid to distract King Joseph.

The British troops began to reach Oropesa on 20 July and rested there on the 21st, when General Cuesta passed them and united his Spanish at Velada, further up the Tagus. When Marshal Victor near Talavera received intelligence of the allies' movements he realized there was a danger that he might be cut off from Madrid, and sent to King Joseph for reinforcements. On 22 July the British and Spanish moved up two columns to drive the French outposts from Talavera, where 2,000 French dragoons held Cuesta's leading columns until the British came into view. Then the French fell back on a line between the Alberche and the Tagus, north-east of Talavera.

It had been generally agreed that the French should be attacked early on the 23rd, though the details had been left unsettled. Wellesley was up at 2 a.m. and the British were under arms at 3 . . . but there was no sign of General Cuesta who, when he was eventually roused at 7, refused to move that day. His troops were too tired after the previous days' marches – he had not reconnoitred enough – the bridge at Alberche was not strong enough for his artillery. It was later widely believed that he had refused to fight because it was a Sunday, but as Wellington remarked to Lord Stanhope in 1833, '. . . he made many other foolish excuses, but that was not one of them'.

During the 24th, with the French apparently in retreat before him, Cuesta became eager for pursuit. Wellesley refused to join him, for the Spanish commissariat had let him down badly and despite repeated representations to both the Junta and Cuesta, supplies and transport had not arrived and his troops were on half-rations.

On 25 July General Cuesta continued his pursuit of Marshal Victor's forces towards Madrid. Wellesley sent two divisions of infantry and some cavalry under General Sherbrooke into the heights above the Alberche as a support for the Spanish in their foolhardy enterprise. Cuesta then took fright and ordered a retreat for the 26th, but the French – Victor having effected his junction with King Joseph's forces on the 25th – recrossed the Guadarrama and attacked the Spanish cavalry, who broke and fled. General Sherbrooke's advance with his divisions stemmed the panic, and the French failed to press their advantage. Wellesley tried to persuade Cuesta to withdraw to Talavera, but the stubborn old man refused to do so until, early the next day (27 July), the French cavalry came into sight and Sherbrooke prepared to retire. General Mackenzie's division plus a brigade of light infantry were posted in the plain to cover the Spanish retreat, while the rest of the allied troops marched to take up their positions in the line determined by Wellesley.

The allied line was roughly along a narrow stream, the Portina, flowing into the Tagus near Talavera. Sir Arthur put the Spaniards on the right of his line, between the town and a mound on which a field redoubt was constructed; covered by outworks, mud walls and felled trees, half his line was thus nearly impregnable and might be held by his worst troops. The British, including the King's German Legion, covered the rest of the position, from the redoubt and straddling a hill, the Medellin, overlooking the west bank of the Portina.

The British cavalry were behind the redoubt and in the plain to the left of the line, with Spanish cavalry beyond the rising ground on the extreme left to block any outflanking movement.

Wellesley was out in the plain between the Portina and the hills to the west, the Heights of Salinas, surveying the area through his telescope from the tower of an isolated building, the Casa Las Salinas, when he caught sight of a party of French light troops under the walls of the house. Dashing to their horses, Wellesley and his staff spurred to safety under a hail of random shot from the French – who, happily, had no idea at whom they were firing. One of the brigades covering the Spanish retreat, snatching an untimely siesta, was surprised and badly cut up by the advance skirmishers of two columns of French infantry who had managed to sneak up through the woods. The British brigades fell into some disorder, but were rallied by Wellesley and, having checked the French, retired to their own lines.

The battle of Talavera began inauspiciously on the evening of 27 July when Cuesta's front-line infantry attempted to repel some French skirmishers probing their positions with a single massive volley. The echo of this tremendous discharge had hardly died away when four Spanish battalions broke and fled back through Talavera and down the road to Portugal, looting the British baggage park as they went. Two hundred of those who fled were rounded up and sentenced to death, and Cuesta later had forty of them shot. This precipitate retreat was observed by Victor, who promptly ordered a general advance on the Allied line. As the sun went down on the 27th, dark masses of French infantry began to roll across the plain towards the British position and the battle began just as dark was falling.

Victor was determined to take advantage of the turmoil caused by the Spanish flight, and three French columns began the attack the night of 27 July. One got lost, one withdrew after a brief exchange of fire, but Victor's advance guard from the 9th Léger surprised some Hanoverians on the Medellin who, thinking they were in the second line, had neglected to post pickets. They fell back firing, alerting their comrades with cries of 'The hill! The hill!' General Sir Rowland Hill ('Daddy' Hill to the troops) was not yet in position in the front line on the Medellin but, attracted by the firing and the shouts and thinking that it was '. . . just the old Buffs . . . making some blunder', he went to investigate and was nearly captured by the first French skirmishers topping the hill. When he realized that the British were facing an all-out French attack, Hill ordered his division forward. The 2nd Division included the 29th Foot, which had fought the French before at Roliça and Vimeiro, and these troops drove the French off the Medellin with a spirited bayonet charge. The French reformed and advanced up the hill again, 'but soon', says W. F. P. Napier, 'the well known shout of the British soldier was heard, rising above the din of arms, and the enemy's broken troops were driven once more into the ravine below.' But for them, this crucial ridge, and therefore the battle, might have been lost.

About daybreak, it was seen that Victor was massing his troops for an assault on the Medellin – about 40,000 French to the 20,000 British. Fifty-four guns concentrated their fire on the Medellin, which vanished under a cloud of dust. Adopting the tactic he was to use so often later, Wellesley had ordered his men to flatten themselves just behind the crest of the Medellin. Many of the French cannon balls either skipped overhead or thudded harmlessly into the forward slope. This tactic also demonstrated Wellesley's faith in the discipline of his infantry, for it might have been difficult to get the soldiers up again from safe shelter and forward into a firing position, but he had no doubts that, when the time came, his men would rise and advance on his orders. Until such time, he kept them from harm.

Three French infantry columns, well supported by artillery, crossed the Portina three times on the morning of 28 July, charging up the Medellin slopes to the sound of drums. Each of the three attacks was met by a line of redcoats, who sprang from the ground at the last moment to man the crest and deliver close-range, rolling volleys which threw back the French with great loss. Less than two hours of such fighting left wounded men and corpses littered along the banks of the Portina and the forward slopes of the Medellin.

At 10 o'clock, in the glare of the July morning, a truce was called during which the French and the allies came forward to retrieve their wounded, fill their water bottles and drink from the stream. The soldiers on both sides mingled freely, exchanging jokes and tobacco, before French drums beat the recall at 11 o'clock. The soldiers took up their former positions and prepared for battle again.

During the pause the French generals held a council of war on the Cascajal. King Joseph and Jourdan wanted to withdraw, but Marshal Victor was certain that he could carry the Medellin on the left if the French IVth Corps would attack the right and centre of the allied line at the same moment. Victor's vehemence won the argument, and he made his dispositions. He was now joined by Sebastiani's corps and a division under General Lapisse, 15,000 men in all, supported by 80 cannon.

The first French onslaught, on the right, was pushed back with terrible carnage, leaving ten guns behind. The French rallied for another attack, but were seen off by British artillery and musketry, and a Spanish cavalry charge on their flank. Meanwhile, on the left, Wellesley had directed Anson's brigade of Light Dragoon Guards and German hussars forward against nine French battalions advancing against his northern flank. The Guards and hussars, charging headlong against the enemy, encountered a hitherto unsuspected gully. The French formed themselves into squares and opened fire and the hussars managed to pull up, but the Guards continued their charge into the gully. The survivors charged piecemeal up the opposite bank through French infantry fire, fell upon a brigade of French *chasseurs* in the rear, and were broken by Victor's Polish Lancers and Westphalian Light Horse. Of the 450 British cavalry who went into action, 207 were killed or wounded.

At the same time, a French attack against the Medellin was repulsed and the Guards and the King's German Legion, chasing the French, came up against their supporting columns. The Hanoverians were thrown into confusion, 600 of the Guards fell, and as the British fled in their turn, they masked the fire from their own line. Their impulsive charge had also left a gap in the British line, through which French columns and light dragoons were poised to pour. Wellesley, observing this from his position on the Medellin, ordered General Hill down from the hill with the 48th (Northamptonshire) Regiment. It seemed as though they would be pushed back by the fleeing Guards and Hanoverians but, wheeling back by companies as if on parade to let their comrades through, they resumed their line. To their lasting credit, the Guards and the King's German Legion immediately rallied behind the 48th, the French wavered, and as they retired were harried by Major-General Cotton's Light Dragoons. The combat at the centre petered out, General Lapisse was killed, and General Sebastiani retired. About 6 o'clock hostilities ceased, but flaring musket-wads had set the grass on the Medellin alight, burning dead and wounded men and horses in its path.

The French had lost more than 7,000 men, a sixth of their force, the British about 5,000 killed and wounded – proportionally greater, a quarter of the army – and there was no pursuit. The French withdrawal was covered by skirmishers and artillery fire, the British were exhausted by their efforts and want of food. General Cuesta's men were fresh enough, but Wellesley could not move them. By the morning of 29 July the French had withdrawn to the Heights of Salinas, beyond the Alberche. The British army tended the wounded, French and British, as well as they could, protecting the French from the savagery of the Spanish peasants and burying the dead. The troops were encouraged, the day after the battle, by the arrival of Robert Craufurd's Light Brigade, which had marched more than forty miles in 26 hours hoping to play a part in the fighting, arriving only in time to help bury the dead and take over the outposts.

The British stayed at Talavera for five days, Wellesley attempting to procure provisions and assistance from the Spaniards to prevent his wounded from dying and his troops and horses from starving. Then disquieting news began to come in from the north. Marshal Soult was nearing the Baños pass – Soult had entered Plasencia, with forces estimated at about 25,000 men. Wellesley was inclined to discount the threat from Soult, but from Plasencia he could threaten the road to Portugal. Wellesley therefore arranged with Cuesta that the British would march to attack Soult, while the Spanish held Talavera and looked after the British wounded.

On the evening of 2 August came information that Victor was aiming to cross the Alberche at Escalona and join Soult in the valley of the Tiétar. This would threaten Cuesta at Talavera.

The French cavalry were already at Navalmoral, just 34 miles to the west of Talavera, and their infantry were close behind. This trap would close on Wellington within days, and since the Spaniards still refused to fight, and were preparing to flee before Soult arrived, Wellesley had no choice but to retire. He sent Craufurd's Light Brigade to seize and hold the vital crossing at Almàraz, left his 4,000 wounded in Cuesta's care and marched the rest of his little army – some 15,000 men – hurriedly back to Portugal. Wellesley reached safe ground around Badajoz by the end of August. There he turned again, ready to fight if need be; but the campaign of 1809 was over.

As soon as Wellesley left Talavera, Cuesta promptly abandoned the British wounded. They fell into the hands of the French, who took good care of them, while Cuesta withdrew to the south. There was then a great outcry from the Spanish Junta, for the Spaniards chose to regard Wellesley's retreat to Portugal as they had that of General Moore to Corunna the year before, as an act of betrayal and wilful desertion. Wellesley, unlike Moore, had kept the British Minister in Spain, Hookham Frere, well informed of his difficulties and of the continual problems with the Spanish in general and Cuesta in particular. The Spanish complaints therefore did Wellesley no harm. A month after the battle he was created Viscount Wellington of Talavera.

If the Spaniards were really furious with the British, they soon regained their composure and appointed Wellesley Captain-General of their forces, albeit without pay and with little real authority. Though he accepted the post, Wellesley was far from pleased with his

Spanish confederates. Had Cuesta co-operated at Talavera or afterwards, much more might have been achieved in 1809, but without
such co-operation Wellesley had been forced to retreat to Portugal.

> I lament as much as anyone the necessity of separating from the
> Spaniards [he wrote to Frere on 1 September 1809], but I was
> compelled to leave and there was not a man in the Army who did
> not think I waited too long. The fault I committed was in trusting
> the Spaniards, whom I have found unworthy of all confidence.

By the first week in September he had established his headquarters at
Badajoz, and his army was spread out along forty miles of the Guadiana Valley, straddling the Portuguese–Spanish border.

The campaign of Talavera was instructive. Wellesley learned that
he could not rely on Spanish promises and that while given good
leadership, firm discipline and regular pay Spanish troops might fight
well, Spanish generals and politicians made his task impossible. In
October he wrote frankly to the Junta of Estremadura:

> Spain is either unable or unwilling to furnish supplies of Provisions
> and Forage for the Armies necessary for her defence, and in either
> case it is impossible for me to risk the existence of His Majesty's
> Army in a country so situated.

For their part, the French should have learned that British infantry,
if drawn up in a defensive position of their own choosing, would not
be easily dislodged. British infantry were quite undismayed by drums
or cheering or the colours and eagles, or by massed infantry columns
advancing at the *pas de charge*. The French generals did not learn that
lesson at Talavera. Their Emperor had still not learned it by the time
of Waterloo, six years later.

It was now the end of August. In Austria, Napoleon was rebuilding
his shattered forces after the battles of Aspern-Essling and Wagram.
In Badajoz, Wellesley also began to rebuild his army. Reinforcements were now coming out from Britain in useful numbers, and his
achievement at Talavera had been recognized with a peerage. The
Heralds at the College of Arms would not allow time for the General
to be consulted over the matter of his title, and his brother William
had to decide. William wrote: 'I . . . determined upon Viscount Wellington of Talavera . . . and Baron Douro of Welleslie in the County
of Somerset – Wellington is a town not far from Welleslie . . . I trust

that you will not think there is anything unpleasant or trifling in the name of Wellington.' The new Viscount Wellington approved, declaring his new title '. . . exactly right', and it is as 'Wellington', which he signed for the first time on 16 September 1809, that he is best remembered.

By the autumn of 1809 there were some 350,000 French troops either in the field in Spain or ready to cross the Pyrenees. This formidable force was a drain on Napoleon's resources, but large as it was, it was scarcely sufficient. The French might – and did – win victories over the Spanish armies; they could not pacify the country. Napoleon's strategy hitherto had always been to concentrate his armies in overwhelming force at the start of a campaign. The enemy's field army would be destroyed, his ability to resist would be compromised, and peace could usually be concluded – on the Emperor's terms – within a few weeks. Such a strategy would not work in Spain, and Wellington knew it. He wrote later:

> Napoleon's plan was always to try and give a great battle. There he would gain a great victory, patch up a peace, such a peace as might leave an opening for a future war, and then hurry back to Paris. We starved him out. We showed him that we wouldn't let him fight a battle except under disadvantages. If you do fight we shall destroy you; if you do not fight we shall in time destroy you still.

In Spain, after the summer of 1808, Napoleon had to deal with an entire nation in arms. Concentration of force was impossible when merely to hold what they had and keep communications open it was necessary to disperse the French army by corps, division, battalion, even by companies, to hold strategic cities, villages, castles, bridges and passes against the guerrillas. To escort one despatch to Madrid took a full squadron of cavalry. There was no Spanish field army, as such; the various juntas sometimes gathered forces together, which could be defeated – if they could be brought to battle. Their generals usually decided to stay out of French reach but, nevertheless, their existence meant that the French forces must be further dispersed. To contain resistance in Aragon and Catalonia required 80,000 men, under Marshal Suchet; 14,000 were needed to keep King Joseph in Madrid; at least 60,000 were necessary to hold the passes through the Pyrenees and secure the roads to Madrid and Salamanca. In the south, in 1810, a further 60,000 men under Marshal Soult invaded

Andalucía, but the advance ground to a halt at Cadiz, a town stoutly defended by the Spanish and 8,000 British troops, fed and supplied by the British fleet. The French sat down before Cadiz for the next two years, a stalemate which reflected the situation elsewhere.

Given the right battlefield and the right tactics, there remained available a French force theoretically more than sufficient to smash Wellington's army. Napoleon had been able to reverse the early French defeats of 1808 and drive Moore back to Corunna in a matter of weeks: it was widely believed that he would return to the Peninsula with the *Grande Armée* in 1810, and again drive the British into the sea. That he intended to do so after the victory at Wagram need not be doubted: he sent his carriages ahead to Madrid, and the Imperial Guard, the élite of his army who always went where the Emperor went, were ordered from Vienna to Bayonne. Yet he did not go, and the conduct of the war beyond the Pyrenees remained in the hands of his marshals.

10

Busaco:

1810

Though it is possible that the armies might be lost and the
authorities dispersed, the war of the partisans may continue.
Lord Wellington to Lord Liverpool
January 1810

THE EMPEROR NAPOLEON had no children by his Empress, and
therein lay a problem, for the Emperor needed an heir. In January
1806 he had adopted Josephine's son, Eugène de Beauharnais, who
became one of his most trusted subordinates. But the birth of a son
to one of his mistresses in December 1806 reassured him. He was
anxious to found a dynasty and while the fate of his Empire rested on
him alone, a single bullet from a lone assassin was capable of bringing
all his ambitions to an end. The most recent of several attempts on
his life had been that of an Austrian patriot at Schönbrunn in October 1809, and at least one would-be assassin had told Napoleon to
his face that while he was without an heir these attempts would
continue. Securing the succession to his Empire became a matter of
personal security as well as of dynastic ambition.

It seemed, however, that Josephine would bear no more children,
and when he returned from Austria in 1809 Napoleon told her that,
although he still loved her, he must, for the sake of the Empire, end
their marriage. The door between their apartments at Fontainebleau
was bricked up, a civil divorce was announced by the Senate on 16
December, the religious separation was pronounced on 12 January
1810, and Josephine retired to Malmaison.

Napoleon now needed another wife and to help secure his position
in Europe he sought her among the Imperial families. Overtures were

first made to Czar Alexander for the hand of his sister, the Grand
Duchess Anna. Since she was just sixteen to Napoleon's forty-one, the
Czar had a plausible excuse for refusing. In reality, the pride of the
Imperial Russian family baulked at a connection with a parvenu
Corsican adventurer, and in any case Alexander was gradually seek-
ing to disengage from the alliance with France.

Napoleon, having anticipated this rebuff, was already in negotiation
with the Emperor of Austria. Eugène de Beauharnais requested the
hand of the eighteen-year-old Archduchess Marie-Louise, as Napoleon's bride. The Austrian Foreign Minister Metternich may have
been behind Emperor Francis's agreement to the match, for he was
inclined to put his faith in the balance of power and until such time
as Napoleon should overreach himself, Austria had need of his friendship. In exchange for the Archduchess's hand, the Emperor of the
French might feel disposed to return some of the Austrian territory
ceded to him by the Peace of Schönbrunn.

Napoleon's determination to secure a bride of Imperial lineage and
thereby forge an international alliance seems strangely old-fashioned.
He may have believed that the royal families of Europe lived on a
more exalted plane than other men, to which he perhaps aspired. The
Emperor was quite wrong in imagining that he might derive political
advantage from a dynastic marriage. By the early decades of the
nineteenth century, such marriages made little or no difference to
national interests or political ambitions.

The marriage was agreed upon in February 1810. In his delight
Napoleon ordered new clothes, went on a diet, took up dancing
again, learned to waltz – and removed the pictures celebrating his
Austrian victories from the walls of his palaces. The wedding took
place by proxy in Vienna on 11 March 1810, and the civil ceremony
was repeated on Marie-Louise's arrival at St Cloud on 1 April, Napoleon galloping out of Paris to meet his bride. He had consummated
the marriage before the religious ceremony took place on 12 April.

At this point in his career, Napoleon had more enemies than
friends, and one of the looked for results of the Austrian marriage was
peace in the east – a pre-requisite for settling the war in Spain.
Equally, an end to the war in Spain was the essential precursor of
Napoleon's long-held ambition to make use of Spain's sea-power to
advance his projects against Britain in India and the Far East. It soon
became clear, however, that such a peace had not been achieved.

Among the causes of the Czar's growing desire to break with Napoleon was the discontent of his mercantile classes over the disruption
of trade which resulted from Napoleon's Continental System. Weav-

ing the Habsburg alliance into his schemes, Alexander feigned fury at the discovery that Napoleon had been asking to marry his sister Anna while actively seeking the hand of Marie-Louise. Napoleon widened the breach thus created by declining to grant Russia more land in Poland, but it was his annexation of the whole Baltic coast in December 1810, including not only the free city of Lübeck but also the Duchy of Oldenburg, a territory belonging to the Czar's brother-in-law, which finally shattered the friendship forged at Tilsit and made the war of 1812 inevitable.

It was clear that, for the time being at least, Napoleon would not be returning to Spain. On 17 April 1810 he gave the command of the Army of Portugal to one of his most able marshals, André Masséna, Duke of Rivoli and Prince of Essling. Masséna was no longer young – he was 55 in 1810 – but he was a professional soldier, having served in the Royal Army in his youth. He then became a successful smuggler, before resuming his military career in 1794, when he continued to increase his fortune. He was well known for being both extremely avaricious and very careful with money: it was said that he missed the battle of Austerlitz in 1805 because he was busy looting Venice. He was also fond of women; his current mistress, the sister of a member of his Staff, accompanied him in Spain, wearing the uniform of a hussar. Her presence was perhaps some compensation for an assignment which he had not sought, and thoroughly detested – and indeed Spain brought him nothing but the hard knocks which he perhaps foresaw. He was shrewd enough to know that victory in the Peninsula would not be achieved easily in view of the terrain, the climate and the intransigent local population. Masséna was also shrewd enough to be very wary of Wellington's Anglo-Portuguese Army, now mustering in ever-growing numbers just across the Portuguese frontier.

Wellington's forces had expanded somewhat since Talavera. In September 1809 he could muster about 26,000 British and Hanoverian troops, most of them infantry. Of about 10,000 sick or wounded, most were victims of 'Guadiana fever', a form of recurrent malaria picked up at Badajoz which was to plague the Peninsular Army for years. As these recovered and returned to their units his numbers grew, but he knew he could never hope to match the French until more men arrived from Britain.

Of rather more concern to Wellington was the quality of his troops. The majority in the Peninsular Army came from the second battalions of their parent regiments, initially raised as militia in Britain as replacements and reinforcements for the first battalions. The men were good enough but Wellington was not impressed with the standard of the officers, who were ill-trained, lacked discipline, and had little idea of leadership. The vital non-commissioned officers, the sergeants and sergeant-majors, were little better.

Another major problem was a general feeling of *malaise*, common to officers and men, a sense of purposeless exertion and suffering, not helped by the widely-held belief that the Spanish and Portuguese were unreliable and untrustworthy, and that the British troops, let down by the Spanish before and after Talavera, would certainly be let down again in the future. Letters home spread the feeling of discontent, and in Parliament demands were made that the army be called home. Wellington, however, was confident: 'I am in no kind of scrape,' he wrote cheerfully to Castlereagh, the Minister for War, 'and if this country can be saved, we shall save it.'

Wellington was now Commander-in-Chief of all the Peninsular Armies, Spanish, Portuguese and British. The new Portuguese battalions under William Beresford had completed their training and were now joining the army. Beresford, a man of no great skill as a field commander but a gifted trainer of men, was created a Marshal of the Portuguese Army and with a cadre of British officers and senior NCOs descended like a hurricane upon the Portuguese Army and set about getting the soldiers into shape. This did not prove too difficult. The sturdy, patient Portuguese peasant had all the makings of a good infantryman, once he had been persuaded to drop what one British officer described as 'his insolent and slovenly habits'. Wellington came to be well pleased with his Portuguese battalions, and from 1810 the standard Peninsular Army division contained one Portuguese brigade and two British. Each British brigade also had a company of riflemen or their Portuguese equivalent, the *caçadores*.

Wellington's army contained troops of many nationalities – British, Portuguese, Spanish, even Swiss and *émigré* French – but among the finest were the Hanoverian troops of the King's German Legion, or KGL. King George III of England, Scotland and Ireland was also Elector of Hanover, and troops from the Electorate made up about a tenth of the army, mustered into four infantry battalions, a splendid regiment of hussars and two field artillery batteries, while the KGL hussars made a useful addition to Wellington's small force of cavalry. The Portuguese supplied several regiments of dragoons, but the British cavalry element boasted no more than three regiments of light cavalry and three of dragoons. There was also a shortage of field and horse artillery, and no siege train.

Wellington's confidence in the success of future campaigns was based on solid foundations. His previous experiences in the Peninsula had taught him to shun elaborate plans and grandiose promises. He relied only upon what he was sure he could count upon, and adapted his ends to his means. His army was good and improving, and the British fleet held Lisbon, through which his army could be supplied, but his greatest allies were the climate and terrain of the Iberian peninsula, and the roving Spanish and Portuguese guerrillas, implacable enemies of the French.

There is a saying, attributed to Henri IV of France and quoted frequently by Masséna: 'Spain is a country where small armies are defeated and large armies starve.' In India Wellington had learned a great deal about the necessity of maintaining supplies and saw no way in which a large French army could maintain itself in Spain, where it was almost impossible for such an army to forage for itself and live off the countryside. Even in peace, the country provided a scanty living for its own people; in time of war, French foraging parties tended to get their throats cut, while should Napoleon decide to feed this army from France, the wall of the Pyrenees, the dreadful state of Spanish roads and the relentless *guerrilleros* would prove effective barriers.

A French army, like a plague of locusts, consumed supplies from the ground it sat on, and had to move to live. Wellington, supplied by the Royal Navy, might move into Spain when he was ready, and draw the French down into a position of his choosing, to defeat them there if he could. If not, he could retire behind his lines, before which the French might starve or retreat, as they chose.

As to these lines – Wellington, a soldier who thought ahead, had ordered the construction of the Lines of Torres Vedras as early as the autumn of 1809. In September 1809, when his army was at Badojoz, following the retreat from Talavera, he had quietly visited Lisbon, and spent several weeks riding over the 'Lisbon Peninsula' – the hilly countryside between Lisbon, Torres Vedras, the coast and the Tagus – with his chief engineer, Lieutenant-Colonel Richard Fletcher. A memorandum of 20 October 1809 outlined his plans for the defence of Lisbon. His first line of fortifications ran for 29 miles from the coast to the Tagus at Alhandra, and was intended to hold up the French while the army fell back to the more impregnable defences of the second line. This, about six miles to the south of the first, stretched 22 miles from the coast to the Tagus, roughly parallel with the first. The Lines consisted of a mixture of strong-points and artillery positions, trenches and redoubts, ditches and palisades. Skilled engineers, aided by the able-bodied peasantry of Estremadura, were completing the fortifications during the summer of 1810. The ground in front was cleared of all cover; slopes were scarped away at the more exposed points; a group of redoubts on the end of the second line gave cross-fire with Admiral Berkeley's gunboats on the river.

The third line of fortifications, at the mouth of the Tagus, was designed to enable the army to embark safely in the event of a disaster. With the frigates and gunboats of the Royal Navy securing the flanks, the Lines could not be turned. Masséna was to learn that neither could they be stormed.

As part of his plans, Wellington had received permission from the Portuguese Regency to order the people of the districts open to invasion to retire from their homes after destroying everything which might be of use to the French – transport vehicles, livestock, food and fodder. He intended that the French should march through a desert and face a siege.

Viscount Wellington was therefore ready for the campaign of 1810. His Anglo-Portuguese Army, having reached a strength of 50,000 men, was a force to be reckoned with, even if some elements, notably the cavalry, were still weak. The command structure had been strengthened by the introduction of the division, a new formation at the time, made up usually of three or more brigades. The élite of the Peninsular Army was Brigadier-General Robert Craufurd's Light Division. There were five divisions of infantry, which it will be convenient, if not strictly accurate (since they contained troops of the King's German Legion and the newly-raised Portuguese battalions), to refer to as 'British'. These divisions were the 1st, under Major-General Sir Brent Spencer; the 2nd, commanded by the redoubtable General Sir Rowland Hill; the 3rd, under General Thomas Picton, a Welshman; the 4th, commanded by Major-General Lowry Cole, one of Wellington's most reliable subordinates; and the 5th under Major-General James Leith. These divisions varied somewhat in strength. While the accepted composition was three brigades to a division, the 1st consisted of four brigades, while the 5th had only two. It was Wellington's intention to strengthen the weaker divisions as more troops became available.

The Portuguese militia must not be forgotten. The *ordenança* were as effective as the Spanish *guerrilleros*, and Wellington was happy to supply them with muskets and cartridges. By their constant harrying of the French, the *ordenança* and the *guerrilleros* played a significant part in destroying French efforts in the Peninsula.

With his reinforced and well-trained army, Wellington advanced to the Portuguese frontier and prepared to meet the Army of Portugal which Masséna was mustering against him.

Masséna's army was widely dispersed: Marshal Ney was at Salamanca with the powerful VIth Corps; the IInd Corps, under the veteran of Maida, General Jean-Louis Reynier, lay near Alemtejo; General Junot with the VIIIth Corps was consolidating his capture of Astorga, in the north; and reinforcements from Germany were still making their way across Spain. Furthermore, Masséna had no clear idea of what force confronted him. Robert Craufurd's Light Division and the hussars of the King's German Legion with five battalions of infantry had kept a tight watch over the Portuguese frontier east of the Sierra de Gata, deterring French patrols, but from the little information Masséna could glean he estimated Wellington's total forces at more than 50,000. In fact, allowing for a garrison in Lisbon and a detachment of 12,000 under Sir Rowland Hill to cover the south, Wellington's field army numbered about 33,000 men.

At the beginning of June 1810 Marshal Ney led his VIth Corps out of Salamanca and laid siege to Cuidad Rodrigo. After a determined defence the town fell on 10th July and Craufurd's light infantry, which had been harrying the French outposts around the town, fell back to Almeida and the valley of the Coa. On 24 July Ney's cavalry, supported by an overwhelming force of infantry, surprised and trapped Craufurd's brigades against the river and the Light Division was severely mauled before Craufurd could withdraw over the only bridge. Wellington, displeased by the loss of 300 good men he could ill spare, told Craufurd bluntly that he might have withdrawn his men twice over before Ney attacked.

Encouraged by this victory the French beat off a British counter-attack and on 26 August began shelling Almeida. This, the main Portuguese strong-point on the road to Coimbra and Lisbon, was a Vauban-style fortress, well equipped with artillery and infantry. Wellington could have expected it to hold out for a month or more, and he needed every moment he could gain for the completion of his plans for the defence of Lisbon, but on 27 August a French shell ignited a powder train and the main magazine exploded, causing great destruction and loss of life. Almeida surrendered the following day, and the French crossed the Coa.

Wellington's plan was to lure Masséna into the barren, wasted valley before Torres Vedras, where there was neither food nor forage and where the *ordenança* could fall on the French rear. As Masséna's troops came forward, so Wellington fell back down the road to Coimbra.

Retreats, as so amply demonstrated on the road to Corunna, were bad for morale so, should the opportunity present itself, Wellington intended to teach Masséna a sharp lesson, which would have the additional advantage of 'blooding' his as-yet-untried Portuguese troops. The opportunity he sought came when the Anglo-Portuguese Army reached the heights of the Serra de Busaco, a long, steep ridge, 400 to 500m (1,200 to 1,500ft) high, running due north for ten miles from the banks of the Mondego river. This ridge is now thickly wooded, but from its crest Wellington was able to observe the French army far below. There were two roads up the steep eastern slope of the Serra: the main road to Coimbra ran over the northern end of the ridge, while a minor and much rougher road ran through the village of San António de Cantaro, up and over the centre. On the top of the ridge another track (today a forestry road) ran north to south, just behind the crest.

Wellington's army formed up on the Busaco heights on the evening of 25 September 1810. Once Masséna had committed himself to the Coimbra route into Portugal, Hill's and Leith's divisions were summoned from the south. The Anglo-Portuguese Army now numbered about 50,000 in seven divisions, with two independent brigades of Portuguese line infantry and riflemen, and a small force of cavalry.

Occupying a position ten miles long, Wellington could not be strong everywhere, but that track behind the top of the ridge enabled him to switch his troops swiftly from one point to another as the situation developed, unobserved and in complete safety. The flat ground behind the crest afforded space for the deployment of his battalions, and gave cover from artillery fire.

Thinly deployed along the entire ridge, the bulk of his force held the left, around the main road to Coimbra. In the south, Rowland Hill had his own 2nd Division and Major-General Hamilton's brigade, plus a strong Portuguese brigade of which one battalion, south of the Busaco ridge, guarded the fords across the Mondego at the village of Penacova. Next to Hill came the two brigades of the 5th Division, then Picton's 3rd Division astride the top of the track leading up from San António, roughly in the centre of the British line. Finally, astride the main Coimbra road as it wound up the eastern slope through the hamlets of Moura and Sula to the village of Busaco were the 1st Division, the Light Division, the King's German Legion and Lowry Cole's 4th Division. The Light Division had sent skirmishers down the eastern slope to occupy the villages of Sula and Moura; the rest of the riflemen were out of sight behind the crest.

The French had no clear idea of the whereabouts of the British divisions, or their exact strength. Just after dawn on the 26th, Marshal Ney came forward towards Moura and examined the British position. They were clearly on the Busaco ridge, for there were horsemen to be seen on the hill, some advance clumps of riflemen and the occasional glint of a bayonet. Exactly where they were, in what numbers, and what they were doing, was more difficult to gauge. Ney's conclusion was that the British were withdrawing north along the Coimbra road, and that since their main strength lay to the north end of the ridge, a frontal assault on the centre would turn their withdrawal into a rout.

It proved difficult to convey the results of this rather cursory reconnaissance to Masséna, who was ten miles further back and in bed with his mistress. Ney's aide-de-camp had to shout his news through the bedroom door, and it was two hours before Masséna emerged to ride to the front, examine the position and give his approval for a general assault on the Busaco ridge the following day.

Masséna's plan was simple: the face of the Busaco ridge being very steep, the assault columns of Reynier's corps were to attack the supposed right of the British line by advancing astride the track leading to the centre of the ridge from San António. When Reynier's divisions had taken the crest they were to turn right (or north) and sweep the ridge clear as far as the main Coimbra road at Busaco. The British positions here, if any, would meanwhile have been assaulted by Ney's corps. Junot's VIIIth corps would wait in the rear with the cavalry, ready to come forward and pursue the British after they had been dislodged.

The French estimated Wellington's strength at about 25,000 men and assumed they were mustered astride the Coimbra road at Busaco. Wellington had imagined that Masséna himself would attack along this road, but his Quartermaster-General Colonel George Murray having observed Masséna and his staff inspecting the track through San António, he adjusted his dispositions accordingly. The point that Reynier was to attack, beyond the supposed British right, was in fact barely right of the British centre.

It was a cold bivouac that night on the Busaco ridge, without fires or hot food, and at dawn on the 27th the valley to the east was filled with a thick mist. Reynier's assault began at 6 a.m. when two division columns, commanded by Merle and Heudelet, each column screened by a cloud of skirmishing *tirailleurs*, soon ran into the advanced pickets of Picton's 3rd Division. The first British troops to become engaged were on the right of Picton's line, astride the track up from San António, where the French 31st Ligne from Heudelet's division ran into two British and two Portuguese battalions supported by a battery of field artillery. Crashing cannon-fire and close-quarter volley-fire brought the French to an abrupt halt, but they hung on just below the crest, exchanging volleys with troops dimly seen in the mist ahead.

General Merle's column on the right, twelve battalions strong, now blundered upon the left of Picton's line, where three British regiments, the 45th, 74th and 88th Foot, held the ground. Merle's men were able to force themselves through this position, but having heard the firing, Picton sent reinforcements in to plug the gap. A furious charge at the heart of Merle's column by the 88th (the Connaught Rangers) and the 45th (the Sherwood Foresters) sent the French fleeing back down the hill. Within an hour of the first shot being fired, most of these two French divisions were in full retreat.

The right of the British line was still not secure, for in the mist and confusion Foy had been able to establish his seven battalions of Reynier's corps on a knoll just north of the San António track. An attack from the Portuguese of Leith's 5th Division dislodged Foy's men and eventually tumbled them back and Reynier's assault on the allied centre petered out. Twenty-three of his battalions had climbed to the crest, only to be roughly handled and flung back.

Over on the French right, as soon as firing from the left indicated that Reynier's men were engaged, Ney's corps had advanced up the winding Coimbra road through Moura and Sula, where they were immediately engaged by five battalions of the Light Division and two batteries of horse artillery, which did grim work on the close-packed files of General Loison's right-hand column. Somewhat chastened after the fight on the Coa, Craufurd was now handling his division with great skill, passing his forward battalions back steadily from point to point and keeping the bulk of his division out of sight behind the crest of the ridge above Sula. Up on the ridge, he stood in full view upon a rock, in plain sight of the advancing French, ignoring the spattering musket balls and waiting for the right moment to commit his reserve. When the head of the French column was only fifty yards from the crest, Craufurd turned, took off his hat and cried, 'Now . . . 52nd! Avenge the death of Sir John Moore . . . .' Two thousand riflemen appeared on the crest and fired one terrible volley into the French column. Then, cheering, the 52nd came flooding down the hill with the bayonet. The 52nd and 43rd outflanked the French column on either side and, having lapped around it from both flanks, they set out to demolish it, firing volleys into the close-packed French ranks, '. . . and the slaughter was great.' When the French broke, the

52nd and 43rd followed at their heels, shooting and bayoneting them all the way down the hill to Moura. Ney's left-hand column fared no better. They came against Colonel Pack's Portuguese brigade and the 4th Portuguese Rifles, supported by three batteries of field artillery. As steady and deadly as their British allies, the Portuguese greeted the French with a blast of musketry and canister, driving them back with great loss.

Having driven off the French at every point and held their positions long enough to ensure there would be no pursuit, the triumphant British and the jubilant Portuguese renewed their withdrawal towards Lisbon. This was no retreat and the troops were well satisfied: they had thrashed the French and they knew it, and if the French came after them, they would thrash them again.

The French were in no position to pursue. Their divisions had been badly mauled and the confidence of their commanders severely shaken. Masséna had lost 4,600 men in three hours of fighting, including nearly 1,000 killed. General Merle and two brigade commanders had been wounded, another general and many officers had been killed. Wellington's casualties were much lower, about 1,200 men, half of them Portuguese, and only 200 men had been killed.

Busaco was a great blow to the self-esteem of the French army, and a fine tactical victory for Wellington. He had kept his men in hand, chosen the perfect terrain, anticipated the enemy's reaction, and dealt them a terrible blow at no great cost to himself. The French had come on in their usual imperious fashion, expecting their massed columns and pounding drums to overawe the British and Portuguese before they punched a hole in the allied line. The failure of such tactics at Maida four years before had taught Reynier nothing.

On the following day the French took the obvious step of trying to turn Wellington's left wing, but by that time the British had slipped away down the Coimbra road. Laden with their wounded and surrounded by sniping *ordenança*, the French followed the Anglo-Portuguese army towards the hills of Torres Vedras. Masséna occupied Coimbra, and found food which – contrary to instructions – had not been destroyed, enough to enable him to resume his advance. He left 5,000 sick and wounded behind under the guard of half a battalion. They were surprised by Colonel Trant, leader of the local militia brigade, who captured both garrison and wounded – compensation of a sort for the British wounded abandoned by General Cuesta in Talavera.

11

Problems with Russia:

1811–1812

> At Tilsit, Russia swore eternal friendship with France, and
> also war against England. Today she has broken her
> undertakings. . . . She places us between dishonour and war.
> There can be no doubt which course we shall choose.
> Napoleon Bonaparte: Imperial Decree,
Paris, 1812

BY 1811, DESPITE his success at Wagram and the coup of his marriage
to the Emperor of Austria's daughter, all was not well with Napoleon's Empire. The campaign of 1809 had shaken the faith of his
marshals and senior officers in Napoleon's judgement, and the difficulties he had experienced in conquering Austria had not gone unnoticed by his enemies or his allies. The French economy had suffered
in unforeseen ways from the effects of the Continental System and
was debilitated by many years of raising, training and equipping her
Emperor's vast armies. The economies of other nations of the Empire
were in even worse case; and the war in Spain dragged on.

On the face of it, Napoleon had now imposed his will everywhere
east of the Channel coast and north of the Pyrenees, but closer inspection reveals a different picture.

For all his titles and territories, for all the kings, princes and dukes
who acknowledged his power or gathered about his throne, the position of Napoleon, who had shattered the pretensions of those who
saw themselves as mankind's natural rulers, was different from that of
the other emperors and kings of Europe. The French Revolution of
1789, with its flood of new and exciting ideas – freedom of speech,
equality of opportunity, education – had terrified the princes of
Europe, threatening as it did their *status quo*. They feared – even

when, like Czar Alexander, they flirted with liberal ideas – the spread to their own realms of the theories which had produced the Revolution and Napoleon.

Napoleon came to power at a time when the Revolution was faltering at home and the wars were at their height. He won battles, imposed order, put France back together. At first, in practice as in theory, his philosophy broadly maintained the ideals of the Revolution, which spread as his Empire grew. In his view Britain, in her stubborn opposition to his revolutionary will and the military power with which he enforced it, was prolonging the old corrupt institutions and discriminatory laws which repressed human energies and preserved inequalities. She alone stood out against the reforming Emperor and the great 'natural force' he embodied. As he, having risen by natural law, came to think himself above it, and to regard all opposition as treason to be crushed without mercy – a view as autocratic as that of any hereditary prince – Britain became the beacon of hope for all who resented injustice and oppression.

In 1811 there was no sign that Britain was willing to compromise or come to a peaceful settlement. Hitherto the British had fought mainly by means of subsidies or supplies of arms to their allies, and their fleet had nullified the effects of the Continental System. Now they had an army campaigning successfully in Spain.

Napoleon needed peace on his 'Central Front', with Austria and Russia, before he could deal with 'the Spanish ulcer', but peace was not to be had. Czar Alexander of Russia and Emperor Francis II of Austria both had grounds for complaint against the Emperor of the French. While his marriage to Emperor Francis's daughter had apparently settled the question of Napoleon's relations with Austria – temporarily, at least – Russia was another matter.

At Tilsit, it had seemed that Napoleon and the Czar might become partners, sharing the balance of power in Europe, but Alexander was not entirely his own man. His mother and his nobles detested the French Emperor and French ideas. The interests of the Russian nobility were not to be dismissed lightly – these same nobles had been responsible for the murder of Alexander's father, Czar Paul. Although at first Napoleon carefully avoided interference in Russian spheres of influence in Eastern Europe, especially in Poland, this did nothing to mollify the Czar's resentment when the French blocked Russian designs on Constantinople, and there remained, as a perpetual source of contention, the philosophy and the political doctrines of the French Empire. Alexander had, indeed, put forward a proposal to introduce a form of parliamentary government into Russia, but this roused blazing hostility. Members of his entourage who shared the Czar's liberal leanings were forced into exile by ministers whose prosperity depended on the labour of millions of serfs, and Alexander abandoned the idea of reform.

Despite his early admiration of Napoleon and the mutual amity displayed at Tilsit, Alexander was uneasy about the Emperor's treatment of Prussia, and even more so about his encouragement of Polish national aspirations by the creation of the Grand Duchy of Warsaw. Finally, if the Treaty of Tilsit was unpopular with the Empress Dowager and the Russian aristocracy, it was even more unpopular – bringing with it as it did the Continental System – with the Russian merchants.

Slowly, Alexander began to distance himself from Napoleon. Russia's lukewarm assistance during the Austrian war was rewarded, under the terms of the Peace of Schönbrunn, with part of Austrian Galicia, but most of this territory was granted to the Grand Duchy of Warsaw. Napoleon, having clearly discerned the Czar's changing attitude, first at Erfurt, then during the Austrian war, was already thinking that the Polish lancers would be useful in any war against Russia. This augmentation of the Grand Duchy was seen in St Petersburg as fraught with evil omen, and in January 1810 the Russiäns drafted a convention by the terms of which Napoleon was to agree that he would never consent to a revival of the Kingdom of Poland. As soon as his marriage to Marie-Louise had been arranged, Napoleon refused to ratify the convention.

In August 1810 the adoption of the French Marshal Bernadotte as Prince Royal of Sweden – a Swedish attempt to secure French support against Russian expansion in the Baltic – was viewed in Russia as another example of French encirclement, though in fact Napoleon detested Bernadotte.

The war of 1812 really stemmed from the fact that, for financial reasons, Russia could no longer adhere to the Continental System, to which Napoleon had devoted his energies during 1810 and 1811.

His annexation of Holland, the Hanse towns of Germany and the Duchy of Oldenburg, the property of the Czar's brother-in-law, caused general resentment and alarm. In mid-October 1810 the Czar refused Napoleon's demand that all ships under neutral flags in Russian waters should be embargoed. This was followed in December 1810 by an order facilitating the entry of neutral shipping to Russian ports, and the imposition of heavy import duties on 'luxuries' like French wines and silks – a severe blow to the fragile French economy. Even now, war was not inevitable – except that Napoleon chose to regard any breach in the Continental blockade as a blow against his Empire and its security.

The prospect of war with France did not, apparently, bother the Czar. The Spanish resistance had given him confidence and as he said to the French Ambassador, Caulaincourt, early in 1811, 'If the Emperor decides to make war, we may be defeated, assuming that we fight, but that will not bring peace. The Spaniards have often been defeated but they fight on, and they are not so far from Paris as we are, and without our space or climate or resources. Our climate and our winter will fight on our side.'

A *rapprochement* between the Czar and Bernadotte, now Regent of Sweden, resulted from Napoleon's occupation of Swedish Pomerania in January 1812 and secured Russia's northern flank, while the Treaty of Bucharest between Russia and Turkey in May 1812 released many thousands of Russian troops and secured the country in that direction. In April, Czar Alexander sent Napoleon an ultimatum: 'The Emperor must withdraw his troops from Prussia and compensate the Duchy of Oldenburg.'

The Czar's demands for territorial concessions in Poland led to a stormy scene at the Tuileries with the Russian Ambassador, Kurakin, in which Napoleon threatened Russia with a *Grande Armée* of 500,000 men, adding that even if the Russian army was on the heights of Montmartre, he would not cede an inch of Polish soil.

Napoleon was clearly undeterred by Alexander's stance. Any concession now would lead inevitably to other demands, eventually to the collapse of his Empire, and he had been pushing forward his preparations since the beginning of 1811. In June 1812 the *Grande Armée* began its march towards Russia, but away in the west, the 'Spanish ulcer' remained open. By attacking Russia before ending the war in Spain, Napoleon repeated his mistake of 1809 – he engaged himself in war on two fronts.

12

The Spanish Frontier:

1811–1812

'It is very difficult to starve a Frenchman.'
General Rowland Hill
Torres Vedras: 1810

WELLINGTON'S ARMY, ESCORTING most of the non-military population of Estremadura, entered the Lines of Torres Vedras on 11
October 1810. Masséna had heard of their existence only days previously, and had no idea of their strength. Coming up the next day,
he surveyed them with his own eyes and with his advance troops
probed several outlying positions – enough to convince him that, with
no more than 50,000 men, his entire siege train still at Almeida,
and the onset of winter rapidly rendering difficult roads all but impassable, an attack was impossible. He had already discovered that
the Portuguese militia, the *ordenança*, had not entered the Lines but,
having allowed the French army to pass, had cut his communications
and were engaged in harassing his rear, enclosing his army in a net.
Wellington had ordered the *ordenança* to avoid any major engagement
and concentrate on cutting off stragglers and convoys, destroying
small detachments, and preventing the French from foraging.
Throughout his pursuit of Wellington, Masséna had found himself
caught up within a sort of mobile blockade, hemmed in on all sides
by an active but intangible enemy. Sitting down before Torres Vedras
he became the besieged rather than the besieger. When the *ordenança*
of Beira closed in on his rear, he was in command only of the ground
on which his three army corps were encamped. With his communications cut, he had no idea whether his reserves were on their way; and,
thanks to Wellington's 'scorched-earth' policy, heroically carried out

at great personal sacrifice by the Portuguese, he was short of food and fodder.

After a month outside the Lines, losing men by the thousand through sickness, Masséna withdrew thirty miles up the Tagus to Santarém, where he stayed for four months. Wellington and his army, snug within the Lines, were victualled by the Royal Navy; it was rumoured that the French were eating cats and donkeys.

Napoleon had intended that Soult should co-operate with Masséna by advancing into the Alemtejo and threatening Lisbon from the south. There was no love lost between the two marshals and Soult began late and moved slowly. In February he defeated the Spanish army of Estremadura at the Gebora and moved on to besiege Badajoz, which surrendered on 11 March 1810. On the 5th Masséna had abandoned Santarém and begun a plodding retreat across the mountains of central Beira. Most of his horses were dead, and his starving troops deserted by the thousand, hunting the Portuguese peasants in the mountains to demand food, and committing hideous atrocities which provoked equally hideous retaliation.

The British within the Lines had almost given up expecting Masséna to move, and his departure took them by surprise, winning him a thirty-mile advantage. Wellington set off in pursuit with five divisions, sending another two under Beresford through the Alemtejo into Spanish Estremadura with orders to relieve Badajoz. This proved fruitless, as the fortress surrendered to the French two days before Beresford's arrival.

Masséna's intention had been to stay in Portugal, withdrawing only as far north as the Mondego river where he hoped to feed and refit his army in the fertile country around Coimbra, but he was harried by the *ordenança* under Trant, and the Light Division were close upon his heels, skirmishing with the rearguard under Ney. Though without General Craufurd who was on leave, and hampered by the fumbling efforts of their temporary commander, General Sir William Erskine, a very senior officer known to be intermittently insane, the Light Division and their Portuguese comrades of the *caçadores* were able to make life unbearable for the French. Masséna abandoned his position on the Mondego, destroyed his baggage train, shot his mules, and made a dash for the Spanish frontier. On the way he quarrelled with Ney, who refused a direct order to take his corps into the wilderness of central Portugal without supplies or support. Ney was relieved of his command and sent back to France in disgrace, and Masséna fell back on the River Coa, where his starving men were supplied by the garrison at Cuidad Rodrigo.

Masséna's withdrawal towards Cuidad Rodrigo was not unskilful. The only occasion on which the French were severely punished was early in April, when the IInd Corps under Reynier, left to cover Masséna's withdrawal at Sabugal just behind the Coa, became cut off. Sir William Erskine, who was currently enjoying one of his less lucid periods, managed to send the Light Division marching in one direction while he galloped off into a thick mist with the cavalry, not to be seen again that day. The four divisions attacking in the centre drove the IInd Corps out of their position, then out of the country, and the only French force now left in Portugal was the garrison of Almeida.

While Masséna began regrouping and refitting near Salamanca, Wellington prepared to lay siege to Almeida where the garrison was nearing starvation. Expecting Masséna to send relief any day, Wellington nevertheless dashed south to Badajoz to give Beresford instructions regarding its investment.

Masséna might have left Almeida to the British but he chose to lead his exhausted army forward once more. He appealed to Bessières, the commander of the Army of the North, for all his artillery and as many squadrons as he could spare and Bessières, showing no great zeal, brought 1,500 horse and a single battery to Rodrigo on 1 May. With 48,000 men and 38 cannon Masséna marched to the relief of Almeida, and on 3 May he encountered Wellington's army on the heights of Fuentes de Oñoro, some miles south-east of Almeida. Fuentes de Oñoro is a small village set on a rocky hillside overlooking a shallow river, the Dos Casas, just inside the Spanish frontier beside the main road from Almeida to Cuidad Rodrigo. A jumble of stone walls and houses, narrow lanes and small fields, all overlooked by a stone church, it was the key to this part of the frontier. Masséna, having failed to learn from Busaco, made a frontal attack, but could not prevail against Wellington's five battalions from the 1st and 3rd Divisions, reinforced by the Highlanders of the 71st and 79th Foot. The vicious street-fighting which took place in Fuentes is still talked about by the older inhabitants: 'Cannon balls bouncing over the walls and blood from the dead Scottish soldiers running into the river ... this we were told by *los abuelos* – our grandparents.' Masséna was more skilful in his second assault, which began shortly after dawn on 5 May.

This time he first feinted to the front at Fuentes, then made an outflanking sweep to the south with three infantry divisions and a cavalry brigade. The right of the British line was thinly held by a troop of horse artillery, 1,500 assorted cavalry, the newly-formed 7th Division and some Spanish *guerrilleros*. Considerably outnumbered, this mixed formation was soon cut up and isolated and Fuentes exposed in flank and rear.

Most opportunely, General Robert Craufurd had returned to his Light Division on the evening of 4 May. Wellington ordered them forward from Fuentes de Oñoro to cover the retreat of the 7th Division. This left his road to Portugal uncovered but, as Lady Longford says, 'he trusted his troops not to need it.'

Craufurd formed his men into battalion columns, each ready to form square when the French cavalry came thundering in. Supported by horse artillery, the cavalry and the hussars of the King's German Legion, the Light Division came back for three miles across the open plain to rejoin Wellington's army west of Fuentes de Oñoro, while the 7th Division reformed. Napier describes an incident of the engagement in epic terms: Captain Norman Ramsay, in command of a pair of guns, lingered too long firing at the French cavalry and became engulfed, but

> . . . a great commotion was observed in [the] main body [of the French]. Men and horses there closed with confusion and tumult towards one point, a thick dust arose, and loud cries, and the sparkling of blades and the flashing of pistols, indicated some extraordinary occurrence. Suddenly the multitude became violently agitated, an English shout pealed high and clear, and Norman Ramsay burst forth at the head of his battery, his horses breathing fire, stretched like greyhounds along the plain, the guns bounded behind them like things of no weight, and the mounted gunners followed in close career.

This fighting retreat enabled Wellington to swing his forces round to more secure positions against Masséna's advance on his right and, after a heavy cannonade, the French attack subsided. Meanwhile, there was more vicious fighting in Fuentes de Oñoro. The Highlanders of the 71st and 79th were in the thick of it and again it was the 'ragged rascals' of the 88th Foot (Connaught Rangers) whose ferocious charge ended the engagement. It had been a close-run thing and, as Wellington himself said later, 'If Boney had been there, we would have been damnably licked.' Wellington, having lost 1,500 men, held his ground for another day and then resumed the siege of Almeida, but Masséna had some slight grounds for claiming – as he did – a victory. The governor of Almeida, Brennier, hearing of the result of the battle of Fuentes de Oñoro, resolved to break out, Wellington's orders designed to counter such an eventuality were inefficiently carried through, and the garrison were able to blow up the fortress and make good their escape to Masséna's outposts.

Masséna withdrew to Cuidad Rodrigo and a week later received news of his recall to France. The new commander was the 37-year-old Marshal Auguste Marmont, Duke of Ragusa. Like Napoleon, Marmont had entered the army as an artillery lieutenant; he had been with Bonaparte at Toulon, and received his Marshal's baton after Wagram in 1809. He was a good soldier, with one virtue uncommon among Napoleon's marshals; Marmont was willing to co-operate with his colleagues.

Marshal Soult's departure with the Vth Corps for Estremadura and Badajoz had been the signal for the British and Spanish troops in Cadiz to attempt a disruption of Marshal Victor's blockade of the city, and 4,500 British under General Sir Thomas Graham routed 7,000 French at Barrossa.

Meanwhile, at Badajoz, Beresford succeeded in driving off the Vth Corps left by Soult and investing the fortress. There he was reinforced by the remnants of the Spanish army under Castaños and Blake which had been crushed at the Gebora. Soult, hearing of this, came up from Seville with 23,000 men, the reserves of the Army of Andalucía. Beresford had been attempting to reduce Badajoz using ancient Portuguese cannon – a fruitless task which he was probably not sorry to abandon when news came of Soult's approach. Leaving a small force to maintain the siege of Badajoz, Beresford marched south on 15th May. Beresford was able to concentrate 32,000 men against the French, at Albuhera, but only 8,000 were British. Albuhera is a jumbled village of whitewashed houses lying at the foot of a long ridge, the last outcrop of a line of hills which run south from Badajoz, fourteen miles away. This ridge is traversed by the road leading to Badajoz, and surrounded on its southern flank by the Albuhera river. Beresford deployed his men astride the road where it overlooks the river. The Albuhera position is commanded by other, higher ground to the left and right but Beresford did not occupy this, later giving as his reason that there was higher ground beyond that, and beyond that yet again, and since he was sure the French would attack his centre wherever he happened to be, he might as well make a stand astride the road.

On the morning of 15 May, crossing the river high up under cover of some woods, Soult was able to fall upon Beresford's right wing, composed entirely of Spanish troops under Blake. These gave way, but Beresford came up with the 2nd Division and attacked the head of the French column. As the troops were closing, a heavy rain storm swept the hillside, under cover of which a brigade of French cavalry was able to charge the British flank and rear, annihilating the three leading battalions. The French lancers galloped on, spearing the gunners of the 2nd Division artillery and reaching Beresford's position. His Staff drew their swords and fought them off, Beresford saving himself by knocking an attacking lancer from the saddle.

Three British brigades now came forward to occupy the Albuhera ridge, before the massed advance of two French divisions now flooding up the slope.

> Silently and steadily [the remaining seven battalions] advanced, to within sixty yards of the enemy, unsupported as yet by any artillery, and opened fire . . . Then followed a duel so stern and resolute that it has few parallels in the Annals of War . . .

Fortescue's account, though written a hundred years after the battle, gives a vivid impression of that confused and bloody fight. Deafened by gunfire and musketry, enveloped in clouds of smoke, those involved were too busy with musket, cartridge and ramrod to see much of what was going on. They fell in swathes, but nothing could break that indomitable line; the survivors fired, reloaded and advanced again. In one battalion every officer was killed or wounded. General Stewart, though wounded twice, refused to leave the field. General Houghton refused even to dismount, and cheered his men on until he fell dead. Colonel William Inglis of the 57th Foot (later the Middlesex Regiment), lying wounded among his soldiers, urged them on with cries of 'Die hard, 57th . . . Die hard!' The Middlesex Regiment are still known as The Diehards. Colonel Inglis survived to become a lieutenant-general, but Colonel Duckworth of the 58th died, as did the Colonel of the 29th, but still the line held. Four-fifths of General Houghton's brigade were down, yet still the survivors stood and fired and fought, advancing now to within twenty paces of the French. Marshal Soult had never seen such infantry. 'They could not be persuaded they were beaten,' he wrote later. 'They were completely beaten, the day was mine and they did not know it and they would not run.'

All sense had gone from either side. These soldiers, French and

English, had set their teeth into each other. They were going to fight this to the finish, whatever the odds or the casualties. On the French side those crashing British volleys had done fearful execution. Four French generals were killed or wounded; all the colonels and company officers of the leading battalions in the French columns were struck down by volleys from that dimly-seen red line which, extending beyond their column heads, was firing into it from either flank. The dead lay in heaps, the muskets grew hot, their barrels thick with fouling, and still the fight went on. Neither of the commanding generals had control of the battle, and Beresford was rapidly losing control of himself. He tried to send a Spanish brigade forward, dragging its colonel along by the scruff of his neck, but the men would not follow. He sent out various contradictory orders to his brigade commanders, most of which they ignored. With Soult's rear brigades coming up, he was on the point of ordering a withdrawal when the smoke on the right wing drifted away for a moment and the French were seen to be in full retreat.

General Lowry Cole had been persuaded by Colonel Henry Hardinge to throw his last troops, three British and three Portuguese regiments of the 4th Division, against the left flank of the French columns. Soult's reserve were thrust aside by the Fusiliers, who with the Portuguese *caçadores* drove the Vth Corps from the field.

> ... then was seen with what a strength and majesty the British soldier fights [wrote Napier] ... Nothing could stop that astonishing infantry ... their measured tread shook the ground, their dreadful volleys swept away the head of every formation ... the mighty mass [of the French reserve] gave way and like a loosened cliff went headlong down the steep. The rain flowed after in streams discoloured with blood, and fifteen hundred unwounded men, the remnant of six thousand unconquerable British soldiers, stood triumphant on the fatal hill.

Albuhera was the bloodiest of all the Peninsular battles. Of 7,600 British on the field, more than 4,000 were lost; the Portuguese lost about 400, the Spanish more than 2,000. French losses exceeded 7,000, plus a gun, five standards and 500 prisoners. After lingering for a day, Soult retreated towards Andalucía, leaving a thousand of his wounded behind.

When Wellington arrived three days later, he was highly critical of Beresford's choice of terrain and handling of the battle. Beresford, in the depths of despair, poured out his regrets in a report which Wellington promptly rejected, convinced that it would 'have driven the people in England mad. Write me down a victory.' The report was duly rewritten.

If a victory, it was of the Pyrrhic variety. In a letter home Sir Charles Stewart, Wellington's Adjutant-General, wrote of the '. . . inextinguishable, unexampled and (I may say) incomprehensible valour of the British infantry'. The price of that valour had been high; Beresford wrote sadly, 'Our dead, particularly of the 57th Regiment, were lying as they had fought, in rows, and every wound was in the front.'

The two fortress towns of Badajoz and Cuidad Rodrigo commanded the viable routes between Portugal and Spain. Before advancing into Spain, Wellington needed to hold one or the other, preferably both, but his ability to take them was hampered by his lack of an adequate siege train. At Badajoz he had only a platoon of Royal Engineers and those antiquated Portuguese cannon. Two assaults, on the 6th and 9th of June, failed and when Marshal Marmont summoned Soult again from Andalucía, the threat of their combined forces of some 60,000 men forced Wellington to raise the siege. On 17 June he withdrew across the Guadiana and the French must have been well pleased, for the fortress had been on the verge of surrender through starvation.

Stalemate ensued. Wellington took up a strong position on the Portuguese frontier with 50,000 men, inviting an attack. The marshals, having stripped León and Andalucía to muster those 60,000 men, did not feel strong enough for another battle, though it was, as it transpired, almost the last occasion on which they would face Wellington with superior numbers. On 4 July 1811 Soult marched away to Seville and, too weak to fight without him, Marmont drew off to the Tagus valley.

On 1 August Wellington set out with four divisions to threaten Cuidad Rodrigo. Two divisions, under General Sir Rowland Hill, were left in Estremadura to watch Soult. Wellington began to make preparations for the investment of Cuidad Rodrigo, but as he waited for his siege train to come up by river from Oporto, he could do little but blockade from a distance. This caused Marmont to call up the Army of the North which, under its new commander, Dorsenne, brought four strong divisions to join Marmont near Salamanca. On 21 September they again mustered 60,000 men. Wellington's army had been depleted by sickness, and he retired into the Portuguese mountains on 25 September.

Forces over which Wellington had no control began, towards the end of 1811, to change the circumstances under which he was operating. Napoleon ordered Marmont to transfer 10,000 men to Suchet's army in Valencia and Catalonia, which meant that Marmont at Salamanca was slightly inferior in numbers to Wellington on the frontier. More importantly, in January came confirmation of the rumours of an inevitable war between France and Russia. This was also the period when the legendary Spanish guerrilla leaders came into prominence. Their activities in harassing the French garrisons and communications ensured that even the 300,000 soldiers Napoleon had in the Peninsula were never enough to both hold down Spain *and* invade Portugal. They enabled Wellington and his small force to keep the field, since the French could never muster an army of more than 70,000 to meet him.

Calculating that it would take the French three weeks to muster an army from their winter quarters, Wellington began his second advance on Cuidad Rodrigo on 4 January 1812. By the 8th it was surrounded and a battalion of light infantry had seized an outwork 600 yards from the walls. Cuidad Rodrigo boasted impressive defences. The city occupies the crown of a small hill on the north bank of the Rio Agueda, about a hundred and fifty feet above the valley. Before a medieval wall thirty feet high the French had constructed a counter-scarp of masonry twelve feet high, set behind a deep and almost impenetrable ditch. While the garrison could muster only 1,700 men, they also had the entire artillery train for the Army of Portugal which had been stored at Cuidad Rodrigo for the winter, and could mount 150 heavy guns on the walls, if they could find enough gunners to man them.

Four of Wellington's seven divisions took turns in the trenches, while the others provided a covering force in case Marmont should attempt to send relief. The besieging troops had to ford the Agueda from their camp on the west bank, going to and from the trenches under cover of darkness, and spent much of their time in clothing either soaking wet or thick with ice in the bitter winter weather. On 14 January a battery of twenty-four siege guns arrived from Oporto and opened fire on the walls. Three days later a second battery opened fire and within twenty-four hours two breaches had been pronounced practicable for assault. By the strict rules of siege-craft the attack should have been held back some days longer, while the fire of the defence was subdued and the breach widened, but Wellington was in haste lest Marmont should come up to raise the siege.

An assault was generally made under cover of darkness, carried forward by the raw courage of the infantry. At Rodrigo the main breach was to be attacked by the 3rd Division, the smaller by volunteers from Craufurd's Light Division. The night was fine and very cold, with a bright moon. The hour fixed for the attack was 7 o'clock; the two main assaults were to be supported by various diversions, but most of these failed to distract the French, who greeted the assaulting troops with grenades, musketry and cannon firing grape-shot. Major George Napier of the 52nd Foot, who led the storming party of the Light Division, left this account of what happened:

January 19 . . . I went to [the] three regiments . . . and said, 'Soldiers, I have the honour to be appointed to the command of the storming party for the assault of the small breach. I want one hundred volunteers from each regiment; those who will go with me come forward.' Instantly there rushed out half the division, and we were obliged to take them at chance. I formed them into companies of one hundred men each . . . These were preceded by what is called the 'forlorn hope' consisting of twenty-five men, two sergeants and one subaltern, a lieutenant, because if he survives he gets a company. When it was nearly dark the Light Division was formed behind the old convent . . . nearly opposite the small breach. Lord Wellington sent for Colonel Colbourne and myself, and pointing out, as well as the light would permit, the spot where the foot of the breach was, he said to me, 'Now do you understand the way you are to lead, so as to arrive at the breach without noise or confusion?' I answered, and we went back to the regiment, and just before I moved on some staff officer present said, 'Why, your men are not loaded; why do you not make them load?' I replied, 'Because if we do not do the business with the bayonet we shall not be able to do it at all, so I shall not load.' I heard Lord Wellington, who was close by, say, 'Let him alone; let him go his own way.'

Promptly at seven o'clock the storming-party advanced in double column of sections, Lieutenant Gurwood in advance a few yards with the 'forlorn hope'. We soon came to the ditch, and immediately jumping in, we rushed forward to the *fausse-braie*, and having clambered up we proceeded towards the breach. But Lieutenant Gurwood and party having, owing to the darkness of the night, gone too far to the left, was employed in placing a ladder on the unbreached face of the bastion, when he got a shot in the head; but immediately recovering his feet he came up to me, and at that moment the engineer . . . called out, 'You are wrong, this way to the right is the breach'; and Captain Fergusson, myself, Gurwood, and the rest of the officers, and such men as were nearest . . . rushed on, and we all mounted the breach together, the enemy pouring a heavy fire on us. When about two-thirds up, I received a grape-shot which smashed my elbow and a great part of my arm, the men, who thought I was killed, checked for a few moments and . . . commenced snapping their muskets. I immediately called out, 'Recollect you are not loaded; push on with the bayonet.' Upon this the whole gave a loud 'hurrah', and driving all before them carried the breach.

Napier's arm was later amputated.

The attack was not as straightforward as Major Napier's last sentence makes it sound. One assault ladder broke and falling men were impaled on the bayonets of their comrades waiting below. A French magazine exploded during the assault of MacKinnon's brigade at the main breach and sent MacKinnon and many of his Connaught Rangers flying through the air. MacKinnon died, but the rest recovered and came forward, bayoneting French gunners right and left as they ran along the ramparts, fighting their way with great loss down into the streets of the town. Robert Craufurd, going forward with his Light Division, received a mortal wound. His soldiers returned to the attack after carrying his body to safety and he was later buried in the breach.

Whether in reaction to the stress of battle and the death of General Craufurd, or because many had been primed with drink before the assault, the men of the Light and 3rd Divisions, having taken the town, lost all sense of order or discipline. Within minutes, little better than an armed mob, '. . . without warning or reason . . .', they started firing into the windows of the houses, breaking down doors, dragging people into the street, looting whatever they could take, smashing anything they were unable to carry. General Picton rode in to restore order, his voice '. . . crying damnation on everyone', but his troops could not be controlled. Men staggered about the town, crazed with drink, some wearing women's dresses, raping, looting, murdering and burning. Not until daylight was order finally restored.

The siege and capture of Cuidad Rodrigo cost Wellington 1,100 casualties, including 200 killed. This successful action earned Wellington an elevation in status, from Viscount to Earl, and an increase of £2,000 a year in his pension.

Marmont had been prevented by bad roads and worse weather from concentrating at Salamanca before 25 January. Hearing of the fall of Cuidad Rodrigo, he sent his divisions back to winter quarters. On 28

January, Wellington sent General Hill's corps to Almaráz to counter any activity on the part of King Joseph's Army of the Centre at Madrid, and when he was sure Marmont's troops had dispersed, he began the march south to the Guadiana, reaching Badajoz on 16 March 1812.

Badajoz was a more difficult proposition than Cuidad Rodrigo. The walls were twenty-five feet high, studded with bastions rising to thirty feet, screened on two sides by the Guadiana river, 300 yards wide, and its tributary, the Rivillas. There were also three fortified outworks, the Pardaleras, the Picurina and the San Cristóbal, and the position was defended by a garrison of 4,700 under a governor, General Philippon, a soldier of known skill and tenacity.

The government had failed to provide Wellington with a corps of sappers so the infantry again had to play the part of engineers. The Guadiana rose and swept away their pontoon bridge, and the men worked in flooded trenches, but Fort Picurina was taken on the 25th. Wellington's cannon then pounded the walls, and breaches were slowly opened up. The assault was ordered for Easter Sunday, 6 April 1812, before the breaches were really practicable, but speed had again become essential. It was known that Soult was moving up, and Marmont was raiding the thinly defended region between Almeida and Cuidad Rodrigo.

What was not known was how busy General Philippon had been. Walls had been built behind the breaches and covered by cannon, the breaches filled with a *chevaux-de-frise* of sharpened swords hammered through planks and chained to the ground. The steep slopes leading to the breaches were covered with planks of wood set with spikes a foot long, and the walls and roof-tops overlooking each breach were occupied by defenders.

The Light and 4th Divisions were to assault at 10 p.m. and Picton's 3rd Division was to attempt an escalade of the main castle, while Leith's 5th Division created a diversion on the other side of the town. The storming parties were creeping forward in columns of companies to the foot of the ditch when a storm of lights and cannon fire broke upon them. French infantry and cannon took a terrible toll of the attackers who, clearly visible in the light of flares, clawed their way over the first defences and onto the *cheveaux-de-frise* of sword-blades, every gun and musket playing upon them. Again and again the Light Division and the 4th tried to fight their way through the breaches, only to be driven back with terrible losses, each attempt leaving dead and dying in the breach. Every charge was repulsed and Wellington was about to call off the attack at midnight, when victory came unexpectedly.

As the bugles were sounding the retreat, news came that a small party from Picton's 3rd Division had taken the castle. The sound of a English bugle was heard on the far side of the town, where Leith's 5th Division had scaled the curtain wall under heavy fire and were running through the streets to take the breach defenders in the rear. Thus encouraged, the Light Division and the 4th came on again, climbing over the *chevaux-de-frise* and their dead or wounded comrades to crest the broken masonry.

Badajoz was taken. The soldiers were parched with thirst and half-mad with the excitement of battle; another orgy of drunkenness and violence, plunder and rape ensued until, on 8 April, Wellington had a gallows erected in the Plaza Mayor.

The price of Badajoz was high. Over 5,000 fell, nearly 4,000 during the actual assaults. The 95th alone lost twenty-two officers, and there were 1,500 bodies in the main breach. Wellington wept when he saw them, and wrote to the War Minister:

> The Capture of Badajoz affords as strong an instance of the gallantry of our troops as has ever been displayed. But I greatly hope that I shall never again be the instrument of putting them to such a test.

Five thousand prisoners were taken, including those of the garrison who were not killed in the assault or its immediate aftermath. The most famous 'captive' of Badajoz was a young Spanish lady, Juanita de los Dolores de León, who was saved from rape by Harry Smith of the Light Division. She married him within days and, years later, when he became Governor of the Cape, gave her name to the town of Ladysmith.

The siege and capture of Badajoz had taken a month, and when Soult's army came up from Andalucía a few days later, Soult found himself confronted by Wellington's army, drawn up again on that ill-omened Albuhera ridge. There was to be no repeat of Beresford's mistakes, and after a few skirmishes Soult withdrew, leaving the gates of Spain in the hands of the Peninsular Army.

Wellington had achieved a strategic advantage. By seizing the fortresses he had gained the initiative for any advance into Spain, but the tide of war was now turning against the French everywhere. Even as Wellington prepared to advance into Castile, far away on the other side of Europe, the Emperor Napoleon was leading his men into the fatal space of Russia.

13

The Invasion of Russia:

1812

From the moment the first troops crossed the Neiman, the
Emperor was committed to a path leading inexorably to St
Helena.

David Chandler
The Campaigns of Napoleon: 1967

NAPOLEON WAS AWARE of the difficulties inherent in any invasion
of Russia. His spies and embassies were ordered to report on the
terrain and the roads, on the size of the Russian forces and the morale
of the Russian people. His investigations can have left him few illu-
sions, but even so it is likely that he underestimated the extent of the
problems, particularly that of supply.

The subjugation of Russia would require a large army. Russia
was another Spain, but a Spain writ large, a vast, desolate and inhos-
pitable land with a harsh climate. On this campaign, if the *Grande
Armée* was to eat, it must carry its supplies with it, and the number of
men who could be fed would determine the number who could
march. Napoleon initially calculated that he would need at least half
a million front-line troops, with as many more in support. In view of the
opposing numbers, this was a not unreasonable estimate. However,
quite apart from the question of supplies, Napoleon failed to address
the vital question of how such a large force was to be commanded
and controlled, given the generally precarious state of communications, and the disparity of the national contingents. It was also necessary to maintain an army in Spain, and strong garrisons on the
French frontiers and in the territories of his reluctant subject-nations.
The French people were becoming war-weary, and Napoleon

therefore decided that his allies should provide the bulk of the invasion force.

By the end of 1811, his three 'Corps of Observation' in the Grand Duchy of Warsaw gave Napoleon an army of some 200,000 men, as large a force as he had ever commanded. Prince Eugène was instructed to bring 50,000 men from the Army of Italy, and 150,000 Germans were provided by the Confederation of the Rhine and his brother Jerome's kingdom of Westphalia. There were 50,000 willing Poles, and rather less willing contingents from Austria and Prussia. Provision was made to increase the size of the Imperial Guard to 50,000 men and Murat, now King of Naples, brought up two cavalry corps, 20,000 horse. The final total exceeded 600,000 men.

As his first step towards controlling this mighty force, Napoleon introduced a new military formation, the Army Group. The First Army Group, his own army, 250,000-strong, included the Imperial Guard, both Murat's cavalry corps, and three corps of varying sizes commanded by Davout, Oudinot and Ney; a number of the units in this army had been recalled from Spain, thus weakening the French effort in the Peninsula. The numbers mustered under brigades, divisions or corps were rarely constant: Oudinot's IInd Corps totalled 37,000, while the more capable Davout had no fewer than 72,000 in his Ist Corps. The majority of soldiers in this First Army Group were French.

The Second Army Group, intended to protect the lines of communication, guard the frontiers and provide reinforcements, consisted of 150,000 allied troops mustered in two armies, one commanded by Prince Eugène, the other by Napoleon's younger brother Jerome, King of Westphalia. Eugène had 80,000 Italians and Bavarians, while Jerome's 70,000 were his own Westphalians, plus Poles, Hessians and Saxons. Jerome had never commanded an army and Eugène had been defeated by the Austrians in 1809, so each was given an experienced French general as Chief-of-Staff. The flanks of this Second Army Group were to be protected by two independent corps, the Xth commanded by Marshal Macdonald covering the Baltic Coast, and Prince Schwarzenberg's Austrian Corps which guarded the flank to the south.

The third Group consisted of replacements, recruits and auxiliaries, destined eventually for transfer to one or other of the leading formations. Among about 165,000 men were Marshal Victor's French IXth Corps, two French divisions of the XIth Corps, and a large number of Lithuanian and German levies. The final formation, the

Grande Armée Reserve, totalled about 60,000 men and included the balance of the Xth Corps under the command of the veteran marshal, Augereau.

France was stripped of soldiers, every garrison cut to the bone; Napoleon called up all men of military age, and these, mustered into a number of territorial formations from the National Guard, plus the Young Guard and a number of infantry and artillery regiments, were to defend France while the Emperor was in Russia.

It was also necessary to ensure that this vast army should be supplied with food, clothing, arms and ammunition for the coming campaign. Although logistics were never Napoleon's strong point, his almost superhuman energies on this occasion resulted in the creation of twenty-six transport battalions equipped with carts and waggons to carry grain, flour and food. Great herds of cattle were collected to provide meat on the hoof. Two hundred thousand horses were found for the cavalry, the artillery, and the vital transport teams. Throughout the spring of 1812 huge depots were established in the Grand Duchy of Warsaw from where supplies would be sent forward as the army advanced. The plans covered every imaginable eventuality: even sunglasses were included, as protection against the glare from snow − in the unlikely event of the campaign lasting into the winter . . .

Napoleon was aware that time and distance were his greatest enemies, but he could do nothing about the state of the Russian roads and the distance between his depots and his advancing armies; he could lay up great stocks of food and fodder in the Grand Duchy, but even the vast resources at his disposal could not maintain his 600,000 men for more than twenty-four days. The Emperor intended one of his swift campaigns and the Czar was to be brought to heel in just three weeks. It was not to work out like that.

Czar Alexander was no warlord, but neither was he a fool. He recognized the tactical benefits of his country's vast, empty spaces, and he aimed to make full use of them. The Czar was not unduly overawed by the prospect of war with the all-conquering Napoleon. The extent of his resolve may be gauged by a remark he made in May 1812 to the new French Ambassador, Narbonne: 'If the Emperor Napoleon is determined on war, and if fortune does not smile on our just cause, he will have to go to the ends of the earth to find peace.'

Such plain speaking reflected the Russian belief that, if all else failed, time and distance would bring Napoleon down. The Czar had also prepared for war. Having concluded peace or forged alliances with Great Britain, Turkey and Sweden, he was able to concentrate all the military resources of his country against the French. His Minister of War was an experienced general, Baron Barclay de Tolly, who would also command the Russian First Army. By June 1812 Barclay had three armies in the west, ready to meet the anticipated invasion; the total Russian force available numbered about 240,000 men. The First Army, about 126,000 strong, included large numbers of Cossacks, those roving, irregular horse, recruited in the Don Valley and armed with sword, lance and musket, who were to prove one of the most effective, feared and memorable elements of the Russian army. The First Army had also a formidable artillery contingent with more than 500 guns of various calibres.

The Second Army, under General Prince Bagration, another experienced soldier, was considerably smaller, just 48,000 men in two corps, plus 7,000 cavalry and another 4,000 Cossacks, for on the empty plains of Russia, cavalry was the most useful arm. Troops still coming in from Moldavia and Wallachia as the French advanced were formed into a Third Army of 43,000, under General Count Tormassov.

Other Russian forces were or would become available. General Wittgenstein commanded a full corps on the Baltic Coast, and there were numerous garrisons in the major towns and cities. The defence of Russia was therefore adequate and in capable hands, but several factors combined to make it less effective than it might have been. Barclay de Tolly and Prince Bagration disliked one another intensely and were reluctant to co-operate, and their armies were too far apart. At the end of April 1812, Barclay's First Army was at Vilna, Bagration's Second Army at Volkovisk, some 130 miles south, and Tormassov's reserves at Lutsk, about 180 miles south again. In this separation, revealed to him by his spies, lay Napoleon's best chance. He would attempt to beat the Russian armies one by one, before they were able to concentrate.

Following his customary strategy, Napoleon aimed to seek out the enemy's main field army, manoeuvre it onto ground of his choosing, holding it there with one corps or part of his army while his other units concentrated and smashed it to pieces, with cavalry manoeuvring at the rear to prevent any escape. The next element of his strategy was to further weaken his enemies' morale by occupying their capital but was it to be St Petersburg, where the Czar held court, or Moscow, the religious capital of the country? Napoleon had spoken to Narbonne of Moscow as the half-way house to India, and of the Russian war as but the opening stage of a great triumphal progress through the East – there were clearly reasons within reasons for his decision to attack Russia but Napoleon decided that his main axis of advance should be across the Nieman river at Kovno, advancing on Moscow via Vilna, Vitebsk and Smolensk.

The general dispositions of the Russian forces being known, Napoleon had selected Barclay de Tolly's over-extended First Army as his initial objective. Against it he proposed to adopt an enveloping strategy. Having made contact, he would push forward with his left flank while falling back or 'refusing' with his right. This should result in Barclay falling back in his turn, and shifting south to avoid encirclement and to link up with Bagration, who would be held by King Jerome and Prince Schwarzenberg. When Bagration advanced to attack Napoleon's right, as he surely would, the Emperor's more powerful left and centre would circle round, cut the First Army's communications with Moscow, push both Russian armies into a pocket around Grodno, and swallow them up. Napoleon estimated that this part of the operation would take about twelve days.

Dominating the ground south-east of the Nieman are the Pripet Marshes, a vast area of swamp crossed in 1812 by three very poor roads. Napoleon's plan was for Jerome and Eugène to feign a major advance south of the marshes. Once Prince Bagration was fully engaged in pushing back this advance Napoleon would sweep forward through Vilna and wheel south, pivoting on Eugène's IVth Corps (which would protect his right flank during this advance), forcing the Russians near Grodno to either fight or surrender. Jerome and Prince Schwarzenerg would then pin the Russians in position, while Napoleon swept in on their right flank and rear. The execution of this superb concept depended on factors which could not be guaranteed – close co-ordination, accurate timing, and secure communications. Most of Napoleon's battles had been won by the exercise of on-the-spot command and his personal will upon comparatively small, compact armies on small battlefields. Using mounted couriers, it was impossible for him to exercise such control over several armies, spread across a distance of 300 miles. Had he done more soldiering in Spain, he would doubtless have known this. Too much depended upon messages getting through and commanders being willing to carry out commands on time, and to the letter. The plan itself was superb but its execution was lamentable.

The plan also depended upon the Russians reacting in the way Napoleon supposed they would. He assumed that, in their anxiety to defend the soil of Holy Russia, they would give battle as soon as he entered their territory. The Czar and Barclay knew, however, that to fight Napoleon while his forces were strong and fresh would be to invite disaster. Their plan was to unite the First and Second Armies and fall back slowly to the line of the three great rivers which run across Russia from the Baltic to the Black Sea, the Dnieper, the Dvina and the Berezina, where strong defensive lines and fortresses were already being established. Here Napoleon would be at least 200 miles from the Nieman, his army weakened, his lines of communication and supply dangerously extended and open to attack by Cossacks. The Czar had space at his disposal, and intended to make full use of it. With both sides determined to fight, the war with Russia began in early June 1812.

The first patrols of the *Grande Armée* reached the Nieman on 22 June 1812 and found there was no sign of the enemy on the eastern bank. When Napoleon arrived he carried out a personal inspection of both river banks while the two advance corps of the army, under Davout and Oudinot, came up with the Imperial Guard under Lefebvre, Mortier and Bessières. The crossing and the occupation of Kovno began on the night of 23/24 June and the last troops crossed the Nieman on the evening of the 26th. There had been no sign of enemy activity, apart from a few scattered Cossacks, watching from their ponies at a safe distance or essaying an occasional long-range musket shot against a French patrol. The armies of Russia seemed to have vanished.

This was not how it should have been. By Napoleon's calculations, Murat's advancing cavalry corps should already have encountered Barclay's patrols. On the 27th, the Emperor realized that Barclay's First Army was withdrawing steadily through Vilna, probably with the intention of making a stand along the River Dvina. At the same time, news from his right flank indicated Bagration's Second Army was also withdrawing to the north-east, with the clear intention of linking up with Barclay. Napoleon saw a chance to isolate Bagration's army and couriers were sent with orders for Jerome to advance from Grodno to cover the *Grande Armée's* southern flank and rear. Meanwhile, Murat's cavalry, now sweeping towards Vilna, was in danger of outdistancing the rest of the army, which after only four days was becoming extended to the front and rear and to either flank. As it spread out, the problems of command and control steadily increased. Torrential rain reduced the roads and tracks to swamps which the laden waggons of the supply battalions soon churned into quagmires.

Captured documents confirmed that Vilna, fifty miles east and slightly south of Kovno, was indeed the objective of the Russian First and Second Armies; if Napoleon could catch them there, his campaign might be over in a week. Vilna was taken by the French on 28 June but apart from a brief cannonade, the Russians made no attempt to defend the town. Bagration's force was still somewhere to the south and Barclay, having burned his stores and destroyed the only bridge, had continued his withdrawal to the north-east.

Clearly the Emperor's first intention, to trap and destroy both the Russian armies, would have to be abandoned, but – if speed could be maintained and concentration achieved – there might still be time to crush Bagration, who was reported to be near Ochmiana, fifty miles to the south. Murat was detailed to take five cavalry divisions and keep up the pressure on Barclay, while the rest of the *Grande Armée* was deployed to intercept Bagration. Davout was to march south with his Ist Corps to cut off Bagration's retreat to the east, while Jerome was to keep pressing the Second Army from the west. If everyone did their duty, Bagration could soon be brought to battle and with 110,000 French against the Russian's 45,000, Bagration's destruction seemed inevitable.

This second plan fell apart. Both Jerome and Eugène advanced at a very leisurely pace, resting their men for several days at a time. Until Eugène came up to cover their southern flank, Davout's corps had to be held back, which provided both time and space for Bagration to slip between the pincers and escape south-east towards Minsk with his entire army.

Furious recriminations then broke out between Napoleon, Jerome and Davout, culminating in Jerome petulantly throwing up his command and returning to Westphalia. The command of his divisions was given to Davout, but when they entered Minsk on 8 July, Bagration had long since departed. It was clear now that there was no chance of smashing the Russian armies within the planned three weeks. The *Grande Armée* was thinly stretched and shedding men but the die was cast and the march on Moscow continued.

Napoleon had spent more than two weeks at Vilna, the capital of Lithuania, setting up a military government. He then decided to advance upon the Dvina and Barclay de Tolly's First Army. Ordering Davout on his right wing to proceed towards Mogilev, the Emperor planned another encirclement. The First Army's defensive line along the Dvina was believed to have its flanks resting on the fortresses at Drissa and Dünaburg. Not wishing to assault these strongly prepared defences frontally, Napoleon hoped to make Barclay abandon them and fight in the open. To this end Ney, Oudinot and Murat were deployed before Drissa, while the rest of the army crossed the Dvina further south and swung north, intending first to cut Barclay's communications with Moscow, then to prevent any retreat towards St Petersburg. This manoeuvre also failed.

Barclay abandoned the Drissa position on 17 July, leaving a corps of 25,000 under Wittgenstein to guard the St Petersburg road. He was supposed to combine with Bagration at Vitebsk, but Davout's steady pressure in the south forced Bagration to march away from this rendezvous to Smolensk, further east. In the same way, the line of Napoleon's advance from Vilna to Vitebsk, by way of Glubokoye, frustrated Barclay's attempt to march by way of Orsha to join Bagration. A sharp skirmish between the Russians and the French at Polotsk in which Oudinot was wounded won General St Cyr his marshal's baton, but on 2 August the Russian armies, mustering about 125,000 men, combined at Smolensk. When the French entered Vitebsk on 28 July, they found the town empty. Nothing had been achieved but the hindering of the junction of the two Russian armies, when it was to Napoleon's advantage that they should combine and do battle with him.

Meanwhile, the *Grande Armée* was shrinking. More than 100,000 men had vanished from the ranks since the crossing of the Nieman. Some were merely stragglers but most had deserted, to make their way back to the west. Supplies of food were not coming forward and an epidemic of colic in the horses inflicted an unwonted lack of mobility upon the cavalry. They were quite unable to deal with the Cossacks, who swarmed in every direction, never accepting an engagement, but compelling ceaseless vigilance.

Napoleon rested his men at Vitebsk for eight days and the pause proved beneficial. Many stragglers returned to the ranks, and the transport waggons were able to catch up. The Emperor also did some reorganizing and Marshal Victor took over command of King Jerome's troops, now formed into the VIIIth Corps. The French forces were now trying to cover a front some 500 miles long, from Riga on the Baltic coast to south of the Pripet Marshes, and running back for nearly 300 miles to the Nieman – far too large an area, even for Napoleon's original force. The *Grande Armée* was now much less efficient. Losses among the horses were particularly serious. Remounts and replacements were hard to obtain, and yet without horses the artillery could not be moved, effective reconnaissance patrols could not be made, and supplies of food could not be hauled forward.

The Russians began to show themselves increasingly willing to engage. Tormassov's Third Army was now fully operational and skirmishing with General Reynier's corps on the southern flank, and

Oudinot was regularly engaged with a 28,000-strong Russian corps in the north. The main Russian armies, however, still refused to engage and although there were attractions in postponing the completion of the compaign until the coming year, Napoleon needed a success to justify himself in the eyes of the French nation and preserve his prestige in Europe. Since turning back was out of the question, the *Grande Armée* prepared to march on.

The Emperor, with 185,000 men under his immediate and personal command, prepared to march on Smolensk on the Dnieper, about 80 miles east and slightly south of Vitebsk, where he hoped to manoeuvre his forces into the rear of the armies of Barclay de Tolly and Prince Bagration and on 8 August, it was learned that the Russians were advancing, apparently intending to give battle near Rudnia, half-way between Vitebsk and Smolensk.

The Czar, whatever his original plan, had now demanded a counterattack. The order for the advance was given by Barclay de Tolly who it will be remembered was Minister of War as well as Commander of the First Army. Prince Bagration, his rival and subordinate, declined to co-operate, the Second Army remained at Smolensk, and Barclay's advance petered out. The Russian armies then reformed west of Smolensk, and the initiative again passed to Napoleon.

Napoleon's intention now was to encircle Smolensk with two huge columns, commanded by himself and Davout. The latter was to plunge south, then circle east and north, cutting the road from Smolensk to Moscow while Barclay was still out to the west. This, by severing Barclay's communications to the rear, must bring on the long-awaited battle and the 'manoeuvre' was to be concealed from the Russians by a vast cavalry screen. The French, moving southeastwards, cossed the Dnieper during the night of 13/14 August and by dawn were marching at speed for Smolensk, apparently undetected but at Krasnoye, about 30 miles south-west of Smolensk, Murat's cavalry bumped into a mixed force of 8,000 Russian infantry and 1,500 cavalry under General Neveroski.

Barclay de Tolly had sent this force westwards along the south bank of the Dnieper to guard the left flank of his army against just such a French probe and to protect Smolensk against any thrust from the south. Murat, instead of surrounding Neveroski's division with his cavalry and waiting until the IIIrd Corps infantry could come up, attacked the Russian infantry with his cavalry alone. He lost many men in more than forty abortive charges against the stolid Russian squares and Neveroski, keeping his men well in hand, withdrew steadily towards Smolensk. On receipt of news that the French were across the river in force and marching round their flank and rear, Barclay and Bagration fell back on Smolensk.

The element of surprise having been lost, the Emperor indulged in further delay. His forty-third birthday fell on 15 August so he halted and reviewed his army. Meanwhile, some 20,000 Russian troops from Bagration's Seventh Corps under General Raievski garrisoned Smolensk together with Neveroski's indomitable division while Bagration and Barclay deployed their armies behind the Dnieper.

The Old City of Smolensk occupied a large area of the south bank of the Dnieper and was protected by a medieval curtain wall four miles long studded with towers, with an outer ditch and glacis, and a small fort, the Royal Citadel, on the south-eastern corner of the walls. Since the Russians held the city bridges, they could also retreat to the New Town on the north bank if necessary.

After a day of sporadic fighting on 16 August, the real battle began on the 17th when the corps of Poniatowski, Ney and Davout took the southern suburbs after three hours of fighting. The French guns failed to make a breach in the walls, and Barclay and Bagration were able to feed men into the New Town from the north.

By nightfall on August 17 the French had lost 10,000 men and gained very little. The Russians held the Old Town but their losses were high, and they were aware of the threat Napoleon could pose to the Moscow road. Barclay, quite correctly, ordered the Russian garrison to withdraw from Smolensk during the night of 17/18 August though this engendered a row with Prince Bagration, who went so far as to accuse Barclay de Tolly of cowardice. The Russians nevertheless withdrew, destroying the main bridge behind them, and when the French took the New Town on the following day the Russian armies had vanished yet again.

Barclay's decision to abandon Smolensk destroyed his ever-fragile relationship with Prince Bagration, who led his army away to the east, leaving Barclay's still in contact with the French. The bridges having been repaired, Marshal Ney pushed Barclay's rearguard out of the northern suburbs of Smolensk on the morning of 19 August.

For the third time in two months, Napoleon attempted to encircle the Russians. General Junot's comparatively fresh corps was sent to Lubina further east, in the hope that the legendary marching prowess of the French infantry would be too much for the weary Russian soldiers, and Junot could block Barclay's retreat. The French did get level with Barclay's troops but Junot refused to attack, even though Ney and Murat had already brought the Russian rearguard to battle and a general engagement was a distinct possibility. Barclay's army was able to disengage and effect a withdrawal and Napoleon was furious: 'Junot has let the Russians escape and is losing the campaign for me.'

There was now a pause. While Davout, Murat and Junot kept up the pressure on Barclay, the remainder of the French army rested and re-equipped at Smolensk. It was nearing the end of August, and the campaign that was to have ended in three weeks had now lasted two full months. His maps showed Napoleon that he was slightly more than half-way to Moscow, perhaps 235 miles to the east and north, with at least 315 miles of hostile, devastated territory between his troops and the symbolic safety of the River Nieman. Given that a withdrawal was unthinkable, the Emperor contemplated a choice of difficulties.

He might winter in Smolensk, and press on again in the spring, with battle-hardened troops and fresh hopes, the course urged by some of his Staff and generals. Reinforcements could come up, and time might iron out the supply problems. A winter with a French army on his soil might also induce Czar Alexander to think again about renewing the fight in 1813. On the other hand, the Czar would also have the opportunity to bring up fresh troops and deploy Cossacks against the French supply lines. Napoleon had also to consider the Austrians and the Prussians, increasingly restive under the Imperial yoke, and Spain, where General Wellington was now advancing towards Salamanca and Paris, the hub of the Empire. By the late spring of 1813, the Emperor would have been away from Paris for a full year and such a lengthy absence was an invitation to unrest.

From a purely military point of view a withdrawal was the sensible course. The task Napoleon had set himself was simply too great unless the Russians could be engaged, and to follow the Russians further east was to risk the disintegration of the *Grande Armée* – a process which had already begun. The Emperor might choose to consolidate his territorial gains in western Russia and Lithuania, but he needed a victory, not a compromise, to prevent his old foes from rising up again. For the same reasons, any withdrawal would send quite the wrong signals to subject peoples and reluctant allies. Napoleon, in short, had become a victim of his own success. Lesser men might absorb an occasional failure, but only constant and visible military success would keep the Emperor on his throne.

The only course was to advance to St Petersburg, or Moscow. Either route was fraught with hazard, but the Russian army which he must destroy lay between Smolensk and Moscow. It was clear that he must march on that city.

There was no certainty that reaching Moscow would induce either the Russian armies to fight or the Czar to capitulate. It would take a month, and it would place the *Grande Armée* nearly 600 miles from the nearest friendly frontier, totally isolated in desolate country, at the end of a long supply line already harassed by Cossacks, faced by an elusive but formidable army and with a growing awareness of the approaching Russian winter.

In the end, for Napoleon Bonaparte, there could be no other solution. Everything in his nature, every lesson he had learned in twenty years of warfare, made him march on. On 25 August 1812 the *Grande Armée* of Imperial France, 156,000 men with 590 guns, set out on its last great adventure; eleven days later, on 5 September 1812, the Emperor saw what he had been hoping for during the last three months. Ahead, on the heights beyond the Kalotcha river, the armies of Russia were finally making a stand, throwing up defences, massing their infantry, bringing cannon forward. Napoleon was to have his battle at last, by the village of Borodino.

General Barclay de Tolly's Fabian tactics of withdrawal and the avoidance of direct engagements, though entirely right and executed with the Czar's full knowledge and approval, were unpopular with the other Russian generals and the nobility. The Czar therefore decided to leave Barclay in command of the First Army, but to appoint the veteran general Prince Kutusov as Minister of War. Kutusov joined the army on 29 August, the withdrawal continued on the 31st, and the army reached Borodino on 3 September 1812.

The village of Borodino lies in rolling, well-wooded countryside on the west bank of the narrow Kalotcha, where it runs north into the Moskva river; shallow enough for wading, the river presents but a trifling obstacle. It is a pleasant countryside of streams, small hamlets and villages and wooded heights. Opposite Borodino, on the east bank of the Kalotcha and north of the village of Schevardino, the Russians were constructing a defensive position which became known as the Great Redoubt. To the south-east were smaller field works (the Three Arrows); all these positions held infantry and cannon. Barclay's stronger First Army was deployed in a naturally good defensive position behind the Kalotcha to the north of the Smolensk–Moscow road, and it was intended that Bagration's weaker Second Army should take up an equally strong position behind the river south of this road. However, Napoleon, coming up on 5 September, launched his advance guard against a small redoubt at Schevardino, forcing the Russians to abandon it in the

1. Sir Arthur Wellesley painted by an unknown artist in 1804, shortly before the beginning of the Peninsular War

2. Napoleon Bonaparte in 1807, painted by T. Heaphy

3. British infantryman from the 2nd Queen's Royal Regiment

4. Spanish grenadiers, as illustrated in the *Mémoires du Colonel Delagrave*

5. Prussian grenadier of the Foot Guards (print by Wolf and Jügel)

6. A French grenadier of the Old Guard

7. The attack at Busaco: Marshal Reynier beaten off by Picton's Division

8. The village of Fuentes de Oñoro (scene of the action shown on the jacket of this book) photographed by the author

9. The storming of Ciudad Rodrigo, from 'a sketch made on the spot by an officer'

10. The battlefield of Salamanca, photographed by the author

11. Sir Thomas Picton, who concealed a serious wound to fight (and die) at Waterloo. Rarely as smart as shown here, he fought at Busaco in his nightcap (portrait by Shee)

12. Lord Beresford, whom Wellington once called 'the only person capable of conducting a large concern' (engraving after Heaphy)

13. Sir Rowland Hill, later Viscount but always 'Daddy Hill' to his men

14. The Earl of Uxbridge, the ablest British cavalry leader but unwillingly employed by Wellington (with whose sister he had eloped). The painting is by Lawrence

15. Davoût, perhaps the ablest of them all, despite his thick glasses and unmilitary air (engraving after Marzocchi and Gautherot)

16. Ney, 'the bravest of the brave', changed sides twice between Leipzig and Waterloo and was shot by the Bourbons (engraving after Gérard)

17. Soult, difficult, ready to disobey even Napoleon, greatly respected by his British opponents in Spain (engraving by Muller)

18. Masséna, morose, greedy, oversexed and recklessly brave (engraving after Gros)

19. Napoleon watches the burning of Moscow from the Kremlin

20. A desperate French Army crosses the Beresina (from a lithograph by Victor Adam

21. Marshal Blücher stunned by a fall at Ligny (as imagined by Cooke). Had he not quickly recovered, the Prussians would not have fought at Waterloo

22. 'Let's see who will pound longest.' The struggle for Hougoumont on the field at Waterloo (from an aquatint by Sutherland)

23. Waterloo: 'Next to a battle lost, the greatest misery is a battle gained' (engraving after Heaveside)

early evening when Poniatowski's Poles succeeded in turning their left flank.

The Russian armies numbered about 120,000, of which about a quarter were cavalry, including Cossacks. They needed every one of their 500 or so guns for they were somewhat over-extended along a five-mile front, with Grand Duke Constantine's Fifth Corps in reserve about a mile to the rear. Nevertheless, their position was not without advantages, and the soldiers were inspired by the presence of a holy relic, the Black Virgin of Smolensk.

Most of the next day, 6 September, was spent by the French in carrying out a careful reconnaissance of the Russian line, probing their positions and patrolling to mark out their flanks and defences. Napoleon elected to attack the Russian centre at the Great Redoubt, with diversionary attacks on their flanks – a scheme which did not meet with unanimous approval. Davout proposed a more complete flanking manoeuvre, but Napoleon was determined on a frontal attack, despite the inevitable losses.

On the night of 6/7 September the Kalotcha was bridged, preparations were made for a massive opening artillery bombardment and the battle began just after 6 o'clock on the morning of 7 September 1812. Shortly after the initial bombardment five infantry corps of the *Grande Armée*, more than 100,000 men, swept towards the central Russian positions, their drummers beating the *pas de charge*. Prince Eugene took Borodino, Davout gained ground around the Three Arrows, and on the far right Poniatowski was soon in possession of the village of Utitsa. Then the attack faltered. A Russian counter-attack pushed Eugène back from Borodino, and Davout had to fall back from the Three Arrows while Poniatowski suffered huge losses from the cannon fire and musketry of Russian troops concentrated in the woods north of Utitsa.

Thus began a day of fierce and bloody fighting, a pounding match of great courage but no great skill. The same pieces of ground changed hands twice, thrice, and more. On the French left, Prince Eugène took Borodino, lost it, took it again and crossed the Kalotcha, where he deployed against Raievski's battery on the Great Redoubt, between Borodino and Semenovskoye. He took the position at 10.30 a.m., but it was then retaken by the Russians.

Davout, on the French right, three times won and lost Prince Bagration's entrenchments on the Three Arrows before finally capturing them about 11.30 a.m. and driving the Second Army back upon Semenovskoye, where part of the Russian reserve came up. The Second Army had lost nearly all its senior officers, and Prince Bagration himself was mortally wounded. A cavalry attack by Murat failed and it was past midday before the French took Semenovskoye, forcing the Russians here back to the edge of the forest. Murat, Davout and Ney believed they could advance no further without reinforcements and these Napoleon refused to send.

The Emperor was suffering from bladder problems and a severe chill, and these ailments seem to have engendered a hitherto uncharacteristic lethargy. He spent much of the day behind the Shevardino redoubt leaving his marshals to their own devices, and there was no final, decisive leadership, as at Wagram.

An attempt by Russian cavalry and Cossacks to outflank the French left and divert attention from the Russian centre was a failure, and the French captured the Raievski battery soon after they had taken Semenovskoye. The whole Russian centre fell back, and by mid afternoon the battle was gradually dying out – a result of complete exhaustion on both sides – except on the French right, where Poniatowski battled on until nearly 6 p.m.

The day ended with the French hanging on grimly to what little they had gained, barely a mile of ground. Some realignment was necessary as the left flank of the Russian army fell back from Utitsa and took up a fresh position, apparently ready to continue the battle the following day, but dawn revealed the Russians in full but controlled retreat. The *Grande Armée* was in no condition to exploit their 'victory' – which was, in any event, only a technical one. The Russians certainly lost a great many men, and Napoleon held the ground, but he had withdrawn his advanced troops, and the Russian army was still in the field and able to fight another day.

The Russians had lost more than 43,000 men, while French casualties by the Emperor's own admission amounted to at least 30,000, but since he rarely told the full truth in his bulletins the figure of 50,000 French killed and wounded is not impossible. Losses among the general officers had been particularly severe. Davout and Ney had been wounded, and the list of killed and wounded included no fewer than forty-four divisional generals and thirty-seven regimental colonels. Of the 600,000 men who crossed the Nieman in July, only 100,000 were now with the Eagles. The rest occupied towns along the army's 500-mile route from the Nieman, were engaged in the Baltic campaign, or had already deserted. Many were dead, and not a few were prisoners – which for the private soldiers was rather worse than death.

If this was a victory, it brought no tangible results. Prince Kutusov continued his withdrawal, Murat and his exhausted cavalry following as best they might. Napoleon remained near Borodino until 12 September, but no envoys from the Czar arrived, to suggest an armistice or to negotiate a peace. Nor did they appear when, on 14 September 1812, Marshal Murat finally led the French cavalry into Moscow. The *Grande Armée* had fought a great battle, and Napoleon was in possession of Russia's religious capital; but he made his entry into a forsaken city, and what would happen now no man could say.

14

Salamanca:

June and July 1812

I considered that our respective positions would not bring on
a battle, but a rearguard action with a part only of the
British Army, and I should probably score a point.

Auguste Marmont,
Marshal of France: July 1812

HAVING TAKEN CUIDAD Rodrigo in January and Badajoz in April of 1812, Wellington controlled the two viable routes from Portugal and could choose his objective should he advance into Spain. Hitherto a relative deficiency of cavalry had made him reluctant to encounter the French in the Spanish plains but, reinforced in the spring of 1812 by five cavalry regiments, he saw the possibility of some major stroke.

The Army of Spain had by now lost some 30,000 troops, mainly Imperial Guard and Polish cavalry, to Napoleon's Russian campaign. Of Soult's 54,000-strong Army of the South in Andalucía, the bulk were engaged in the siege of Cadiz. Far away in Catalonia and Aragon with 60,000 men, Marshal Suchet had never shown any interest in supporting his fellow marshals, and Caffarelli's Army of the North, mustering 50,000, was fully engaged with guerrillas in Navarre and in keeping the passes to the Pyrenees open. There remained Marshal Marmont and the Army of Portugal.

Wellington decided to advance against the Army of Portugal for in defeating Marmont he would gain two victories in one, as Soult would be obliged to abandon the siege of Cadiz. Thanks to his own reinforcements and Napoleon's withdrawals, Wellington now had a slight superiority in numbers against any one of the French armies in the Peninsula, though not if they were able to combine.

Plans were therefore laid to keep the other French armies occupied while Wellington dealt with Marmont. The Spanish in Andalucía were directed to harass Soult; Napoleon's diversion of Murat's forces from Italy to Russia enabled an expedition of British and Neapolitan troops to sail from Sicily to engage the attention of Suchet in Aragon and Catalonia, where he had hitherto met with comparatively little trouble from the local population.

Caffarelli's Army of the North in Galicia, Cantabrica and the Spanish Basque provinces was already being harried by Commodore Sir Home Popham's squadron of warships, from which Royal Marines were landed by day and night to assault towns and fortresses and attack French communications along the northern coast. The much smaller Army of the Centre, some 18,000 men under Marshal Jourdan, charged with keeping King Joseph on his throne in Madrid and suppressing guerrilla activity around the capital, was to be kept occupied in La Mancha and the Guadarrama mountains by the local Spanish forces.

Having spent the month of May in establishing magazines of food, ammunition and fodder, on 13 June Wellington crossed the Agueda with 42,000 men and 54 guns. The bulk of this army was British, but included a strong contingent of the King's German Legion and several regiments of the resolute and ever-improving Portuguese infantry and dragoons, and a division of Spanish troops (fed and paid for by Britain) under Don Carlos d'Espagne. In the north, the activities of the guerrilla forces and the Spanish Army of Galicia, supplied and armed by the Royal Navy, had already caused Marmont to send one of his divisions to the Asturias. It was intended that the Army of Galicia should now move to lay siege to Astorga, thus covering Wellington's left flank.

Marmont's headquarters were at Fuentesaúco, with one division forward in garrison at Salamanca. His other seven divisions were deployed in a great arc stretching from Oviedo in the Asturias, across the northern *meseta*, east and south to Avila in the northern foothills of the Guadarramas. This deployment was spreading his force extremely thin, and Marmont knew it, but it was in obedience to Napoleon's express orders, which he did not care to disobey. At Wellington's approach Marmont ordered a concentration and fell back across the River Tormes, and the division at Salamanca withdrew north to Fuentesaúco, leaving a garrison of 1,000 men in three fortified convents commanding the bridge across the Tormes on the southern side of Salamanca. Leaving General Clinton's 6th Division to attack the convents, Wellington drew up the rest of his army in a good defensive position along a line of hills just north of the city, between the villages of San Cristóbal and Cabrerizos, to await Marmont's next move.

Marmont had sent to Caffarelli's army for the two divisions he had been promised in the event of an advance by Wellington. In the meantime, his advance guard probed the British positions, and on 20 June he came forward for a personal examination. An attack by Marmont on the San Cristóbal position would have suited Wellington well enough, but Marmont, taught by experience that it was unwise to attack British infantry on their chosen defensive positions, and having received only a brigade of cavalry and a battery of field artillery from Caffarelli, consulted with his generals and declined the offer of battle.

For his part, Wellington was too well satisfied with his defensive position on the reverse slopes of San Cristóbal to go onto the attack and after four days of stalemate, Marmont withdrew behind the River Duero.

Marmont's caution in this encounter stemmed from a growing respect among the French for the stubborn resistance of British and Portuguese infantry in defensive positions, and for the devastating power of their musketry. For Wellington himself, the French had much less regard: he was not their sort of general. He lacked dash, and *élan*. A French general led from the front, sword in hand. A French general believed in the crushing power of artillery, and of infantry columns storming to the attack, carrying all before them. Wellington was not like that. He husbanded his men carefully, because he had none to spare. He hid his men behind reverse slopes, or bade them lie down, common sense indicating that to set them up as targets for the French artillery was stupid. Although he galloped about the battlefield he stayed to the rear because that was the most efficient way of exercising command, but he was often to be found where the fighting was heavy, and was no stranger to close-range shot and shell. Fighting on the defensive both compensated for his shortage of numbers, and made the most of the line formation which, in turn, provided the most telling use of musketry. A fine battlefield tactician and a flexible general who rarely did the same thing twice, Wellington would attack without hesitation, if he could do so with advantage. This his opponents had yet to learn.

Wellington was later criticized for not attacking Marmont at San Cristóbal. He had been tempted, but the Salamanca convents to his rear had not been taken, and the San Cristóbal terrain favoured the defence. In addition, while he enjoyed a slight superiority in numbers, his force was not large enough to ensure a complete victory and leave him strong enough to then deal with Soult. An unlooked-for benefit arising from his refusal to engage at San Cristóbal was its apparent confirmation of the French conviction that Wellington was a 'cautious' general. Marmont now believed that Wellington would never attack, and that he might therefore be shepherded back to Portugal without undue risk. Risk must be avoided because Marmont, too, now had to husband his resources: troops from those marshals in Spain who had not refused to send them would now arrive too late to affect any coming engagement.

Following Marmont's withdrawal, the Salamanca forts surrendered on 27 June and Wellington and his men made a triumphal entry into the city – the first Spanish city to be liberated from the French. He then set off after Marmont across the León plain, concentrating around Medina del Campo.

On 1 July Marmont's last division came up to his position near Tordesillas, after a long and guerrilla-plagued march from Oviedo. This raised his strength to some 50,000 men, a parity of force which he considered sufficient to begin hustling Wellington away from Salamanca. He pushed two divisions across the Duero at Toro in a feint against Wellington's right flank, and in parrying this stroke Wellington was promptly wrong-footed. Marmont quickly pulled his divisions back across the river, counter-marched, and at dawn on 18 July crossed again at Tordesillas where some of his cavalry caught Wellington's Reserve, the 4th and Light Divisions, completely by surprise.

They nearly caught Wellington. He was visiting his Reserve that morning when the French came up. He and his Staff, swords drawn, galloped into the safety of hurriedly-mustered Light Division squares as a confused and hopelessly intermingled mass of British and French cavalry and horse artillery thundered past on either side, slashing at each other with their swords. Wellington, less than pleased with this sudden and unexpected alarm, took no further risks that day and the Reserve joined the rest of the army during the afternoon.

Marmont's army came up on the 19th, and the two armies watched each other across a shrinking summer stream until the afternoon, when Marmont again seized the initiative and began to march towards Salamanca. Wellington fell back along a parallel route, and the two armies marched side by side, almost within cannon shot, every man's head turned on his shoulder to watch the enemy columns on his flank. Marmont's intention was now clear: to get ahead of the British, then hook across their front and cut their communications from Salamanca to Cuidad Rodrigo and Portugal. This had to be prevented, for not only did his supply waggons depend on that route, but Wellington had learned that King Joseph was preparing to march from Madrid with 15,000 men from the Army of the Centre. Whether or not Marmont was aware of this did not matter: either way, Wellington had to safeguard his communications with Portugal.

On 20 July the French infantry succeeded in outmarching the British, leaving Wellington the choice between engaging now, on Marmont's ground, or swinging away to the south-west to pick up the Cuidad Rodrigo road. To the disgust of the army, who were anxious to fight, Wellington elected to fall back again, and while the British were marching south-westwards the French pressed on without opposition to ford the Tormes at Huerta, ten miles east of Salamanca, on 21 July. That evening Wellington crossed the river about two miles above the town, to reoccupy the San Cristóbal heights. Marmont had achieved his first objective. He had manoeuvred Wellington out of his defensive position, and moved the British army out onto the rolling plain just south of Salamanca.

Marmont's intention now was, to keep the British moving west by constantly hooking round Wellington's right: sooner or later Wellington must run, and then Marmont would be able to maul the British rearguard and chase Wellington back into Portugal with his reputation in ruins.

By the evening of 21 July 1812, Marmont had eight infantry divisions and a full cavalry brigade, plus 78 guns, mustered in lightly-wooded country five miles south and east of Salamanca, beyond the dried-up valley of the Algabete river. Wellington's army lay along the ridges to the north and west of this valley, masking the southern and eastern approaches to Salamanca. Marmont's plan was to march around the British right flank to the west, where a little pressure should force them to march, or risk being cut off from the Cuidad Rodrigo road. Marmont would thus dislodge Wellington and set him in full retreat towards Portugal. Since Wellington appeared unwilling to attack the risks inherent in a march across his front seemed minimal.

During the night of 21 July Wellington had actually determined upon a withdrawal to Portugal. The two armies were now almost equal in strength and he could not hope for a decisive victory without losses he could ill spare in view of Joseph's advance from Madrid and the possibility of Suchet reinforcing Marmont from Valencia. On the morning of 22 July he ordered his baggage train to start for Cuidad Rodrigo.

The British army had spent the night of 21/22 July in hilly ground south of Salamanca, their left flank on the Tormes with the 3rd Division under Pakenham on the north bank of the river. As they moved off on the 22nd, most were concealed by higher ground from Marmont, who was edging west and south to circle round Wellington's right flank.

In their parallel movement south-westwards towards the Cuidad Rodrigo road, both armies soon came in sight of the two features which dominate this landscape, the steep-sided, flat-topped hills known as the Greater Arapil (Arapil Grande) and the Lesser Arapil (Arapil Chico). In what became a race for possession the swifter French captured the Greater, while Wellington occupied the Lesser, together with the village of Los Arapiles, and the ground to the north. While Marmont was closing up his forces, Wellington altered his dispositions. Directing Pakenham to cross the Tormes at Salamanca and move under cover to a wood near Aldea Tejada, Wellington ordered his forces into a line behind the ridge between Los Arapiles and Aldea Tejada.

About two in the afternoon Marmont observed the dust thrown up by Wellington's baggage train as it lumbered down the Cuidad Rodrigo road. Interpreting this as evidence of a major withdrawal, and taking the 7th Division opposite his position to be Wellington's rearguard, he ordered his left wing, under General Thomières and General Maucune, westwards in a sweep designed to cut off what he imagined to be a retreating army. Thomières marched out smartly, and a gap began to open between his division and Maucune's and another between his left wing and the French centre. This was quickly brought to Wellington's attention as, eating a late lunch, he sat his horse in a farmyard behind the northern ridge.

'The enemy are in motion, my Lord,' said an aide, 'and I think they are extending their left.'

'The Devil they are!' replied Wellington. 'Give me the glass, quickly.'

Observing the enemy with the closest attention for a short space, he said, 'Come . . . I think this will do,' then galloped hard towards Aldea Tejada, where General Pakenham and his 3rd Division had just arrived. Wellington gave Pakenham a brief, clear order:

'Edward, move on with your Division. Take that hill to your front and drive everything before you.'

Pakenham's reply was equally brief: 'I will, my Lord.'

Within minutes, the 3rd Division in two columns supported by d'Urban's Anglo-Portuguese cavalry was marching hard in dead ground towards the unsuspecting General Thomières. Meanwhile Wellington galloped back onto the ridge above Los Arapiles to give his orders to the 5th and 4th Divisions, still out of sight behind the northern ridge. They were to advance over the ridge and cross the Arapile valley to storm the south ridge. On their heels would come the 6th and 7th Divisions, with the two independent Portuguese brigades and the cavalry covering their flanks. Marmont's over-extended army, marching west and led by Thomières, was about to collide head-on with Pakenham's division, while no fewer than four more British divisions swept in on his centre.

It was now about half-past four. Marmont, having realized the danger of the gap between Thomières and Maucune, was (according to his own account) just mounting his horse on the summit of the Greater Arapil, to ride and urge Brennier's division to plug the gap, when a British shell burst beside him. Marmont was blasted from his horse, breaking two ribs and shattering his right arm so badly that it was later amputated. In the rain of British shells it was some minutes before his shaken Staff could gather their wits and rescue their commander. General Bonnet took command but was soon injured and before General Clausel could take command the British attacked.

First into action, d'Urban's Portuguese Dragoons came sweeping over the ridge and cut into Thomières' leading battalion before they could form square. The battalion broke and fled back to their division, who hardly had time to realize what was happening before Pakenham's 3rd Division came into sight, led into the attack by Colonel Wallace's brigade. Wallace's battalions advanced in column and only deployed into line 250 yards from the French. Thomières flung his *tirailleurs* and leading battalions at them, opening with a volley which brought down most of the front rank, but when the smoke cleared, the rest of Wallace's brigade were still coming on. The British came up, fired their muskets in one great volley, then charged in with the bayonet. Thomières was killed, two-thirds of his leading regiments and half his entire division were casualties, and all his guns were taken. The survivors fled back into Maucune's division, arriving just as Wellington's main assault across the Arapiles valley came in onto Maucune's flank.

Leith's 5th Division had taken time to dress their lines carefully and get the various battalions into position behind the northern crest before the light troops went to skirmish ahead and the advance began across the valley, two red walls of British infantry, the second line a hundred yards behind the first, Wellington riding to and fro between them. Pounded by French artillery from the Greater Arapil and the ridge ahead, the 5th swept across the valley and up the slope to the top of the ridge. There Maucune's division awaited them, hastily formed up in square.

This, a good formation against cavalry, was fatal against infantry. After firing one volley, Leith's division went in with the bayonet and within minutes the squares had broken and yet another French division was leaving the field in disorder, the men fleeing to the shelter of Brennier's division. As they ran, the first of Cotton's cavalry brigades, the 5th Dragoon Guards and the 4th and 5th Dragoons under Major-General Le Marchant, swept in, caught them in the flank and drove them in upon Brennier's division. By the time Leith's infantry had come up to finish the attack, more than a third of Marmont's army had been destroyed.

Cole's 4th Division, on the left of the 5th, had a more difficult time advancing across the valley, being severely galled by cannon fire from the Greater Arapil. Pack's Portuguese brigade was detached to take this position and his men got to the top but were promptly driven back with great loss, and the left flank of Cole's 4th Division, now heavily engaged along the crest of the south ridge, lay wide open to a counter-attack.

General Clausel was now in command of the French army and he still had three infantry divisions in hand, Foy's, Sarrut's and his own, plus Boyer's dragoons. He ordered Sarrut to fend off the assaults from the 3rd and 5th Divisions and sent the rest of his force in against Cole's division. Forming into columns of battalions, the French advanced, first driving off the Portuguese and then pushing the British Fusilier Brigade back into the Arapiles valley. Then they faltered. A Portuguese brigade from the 5th Division came in on their right, while General Clinton's 6th Division came on across the valley in support of the troops on the south ridge. A ten-minute exchange of volleys along the slope of the southern ridge left 1,500 French on the ground. Clausel's division broke first, then Sarrut's, then the whole French army began to give ground by battalions and brigades, as Wellington sent the 1st Division wheeling in from the left, and the light companies of the King's German Legion finally took the Greater Arapil.

The French army fell back into the woods south-east of the Arapiles valley, where the 6th Division eventually overwhelmed Ferey and Sarrut's tenacious rearguard. Foy's division, the last of Clausel's formations, now fell back and, the catastrophe complete, the French scrambled away in full retreat to the bridge at Alba de Tormes. The Spaniards of Don Carlos de España's division had been charged with holding the bridge at Alba de Tormes and had Don Carlos not decided to abandon this position without informing Wellington, the survivors of Marmont's army would have been trapped.

The Army of Portugal had still been severely cut up: of 48,000 French involved at Salamanca, more than 14,000 had become casualties. Marshal Marmont and General Bonnet had been wounded, and two divisional commanders, Thomières and Ferey, had been killed. The British had captured twenty guns and taken 7,000 prisoners.

On the following day Foy's division, the only one in any condition to fight after the battle, lost two regiments in a savage encounter with the 16th Light Dragoons and the dragoons of the King's German Legion. It was one of the rare occasions on which cavalry managed to break an infantry square, for a German charger killed by a volley fell across the bayonets of the square, creating a small gap through which the dragoons swiftly leapt their horses, to lay about the square with their sabres. That square collapsed, another square panicked and broke, and the French drew off with the loss of another 1,100 men.

British losses at Salamanca were not insignificant. More than 5,000 fell, 3,000 from the 4th and 6th Divisions, and the gallant Portuguese accounting for a large percentage of the balance. Losses among the general officers were also severe: Le Marchant of the Heavy Dragoon Brigade was killed, and four other generals were wounded.

Salamanca was recognized throughout Europe as a splendid victory. The news reached Napoleon's armies in Russia just before Borodino and did nothing for their morale. Marshal Marmont, though a considerable soldier, had made the mistake of underestimating Wellington's abilities, and was taken completely by surprise. Nevertheless, most of Marmont's colleagues continued to regard Wellington as a cautious general. Salamanca must rank (with Vitoria) as one of Wellington's finest Peninsular victories. He kept his army well in hand, fended off the enemy and, when the moment was right, struck hard and decisively with his full force. Few generals could have done it – but few generals commanded such a flexible and efficient army.

After their mauling, the Army of Portugal fell back eastwards across the *meseta* to the fortress town of Arévalo, below the northern edge of the Guadarrama. As Wellington came on, they retreated northwards, first to Valladolid, then to Burgos, where they arrived on 31 July, their rapid withdrawal preventing any junction with King Joseph, who crossed the Sierra de Guadarrama with the Army of the Centre on 24 July. Learning the outcome of the battle, he promptly returned to Madrid, arriving on 5 August and issuing a direct order to Soult to abandon Andalucía and bring his Army of the South to join the Army of the Centre. Wellington had gained his second victory.

The British army entered Valladolid on 30 July, and paused there while Wellington considered his options. The Army of Portugal had been severely battered, but as it withdrew to the north its lines of communication shortened and its numbers steadily increased. Wellington on the other hand now faced the problem of an over-long supply line from his base in Portugal. Leaving the 6th Division to watch Clausel's Army of Portugal, he therefore decided to march on Madrid.

The march became a triumph. For the first time in this war, the British soldiers saw smiles on Spanish faces. In every town and village the people came out to cheer, offering food and wine in such abundance that the British were almost willing to forget the endless shortcomings of these allies over the past three years. King Joseph fled south to Toledo, on 12 August Wellington entered Madrid, and on the following day he forced the surrender of the 1,200-strong garrison left behind to hold the Retiro forts above the city.

However, within a few days Wellington received news that Clausel's Army of Portugal was displaying surprising resilience. On 14 August Clausel reoccupied Valladolid and Foy's division was soon making advances along the Duero to relieve the beleaguered French garrisons at Toro and Zamora. By the end of August the Army of Portugal was in the field again and the 6th Division were unable to contain it.

Wellington was now in a precarious position, poised between Soult's Army of the South on its way from Andalucía to Valencia, Joseph's Army of the Centre in Toledo, Clausel's Army of Portugal to the north, and Suchet's Army of Aragon in Catalonia. As ever, he felt confident of his ability to defeat any one of these armies separately but not if they should combine, so he decided to deal first with Clausel.

Leaving General Hill with three divisions to secure Madrid and watch Soult and Joseph, he took the rest of his army north to join Clinton's 6th at Valladolid. Clausel fell back unhurriedly to beyond Burgos. Coming up to Burgos on 18 September 1812, Wellington laid siege to the castle, but after the outworks were captured on 19 September, the siege dragged on. As so often, part of the problem lay in the inadequacy of Wellington's siege-train – he had only three 18-pounder cannon and a few mortars, quite inadequate for the task; he had too few engineers; and he was reluctant to mount the sort of assault and incur the heavy losses taking Badajoz had necessitated.

The approach, on 22 October, of the Army of Portugal, reinforced by divisions from the Army of the North and mustering 50,000 men, gave Wellington little choice but to abandon the siege of Burgos; he had only 35,000 troops, and a third of them were Spanish. A few days later, on the other side of Europe, Napoleon decided to withdraw from Moscow, and for a few weeks in 1812 both Wellington and Napoleon shared the common problems of a winter retreat.

To make the British position even more precarious, Soult had finally combined with Suchet and King Joseph at Valencia, and with some 60,000 men they marched upon Madrid. General Sir Rowland Hill, declining to defend the capital against such odds, had already withdrawn to Arévalo when he received Wellington's orders to join him in the vicinity of Salamanca. Wellington reunited his army on the Tormes on 8 November and prepared to offer battle.

Marshal Soult now commanded the combined Armies of Spain but despite his 100,000 veteran troops he declined to attack the British on their chosen ground. Instead he began another turning movement against the British right, threatening the road to Portugal. The Anglo-Portuguese army marched out in pouring rain on 15 November to retire upon Cuidad Rodrigo and though Soult kept up his cautious pressure over the next four days, the campaign of 1812 finally petered out in the snow and rain of a Peninsular winter.

To add to the misery of the soldiers retreating in icy rain down roads little better than quagmires, the rations had gone astray and there was next to no food. Discipline faltered, the men looted and straggled and Wellington lost 5,000 before he reached Portugal. By 19 November 1812 the British were safe behind the Agueda, but it was many weeks before the thousands of sick were restored to active duty.

The glory Wellington had gained at Salamanca was dimmed by his failure to take Burgos and his withdrawal to Portugal, and there were complaints in the British newspapers and criticism of him in Parliament. He was supported by the new Prime Minister, Lord Liverpool, fresh honours were heaped upon him (he was raised to the rank of Marquess), and fresh reinforcements were sent to strengthen his army. Even so, the campaign of 1812 had not achieved any strategic gains. Wellington's main consolations were that Soult had abandoned the siege of Cadiz, the Spanish guerrillas were again rampaging throughout the Peninsula and, far away in the east, Napoleon's *Grande Armée* was dying on the snowy wastes of Russia.

15

Flight in the Winter:

Russia 1812

The regiments began to disintegrate; horses died by the
thousand, so that every day we burned waggons and
supplies, having no means to draw them. The peasants of
Moscow and Kaluga were in arms to avenge the atrocities
perpetrated upon them.

The Ordeal of Captain Roeder: 1812

ON 15 SEPTEMBER 1812, the day after the French entered the city,
Moscow caught fire. The conflagration, which consumed three-quar-
ters of the city in three days, was not their fault. The fires were laid
at the orders of the Military Governor of the city, Count Rostopchin,
aided by convicts released from the city prisons as the French marched in. At the time, however, the destruction of Moscow was seen
by Europe as another example of Napoleonic frightfulness.

Appalled, Napoleon wrote to the Czar at St Petersburg, disclaiming
all responsibility. This, the first of a series of letters sent to the Czar
after the *Grande Armée* entered Moscow, failed to elicit a reply and as
the weeks passed Napoleon began to realize that even with half his
country occupied and his second city in ruins, the Czar would not
come to terms. The Russians were determined upon the destruction
of the French army and the end of the Napoleonic Empire, and all
they had to do was wait. The longer the French lingered in Moscow,
the better.

With every day Napoleon remained there the fearsome Russian
winter drew closer, and his troops were woefully ill-prepared for it.
Most of the stores for the invasion had been ordered with a summer
campaign in view and the soldiers were without the most basic
necessities for winter warfare. A hunt began among the ruins of Mos-

cow for furs and other warm clothing, but there was no hope of
finding enough. Furthermore, there was a shortage of horses for the
cavalry and transport. Thousands had died on the march and there
were no more to be had east of the Niemen.

The Russian forces, conversely, were gaining strength daily. By
early October they outnumbered the French holding Moscow and
were inching forward, concealing their preparations for an attack
behind a thick screen of Cossacks and the appearance of cordiality.
Murat, commanding the French forces to the east and south of
Moscow and now in regular contact with the Cossacks, reported them
friendly and apparently eager for peace. The experience of other
outposts tended to confirm this view, but it was merely part of
Kutusov's strategy for keeping the French lingering in Moscow. A
delegation from Napoleon arriving at his headquarters on 2 October
1812 with proposals for an armistice and letters for the Czar was made
welcome for days, while their despatches went to St Petersburg with
a confidential note from Kutusov advising Alexander, in rejecting all
Napoleon's overtures, to take his time in replying. A second delegation on 15 October was treated in the same way.

Napoleon was in a quandary. His intention of a swift defeat of the
Russian forces followed by a dictated peace with the Czar had not
been achieved, while the forces at Kutusov's command now outnumbered the French on almost every sector of the front. Kutusov's army
alone numbered 110,000, as against the 95,000 the Emperor commanded in Moscow. To the north General Wittgenstein, with 40,000
men, faced Oudinot and St Cyr with just 17,000; the Russian defenders of Riga had a garrison of 24,000 men, while Macdonald's
besieging army numbered only 25,000, half of which were Prussians,
eager to go home. On the southern flank, 65,000 Russians opposed
Prince Schwarzenberg and Reynier with just 34,000 men between
them and, like the Prussians, Schwarzenberg's Austrians wished to be
elsewhere.

The extent and complexity of his problems began to prey on Napoleon's mind. According to General Comte de Ségur, the Emperor
slept a great deal, lingered for hours over meals, tended to brood,
and became increasingly uncommunicative. This is hardly surprising.
There was a decision to be made, and all options were fraught with
risk. What remained of the *Grande Armée* was now isolated in the heart
of Russia, 550 miles from the nearest friendly frontier, and Napoleon
did not know what to do next.

It might have been possible for the French to remain in Moscow
until the spring, but the same considerations applied as at Smolensk:

Napoleon had already been away from Paris for too long, but he needed to return with a peace, or at least a victory, to celebrate. He might force an agreement out of Czar Alexander by marching directly on St Petersburg, but it was as doubtful that his depleted army could get there with Kutusov's forces massing on his rear as it was that the Czar could be brought to terms.

So the Emperor brooded, day after day, until the only solution became too obvious to be longer avoided. He finally accepted the fact that his army had been defeated, and was facing destruction. He must retreat from Moscow with his remaining troops and try to re-cross the Nieman before the snows came. This was not going to be easy. It was already mid-October, and the Chief Commissary of the Army, General Dumas, calculated that the march to the Nieman would take at least fifty days, through Cossack-infested country devastated by the passing of the French army two months earlier.

On 18 October Kutusov's cavalry, hitherto peaceful, suddenly attacked Murat's cavalry corps outside Moscow, and the Russians had almost overwhelmed the French troopers when Murat woke up to what was happening and fought his way clear. Napoleon at once gave orders for the retreat, his spirits and energy revived by the decision, and within twenty-four hours the *Grande Armée* was on the move. Early in the morning of 19 October 1812 Napoleon led his army out of Moscow to begin one of the most memorable and tragic retreats in history.

The Emperor passed out through the western gates of Moscow with 95,000 men and some 500 guns. Had that been all, the story of his retreat to the Nieman might have been different. However, the columns also included some 40,000 waggons of various kinds, '. . . from four-wheeled coaches to wheelbarrows', piled high with loot, camp followers, the French sick and wounded, and a number of Moscow prostitutes who preferred the French to retribution at the hands of their fellow-countrymen. In this they were wise: the French wounded left behind were murdered in the Moscow hospitals. So encumbered was the army, so difficult the roads, that the French covered only sixty miles in the first four days – fine and sunny days, but with bitterly cold nights.

In an attempt to avoid both the worst of the winter weather and a ravaged countryside, Napoleon at first attempted a more southerly route westward. Unfortunately, the southern road proved worse than the main one towards Smolensk, and Cossacks soon informed Kutusov of the Emperor's movements. On 24 October, Prince Eugène's advance guard from the IVth Corps found the town of Maloyaroslavets swarming with Cossacks, supported by a division from Doctorov's corps and several artillery batteries. The fierce fight which ensued for possession of the bridge over the River Lusha involved Eugène's entire corps, and the *Grande Armée* was forced to await the outcome on the north bank of the river. When Doctorov eventually drew off, the French had lost six general officers and 4,000 troops; it was small consolation that the Russian losses were more than 7,000.

On the following day, 25 October, Napoleon himself was nearly captured when some Cossacks galloped out of a wood and were among his personal escort before they could be repulsed. The appalling prospect of falling alive into the hands of the Don Cossacks, to be dragged at a horse's tail to St Petersburg, caused the Emperor to demand from his doctors a strong poison, which he thenceforth kept about his person, to be swallowed if capture seemed imminent.

On 26 October Napoleon gave the order for the *Grande Armée* to retrace its steps and return to Smolensk down the route they had covered so painfully two months earlier. This decision was a terrible mistake. Not only had more than a week of good weather been lost, but it meant a return on roads churned up by the passage of the army, through a countryside swept bare of all provisions where villages burned and wrecked on the advance offered no shelter, and were littered with putrefying bodies half-eaten by wolves.

Other accounts in this book have demonstrated that retreats are not good for any army – and Napoleon's *Grande Armée* was no exception. The French columns were strung out over fifty miles by the time they reached Borodino, haunted by the stinking corpses of 30,000 men, dug up by dogs or left unburied after the battle. Marbot described the battlefield as 'an immense tomb'. The *Grande Armée* crawled across this place of slaughter and by 31 October Napoleon and his advance guard had reached Viasma, where they waited a day for more of the army to come up. In twelve days on the road the French covered 150 miles, an average of less than fifteen miles a day, and some of the stragglers were up to three days' march behind the main body.

The soldiers suffered persistent harassment from Kutusov's cavalry and the ever-watchful Cossacks. Foraging parties were easy prey and most of those attacked by the Cossacks were massacred to the last man, but the fate of any prisoner was worse. All prisoners, even the wounded, were stripped naked and herded barefoot back to Moscow. At night, left in the open, many froze to death. Those who could not keep up were killed on the spot, or handed over to the peasantry and a terrible death by clubbing or burning or drowning. Some parties of French prisoners were buried alive.

Pressing on towards the supplies and shelter he expected to find at Smolensk, Napoleon left those men and camp followers who could not keep up to their fate. On 2 November, as Eugène, Poniatowski and Davout plodded through Viasma, the Russians attacked in force and Davout's Ist Corps was cut off. Surrounded by 20,000 Russian cavalry and infantry, they might have been killed or captured to the last man had not Prince Eugène sent two divisions back to open the road for Davout's troops. From then on there was fighting all day, every day. Kutusov believed that the total collapse of the *Grande Armée* was only a matter of time, and while the main Russian army kept up the pressure on its rear, Cossacks and peasants snapped around its flanks. The constant fighting and marching soon reduced even Davout's usually well-disciplined corps to a rabble, and Eugène's was little better. All depended upon the IIIrd Corps in the rear and their hard-fighting commander, Marshal Ney.

Winter set in late in 1812: the first snow fell on 3 November. When Napoleon reached Smolensk on the 9th, it was to find that the urgently needed supplies of food and ammunition had been consumed by rear-echelon troops retreating ahead of the main army. In an orgy of looting and destruction in which even the Imperial Guard took part, much of what was left in the depots was lost or spoiled. This setback followed Napoleon's receipt from Paris of news of an attempted *coup d'état* in which a General Malet, previously confined in a lunatic asylum, had with his confederates murdered the Military Governor of Paris and arrested several of the Emperor's officials before being arrested himself. Clearly, the sooner Napoleon could return to his capital, the better it would be for his Empire.

That night the temperature plummeted to well below zero. Shelter, clothing, firewood were inadequate and a miserable night spent huddled and shivering in the streets of Smolensk was followed by news of further disaster. A division of troops marching east from Vilna to open the route for the retreating army had encountered a much larger Russian force, and after a brief engagement had been forced to surrender.

By 13 November only some 40,000 soldiers remained of the 95,000 who had left Moscow twenty-five days earlier. Many battalions had been reduced to just a few score men. The Vth and VIIIth Corps could muster only 1,500 men between them, while Ney's vital rear-guard was reduced to 3,000 from its original 11,000. Quite apart from the lack of supplies, the physical state of the remaining troops was terrible. Without proper clothing and boots, they were suffering from frostbite and exposure. Horses were dying from lack of fodder, or unable to move because they were improperly shod for icy fields and frozen roads. There were not enough mounts for the remaining cavalry to reconnoitre properly or to counter the Cossacks, who now came swooping in to make short work of the stragglers and camp-followers, wives and servants and wounded, who made up the long 'tail' of the shattered army.

If anything was to be salvaged, the army must press on as fast as possible towards the Nieman. The advance guard left Smolensk on 12 November, while remnants of the force were still trickling in. Ney did not march his rearguard out for another five days, by which time he had managed to recruit his corps to 6,000 from among the stragglers.

Then the Army's spirits were briefly lifted by an unexpected victory.

On the 17th the Imperial Guard, which led the army, ran into the main Russian army near Krasnoye and caught General Kutusov by surprise. The cavalry of the Imperial Guard struck home and saw off the Cossacks with one thundering charge and the advancing infantry went Kutusov's army reeling back in unexpected defeat. The Russians had become so used to attacking the French columns with impunity that this sudden counter-attack took them completely by surprise and gave a great boost to French morale. Thus encouraged, but without waiting for Ney, who was still several days' march to the rear, the Emperor ordered his troops to march on at their best speed towards the Dnieper and then the Berezina rivers.

Napoleon had reached the Dnieper at Orsha on 19 November. He found the bridges intact, but Prince Schwarzenberg and his Austrians had lost Minsk to the Russians on 16 November and the expected rations had not been sent up from the depots. The Emperor was inclined to suspect the Austrians of treachery, and a Polish division had therefore been sent to hold the crossing of the Berezina at Borisov.

The army, much heartened by Ney's reappearance on 21 November, pressed on to the Berezina. Believing himself to command the crossing at Borisov, Napoleon ordered all unnecessary baggage to be abandoned, including the pontoon trains. Unfortunately, on 21 November the Polish division lost possession of the Borisov bridgehead to a Russian force. The Russians now occupied all the west bank of the Berezina, from Studianka south past Borisov to Usha. They had also destroyed all the bridges. With Tschitschagov's army across the Berezina, Kutusov's army behind them, and Wittgenstein marching upon them from Vitebsk, it seemed that the remnants of the *Grande Armée* were trapped.

The crossing of the hundred-yard-wide Berezina took four days, from 25 to 29 November 1812. The location of the chosen crossing place was concealed from the Russians by means of various feints, and these were so successful that only a small detachment of Russians remained opposite Studianka, and were soon driven off by a brigade of cavalry and some light infantry who crossed the river on rafts. Artillery was then mounted on the heights of Studianka to cover the crossing.

General Eblé and his engineers had fortunately preserved some waggons from the general destruction of baggage ordered after Orsha, and the material for two pontoon bridges was obtained by pulling down the houses of Studianka. The pontoniers worked without stopping, chest deep in icy water, throughout the night of 25/26 November and by the morning of the 26th Oudinot's corps was able to cross the first bridge and expand the bridgehead. Troops continued to cross while work proceeded on the second bridge, a wider and stronger structure for waggons and artillery which was completed by mid afternoon on the 26th. The evacuation of the east bank continued during the night of 26/27, periodically interrupted by the bridges collapsing. In the early afternoon of the 27th Napoleon himself crossed with the remaining 8,000 men of his Imperial Guard, all that were left of 50,000 who had marched proudly eastwards five months earlier. Hardly were they across when the main bridge collapsed again. Victor, Davout and Eugène, together with a great mass of unattached troops and camp followers, and the whole of the baggage train, had yet to cross and, panicking, the crowd of camp followers rushed the remaining bridge. In the ensuing chaos many hundreds were trampled underfoot or fell into the icy waters. Corpses soon blocked the entrance to the bridge or became entangled in the pilings, and the crossing was held up for several hours while some sort of order was restored and the main bridge repaired.

Davout's corps then crossed, leaving Victor to hold the eastern bridgehead while the tail of the army followed. Movement was slow during the night of 27/28 November and long hours of waiting in freezing cold without food or sleep sapped the energy of those still on the east bank. Many huddled miserably in the snow during the hours of darkness had frozen to death by dawn.

General Wittgenstein's Russians began to appear around Victor's perimeter shortly after dawn on the 28th, having snapped up General Partouneaux's division of 4,500 men during their feint at Borisov on 25 November. Reinforced by the Baden brigade, which went back across the river with the greatest reluctance, Victor managed to hold on to the eastern bank for the rest of the day, but by noon the Russians had guns within range of the bridges, and their firing caused further panic and confusion. Women and children were trampled underfoot, the wounded and frostbitten were abandoned, and thousands trying to cross were elbowed off the bridges into the river below.

The Russians on the west bank were driven back by Oudinot and Ney, and from high ground on the east bank Victor held off Wittgenstein's attack and during the night of 28/29 November he too crossed, leaving only his rear-guard behind.

The last of the troops having crossed at dawn, at 9 o'clock on the morning of 29 November, in obedience to Napoleon's instructions, General Eblé's pontoniers set fire to the bridges, a sight which stirred the huddled survivors on the east bank into one last desperate bid. Most of those who now rushed for the bridges fell back before the fire or into the river, or collapsed, weakened by cold, and hunger, and hopelessness. Napoleon's concern had been to evacuate his army; he was not troubled by the fate of non-combatants, camp followers and refugees. Those who could not keep up with the army were left to the Russian armies and the Russian winter, and through the smoke of the burning bridges Russian cavalry and Cossacks, lances raised and sabres flashing, could be seen driving in among the thousands left behind.

Although the French suffered terrible losses – at least half of Napoleon's remaining regular army, some 20,000 or 25,000 – the passage of the Berezina can be seen as the greatest achievement of the retreat, rather than as a dismal failure. It was the magic of Napoleon's name and the prestige – still – of his armies which saved the French from annihilation at this point. Both Wittgenstein and Tschitschagov were afraid of the Emperor and reluctant to come to close quarters, and Kutusov believed that he could attain his ends without a pitched battle.

Wittgenstein's forces continued to harass the retreating French for the next four days. It is not clear why Kutusov did not order his troops to close in and finish the French off, for by 2 December there were fewer than 15,000 French troops still with the colours and able to fight, with a rabble of about 30,000 men, women and children stumbling along behind them. Behind the tail of the army came the indomitable Marshal Ney, still fighting and still commanding the ragged troops of the rearguard, reduced now to fewer than a hundred men.

Since learning at Smolensk of the attempted *coup d'état* in Paris, Napoleon had entertained thoughts of leaving his army. Resolved now upon this course of action he prepared the '29th Bulletin' of the campaign, dated 3 December 1812, in which he confessed to the ruin of his army, blaming the early arrival of the Russian winter. At Smorgoni, fifty-five miles east of Vilna, he announced to his marshals on 5 December his intention of departing for Paris. The command was entrusted to Marshal Murat, the King of Naples, an unwise and unpopular choice. The same day the Emperor, with 'a small party' which included a Polish interpreter, set out by coach for Warsaw. By 14 December he was at Dresden, and four days later he was again in his capital.

Napoleon had left orders that the remnants of the *Grande Armée* should go into winter quarters around Vilna. The last of the troops reached there on 8 December to find, given their scanty numbers, almost a superabundance of stores; but the Cossacks were still on their heels, so on the night of 9/10 December Murat retreated towards Kovno. In the rearguard Ney, with what was left of General Loison's division and Wrede's Bavarians, attempted to check the Cossacks, but his efforts ended in the complete destruction of his forces, and the French were forced to abandon everything, their equipment and stores, even their wounded. On 11 December the army, now slightly augmented by garrisons picked up during the retreat, reached Kovno. Ney attempted to hold the town, but the Russians took Kovno on 14 December, and the French finally limped into Königsburg on 19 December.

This was not, however, the end of the disaster. On 18 December the Russians surrounded a strong force of Prussians under General Yorck, 17,000 men and 60 guns, which had been serving with Marshal Macdonald at the siege of Riga. On 30 December Yorck signed the Convention of Tauroggen with the Russians, declaring the neutrality of himself and his men. A few days later Prince Schwarzenburg came to a similar agreement with the Russian forces in the south and was allowed to retire to Austria with his entire command.

It had been hoped that the Russians would halt on the Nieman, having driven the French from the soil of Holy Russia, but on 13 January Alexander's main army crossed the Nieman and began to sweep the French garrisons out of the Grand Duchy of Warsaw. Murat had fallen back from Königsburg on Posen, where on 10 January 1813 he handed over his command to Prince Eugène. The latter was forced to fall back gradually to Magdeburg, and by March 1813 what

16

The March to the Frontier:

1813

The history of European warfare affords few examples of
battle which have been more important in their results or
more brilliant in their achievement, than that of Vitoria.
                            Captain Robert Batty: 1813

WHEN WELLINGTON RETURNED across the Agueda into Portugal
in November 1812, the Light Division was sent to hold the river line
while the rest of the army went into winter quarters. Discipline had
slackened again during the retreat from Burgos, 5,000 men had been
lost, and there were 20,000 on the sick-roll. Fortunately, in spite of
the demands made by the war with the United States which had
broken out in the summer of 1812, the government, heartened by
Napoleon's Russian disaster and its repercussions in Europe, and
determined to further the campaign in the Peninsula, sent reinforcements. With these, and the recovering sick and wounded, by the
spring of 1813 Wellington could muster about 100,000 men, including
for the first time a full division of Spaniards.

From his headquarters at Freineda, where he stayed from November 1812 to May 1813, Wellington dealt with familiar problems.
There was little money. The British troops had not been paid for
months, the Portuguese for more than a year, and there was not
enough to hire carts, or to buy mules. Relations with the Spanish
remained strained, Wellington's appointment as Commander-in-Chief
of the Spanish forces in September 1812 notwithstanding. Those Spanish generals who were willing to co-operate with him were already
doing so, while those who resented his influence and suspected his
motives intrigued against him.

King Joseph and Marshal Soult had forced Wellington out of Madrid, but the king was finding it increasingly difficult to control what remained of his realm. Wellington's successes had encouraged the Spanish guerrillas, who were now so active and formidable that even with four divisions in Biscay and Navarre General Clausel was fully occupied in trying to keep open the route between Madrid and the Pyrenees. Despatches between Paris and Madrid might take as long as six weeks and it was February 1813 before Joseph learned of Napoleon's arrival in Paris the preceding December.

The defeat of the *Grande Armée* and its terrible losses during the retreat from Moscow meant not just that no more reinforcements could be sent to Spain, but that the remaining units of the Imperial Guard plus veteran NCOs and men to the number of 15,000 were recalled to France to aid Napoleon in the rebuilding of his army. King Joseph was not sorry to see Marshal Soult among those recalled, and he was replaced by an old friend, Marshal Jourdan, an honest and reliable soldier. A realist, Jourdan saw that the south and the north-west of Spain would have to be abandoned, whatever the Emperor might wish – there were not the troops available to control Galicia and Andalucía. The vital area was Old Castile and Navarre, the route to the Pyrenees, Bayonne and Paris, with the ports of Santander and San Sebastián. What remained of Joseph's armies, apart from Clausel's forces in the north and various garrisons, were deployed in a great half-circle stretching from León, west of Burgos, and around to the province of La Mancha, south of Madrid.

In the middle of March 1813 Joseph received orders from Napoleon to leave Madrid and set up his capital in Valladolid. From there, said Napoleon, Joseph and Jourdan were to mount a defensive campaign against Wellington when he crossed the Portuguese frontier. Having moved to Valladolid, the king and the marshal began to consider where Wellington would strike next, and how they might resist him. Discounting Clausel and the Army of the North, the Armies of the South, Centre and Portugal might muster 60,000 men, if they were concentrated. On the other hand, such a concentration would leave the countryside wide open to the guerrillas.

Joseph therefore divided his forces. The Army of the South was deployed between the Duero and the Tagus, with one division from the Army of the Centre patrolling the borders of Galicia. In Valladolid, Joseph had only his Royal Guard of 2,000 men, with the IInd division of the Army of the Centre in garrison at Segovia. The six divisions of the Army of Portugal were scattered about: one lay between Burgos and Palencia; two were chasing Spanish *guerrilleros* in the wilder parts of Navarre, west of Pamplona; one was on the Biscay coast near Bilbao; and two more guarded the vital mountain road from Bilbao to Burgos, along which guerrilla activity was rife. Apart from the ports of Santander and San Sebastián, the north coast of Spain from Galicia in the west to the Basque country in the foothills of the Pyrenees was completely lost to the French.

Joseph and Jourdan both believed that Wellington would enter Spain via Cuidad Rodrigo and head north-east through Salamanca, to Valladolid. It was hoped that the divisions guarding this road would be able to contain him until the other French forces could be concentrated on the Duero, somewhere between Toro and Tordesillas. Joseph was unable to convince Napoleon that Wellington's forces now outnumbered the French armies in the Peninsula, unless Suchet should come to his support – and Suchet was fully engaged in Catalonia and Aragon.

Wellington had 80,000 reliable and battle-tested Anglo-Portuguese, the Hanoverians of the King's German Legion, and 20,000 of the Spanish Fourth Army, a force fed, clothed and paid by the British government. During the early spring of 1813 Wellington's emphasis was on training, with twice-weekly route marches and a series of reviews in the area of Cuidad Rodrigo which served to confirm French impressions that his main thrust would come from that direction. On 22 May 1813 the Peninsular Army duly advanced on Salamanca, and as he crossed the frontier, Wellington took off his hat, turned in his stirrups and bade farewell to Portugal. At the same time the British fleet in Lisbon was ordered to sail north to an undisclosed destination.

Their expectations confirmed, by the end of May Joseph and Jourdan had assembled 50,000 men and a considerable quantity of artillery between Toro and Tordesillas, where they awaited the arrival of Wellington's army.

The British, screened by a great quantity of cavalry and led by the Light Division, reached the outskirts of Salamanca in four days. The single French division in the town withdrew towards the Duero, and Wellington's troops sat in Salamanca for a week. Meanwhile, disquieting news began to reach King Joseph. General Wellington was certainly in Salamanca, and the Light Division were skirmishing ahead as would be expected, but the British force was very small. Where were the rest of them? Joseph soon found out.

On 2 June 1813, troopers from the 10th Hussars charged in on two regiments of French cavalry guarding the outposts at Morales, on the right flank of the French position beyond Toro. The surprise was total and the French cavalry were driven off in confusion, one regiment being cut to pieces. While Joseph and Jourdan were allowing themselves to be mesmerised by Wellington's advance to Salamanca, Lieutenant-General Sir Thomas Graham with six full divisions had crossed the Tras-os-Montes mountains into Spain.

Graham's units had begun to march north through Portugal as early as the middle of April. Quartermaster-General George Murray's scouting officers had earlier assessed roads and mapped river-crossings and noted the availability of fodder, but notwithstanding all this forethought it was an arduous march. By 16 May Graham and his men were through the Tras-os-Montes and descending on the León plain. Wellington, having left Cuidad Rodrigo on 22 May, had no sooner arrived at Salamanca than he left his forces in General Hill's hands and slipped across the river at Miranda del Douro and joined Graham at the Esla. This tributary of the Douro was in spate, but the men crossed chin-deep, hanging on to a stirrup or a horse's tail; and the cumbersome pontoon train which had, somehow, been shepherded from the Tagus to the Douro without any word of its passing reaching the ears of the French, justified its nuisance value. On 1 June the advance-guard entered Lamora, and on 3 June Hill marched up to join Graham at Toro, where the whole Anglo-Portuguese army was now concentrated.

King Joseph left Valladolid for Palencia, but Wellington's army set off north-eastwards towards the Carrión and the Pisuerga, marching in parallel columns with a cavalry screen between it and the retreating French, persistently turning the French right (northern) flank. Joseph abandoned Palencia on 7 June, Burgos on the 12th. On 13 June the British were awoken by a huge explosion; the French had blown up the castle at Burgos. His strength now augmented by troops from abandoned garrisons, Joseph's army numbered about 60,000 men deployed behind the Ebro in the hope of stemming Wellington's advance.

Three days passed with no sign of the British army. Wellington had again hooked north, leaving his cavalry to screen him and shadow the French, and by 16 June was pushing his men across the Ebro beyond the French right at Puente Arenas. Outflanked yet again, Joseph pulled back to the plain west of Vitoria, where his Armies of Portugal, the South and the Centre arrived in some confusion on 19 June 1813. There, in the valley of the Rio Zadorra, with their flanks apparently secure, they turned to fight.

Having covered more than two hundred miles, his soldiers had been ready to halt at Burgos, but Wellington was determined to march on.

The army was in great spirits. The French had been driven out of one position after another, almost without a shot being fired, and it was clear that this time there would be no turning back. There were no problems with provisions, fodder was plentiful, and Wellington's other supply arrangements were working well. Waggons had come rolling forward, laden with provisions, from Cuidad Rodrigo and then, as the army hooked north, from the British Fleet and transports sent from Lisbon and anchored at Corunna.

As early as 10 June, Wellington was confident enough to arrange for the next stage of his advance, ordering the British Naval Commander at Corunna to send ships laden with powder, shot and provisions to the Biscay port of Santander, there to await the arrival of the British army. The French still held Santander, but Wellington had no doubts that he would soon need those stores. 'If Santander is occupied by the enemy I beg him [the Admiral commanding the fleet] to remain off the port till the operations of this Army have obliged the enemy to abandon it.' On 21 June 1813, the next phase of Wellington's campaign began.

Vitoria, capital of the Basque provinces of Spain, lies at the eastern end of a diamond-shaped plain some twelve miles long and eight miles wide which spreads out towards the city from the pass of La Puebla. This pass cuts between the mountains of La Puebla, which lie to the south, and the higher Monte Arrato to the north. Both the road from Burgos and the Rio Zadorra, which winds across the Vitoria plain, run through the pass at La Puebla. The Zadorra, a fast but fordable stream, was bridged in a number of places down the valley.

Having decided that Wellington must come in through the La Puebla pass and make a frontal attack down the road to Vitoria, Joseph placed a strong picket of riflemen on the steep hills to the south of the road, above the pass, and the rest of his army was deployed in depth down the valley before Vitoria, their flanks resting on the Zadorra to the north and on the heights of La Puebla to the south. Joseph held a good, strong position, always provided Wellington did as he expected.

On Joseph's front line, three of the four and a half divisions of the Army of the South under General Gazan straddled the road south of the bridge at Nanclares, with the last in reserve south of the village of Arinez. The second line, a mile to the rear of Arinez, north of Gomecha, consisted of the two divisions which made up the Army of the Centre under General d'Erlon, who was also charged with defending three more bridges over the Zadorra, at Villodas, Tres Puentes and Mendoza. To this task he allocated a small cavalry force of 800 men. Finally, two divisions of the Army of Portugal under General Reille formed a third line, just west of Vitoria. In view of Wellington's tactic of hooking around the French flank to the north, Reille was also ordered to hold the northern side of Vitoria against any advance down the road from Bilbao. The vital escape route from the plain of Vitoria, at the city end of the valley and following the Zadorra through the Salinas pass, was guarded by 2,000 Spanish soldiers ostensibly loyal to the French. Finally, General Tilly with some cavalry watched the southern road from Logrono, and Clausel and Foy's divisions, currently chasing guerrillas in Navarre, had been summoned to the muster. With their main force guarding the likely approaches, the rest sensibly deployed and reinforcements anticipated, Joseph and Jourdan felt their position reasonably secure.

Wellington never permitted tactical considerations to deflect him from his strategic objectives. His strategic objective now – to drive the French out of the Peninsula – would be best achieved by inflicting a heavy defeat on Joseph's army so far east that the French would have neither time nor space to regroup on the Spanish side of the Pyrenees. A simple frontal assault west of Vitoria would not accomplish this purpose.

By dawn on 21 June 1813, Wellington's dispositions had been made. His right-hand corps, under General Sir Rowland Hill, would fulfil French expectations, marching through the La Puebla defile to attack the French front line before the village of Arinez. Hill commanded his own 2nd Division, a Portuguese division, General Morillo's Spanish Division, and two cavalry brigades – some 30,000 men.

On the far left flank was Wellington's second-in-command, General Sir Thomas Graham, with another 30,000: his own 1st Division, the 5th Division, two Portuguese brigades, and a strong brigade of Spanish light infantry. Graham was to swing wide to the north and come in on Vitoria down the Bilbao road. If the French should be seen to be falling back, Graham would continue swinging east until he could cut off their retreat east of the Salinas defile. In boxing terms, these two corps may be imagined as delivering a straight jab and a left hook. The main attack would be delivered between these formations, by two corps moving down onto the north bank of the river and so into the French right flank.

The left-centre column, to Graham's right, under General the Earl of Dalhousie, had the difficult task of making a night crossing of the rugged Monte Arato, north-west of Vitoria, to come down on the

Zadorra at the bridges of Tres Puentes and Mendoza. Dalhousie commanded two infantry divisions, Picton's 3rd and his own 7th. Dalhousie was no veteran of Spain, unlike Picton, who had little time for Dalhousie and little interest in taking his orders.

Wellington attached himself to the right-centre column, made up of the Light Division and Lowry Cole's 4th Division plus four cavalry brigades, which was also to come in via the La Puebla pass, but on the north bank of the river, and hook across the bridges at Villodas and Nanclares. Joseph may have been anticipating a frontal attack from the west, but Wellington intended a two-pronged flank attack from the north. The fact that Joseph's front-line Army of the South was five miles forward of his second-line Army of Portugal made it all the easier for Wellington to insert his forces into that gap and, having done so, destroy the French forces in detail.

Riding out early on the morning of 21 June 1813 to make a final check on their positions, King Joseph and Marshal Jourdan soon noticed the excessive gap between their first and second lines. Before they could order it closed, however, news came in of Hill's advance through the pass at La Puebla – which, since it had been anticipated, caused no particular alarm.

General Hill came on with care. General Morillo's Spanish infantry, sent to secure the heights on the south side of the La Puebla pass and dislodge the French *voltigeurs*, were soon involved in a heavy skirmish along the crest, each side sending in one brigade after another to contest possession of this commanding position. The hill was finally taken by the 71st Highlanders of Cadogan's brigade of the 2nd Division, though not without heavy loss of life, including that of the brigade commander. O'Callaghan's 3rd Brigade then descended the eastern side of the heights, south of the road to Vitoria, and occupied the village of Subijana de Alava, while the rest of Hill's troops marched through the La Puebla pass and began to deploy on the plain.

The 4th and Light Divisions were now in sight on the north bank of the river, moving towards the bridge at Nanclares, but had to pause there: Wellington's plan depended upon careful timing, and he had as yet received no news of either Dalhousie's column, which should have been in sight on his left, marching for the bridges upstream, or Sir Thomas Graham's column on the far left, which should by now have been in action somewhere north of Vitoria. Until they appeared, he would have to wait.

This pause did not help the French, who could not decide which of the attacks developing on either side of the river was the feint. In either case, they should not have omitted to defend or destroy the

Zadorra bridges. Jourdan now decided that the attack on the north bank was the feint and ordered General Gazan to advance and drive the British and Spanish out of Subijana de Alava and off the La Puebla heights – an order which further, and fatally, divided his army.

There was still no news of Dalhousie's division, but Wellington learned from a Spanish peasant that the bridge at Tres Puentes, which gave access to the right flank of the French front line, was both intact and unguarded. Abandoning his plan to surprise the bridge at Villodas, Wellington ordered Brigadier Kempt and three battalions of the Light Division to advance at the double to take and hold the Tres Puentes bridge. Inside ten minutes they were in cover on the French side of the river, supported by some of the 15th Hussars. The arrival of Kempt's brigade on their flank and the loss of the bridge put the Army of the South in a difficult position. Gazan's only reserve, Villette's division, was now engaged with Hill's troops on the heights of La Puebla, where they were at bayonet thrust with the 71st Highlanders, and more British troops were poised to cross the river by the Mendoza bridge.

At Mendoza the 3rd Division, in the right spot at the right time, was eager to cross the river but there was still no sign of Lord Dalhousie, although the leading columns of the 7th were beginning to come up. When an aide-de-camp came from Wellington with orders for Dalhousie to take the bridge when he should appear, Picton's patience snapped.

'No, Sir, I have not seen his Lordship . . . and you may tell Lord Wellington from me, Sir, that the 3rd Division under my command will attack the bridge and carry it, and the 4th and Light Divisions may support us if they choose.'

With that, Sir Thomas placed himself at the head of his division, ordering them forward with a cry of 'Come on, ye fighting villains. . . .'

The arrival of Picton's division on the south bank was a relief to Kempt's brigade of riflemen, who saw 'On our left, the bright bayonets of the 3rd, glittering above the standing corn' as they swept down to the Mendoza crossing. A battalion of Kempt's infantry drove off the French *voltigeurs* lining the south bank of the river, Picton's division crossed without loss, and the rest of Dalhousie's corps were hard upon their heels.

On the far left flank of the British advance, General Sir Thomas Graham had found Reille's two divisions drawn up one behind the other north of the Zadorra. The first was driven off by Pack's Portuguese brigade and some Cantabrian Spaniards, who then advanced to block the road from Vitoria to Bayonne. Meanwhile Graham's own

5th Division fell on the French holding a bridge over the Zadorra at Gamarra. The village soon fell to the British, but the French held the bridge with such tenacity that Graham's men had to continue their assault against it for most of the day.

With the British across the Zadorra and circling round the French right, Joseph and Jourdan realized too late that Hill's frontal assault down the road from La Puebla had been the feint. Completely outflanked by troops advancing from the north bank of the river, they determined to fall back at once on Vitoria. General Gazan remonstrated that his Army of the South was so closely engaged with British battalions to the front and right flank that they could not possibly withdraw; it would be better, he thought, to stand and fight.

King Joseph and Marshal Jourdan prevailed, and Gazan began to withdraw, leapfrogging his brigades back one after another. With the Peninsular Army in hard pursuit this withdrawal, once begun, never stopped. In their path lay the village of Arinez, now held by Picton's 3rd Division, where a fierce fight broke out, but this stand was the last French effort. The 4th Division had now crossed the river via the Villodas bridge, and the riflemen and *caçadores* of Vandaleur's 2nd Brigade took the village of La Hermandad. Then the 4th and 7th drove the French back to a position among four villages west of Vitoria where, his flanks apparently secure, Joseph had hoped to make a stand. Gazan, however, continued to retreat.

With all his troops across the river or through the La Puebla defile, Wellington brought his artillery forward to pound the French regiments. Then his infantry went forward, the 7th Division marching east along the river bank, the other divisions strung out right across the valley to the La Puebla heights. There was little resistance left in the French armies. The Hussar Brigade from the King's German Legion, snaking between the Army of the South and the Army of the Centre, were soon making their way into the suburbs of Vitoria where, with the British swarming all over the plain, near-panic had long since broken out. As Graham's division held the roads to Bayonne and Bilbao, the French rear-echelon troops and their camp followers were forced to attempt the rough track to Pamplona, which soon became a huge and chaotic jam of fleeing men and women, overturned waggons and abandoned guns.

Within an hour of Wellington's general advance, King Joseph's army was in full retreat and the situation in Vitoria was desperate. British cavalry and Spanish *guerrilleros*, slashing and stabbing at the foe, were now well forward in the rout, intermingled with the fleeing French soldiers and a great mob of camp followers. The French were being cut down on every side, and their death toll might have been higher had not many British troops been diverted from slaughter by the chance of plunder.

The booty was vast, and included the entire payroll of the French army: millions of gold francs vanished into the pockets of British, Portuguese and Spanish soldiers, never to be seen again. Gold and silver ornaments, church vessels, jewellery, fine wines, silks, dresses – everything the French had stolen in the last seven years was now stolen from them.

The 14th Light Dragoons and the 10th Hussars nearly laid hands on King Joseph, who had to abandon his coach and flee on horseback, leaving a great quantity of valuables behind. These included, rolled up in the coach, a collection of priceless Old Master canvases, which escaped the attention of the soldiers and were later graciously bestowed on Wellington by a grateful Spanish monarch. Jourdan lost his Marshal's baton, taken as a trophy by the 87th Foot. The fields on either side of the track were filled with survivors of the battle, running hard eastwards and throwing away their possessions to run faster. More than 150 guns fell into British hands, with large quantities of stores and ammunition.

Wellington wanted to capture Joseph's army as well as his guns and his booty, but the distractions of the last combined with torrential rain and a particularly bad road meant that the pursuit up the Pamplona track was called off after five miles. The French did not stop until they had crossed the frontier into France. They had lost comparatively few in battle – about 8,000, two-thirds of them prisoners – but hundreds more fell victim to the *guerrilleros* during the retreat. The blow to their self-esteem as soldiers and the loss of so much wealth and equipment was a heavier burden to bear. British losses were comparatively slight, about 5,000, ten per cent of them Spanish and twenty per cent Portuguese.

Wellington's achievement at Vitoria made a great impression throughout Europe. The liberation of Spain encouraged Austria to abandon her neutrality and declare war on France in August 1813, bringing 200,000 men into the coalition of Britain, Russia, Prussia and Sweden, and as for Wellington, nothing was too good for him. A *Te Deum* was sung in St Petersburg to celebrate his triumph, and Beethoven composed a symphonic piece, *Wellington's Victory*, in honour of the battle. Marshal Jourdan's baton was sent to the Prince Regent, and a few weeks later Wellington received in return the baton of a British Field Marshal.

Although most of the French army had fled back into France,

General Clausel was still in the field with 12,000 men, and there was also Marshal Suchet's corps in Aragon and Catalonia, which had been annexed to France in 1812. Suchet was notoriously reluctant to combine with other marshals but he could not be discounted, and must be masked as the Peninsular Army advanced to the frontier.

There was, however, no immediate prospect of such an advance. The discipline of the British army once again broke down and some of Wellington's most caustic remarks about his troops were occasioned by their behaviour at this time. 'We have the scum of the earth as common soldiers . . . some enlist for having fathered bastard children . . . others for drink.' It is often forgotten that these bitter remarks concluded with: '. . . it really is wonderful that we should have made them the fine fellows they are.' The quantities of loot and opportunities for pillage, above all the drink, led to an almost complete disintegration of the army in the days after the battle. Had the French been in any condition to counter-attack, matters might have gone badly for the British. Discipline was gradually restored with the lash and, in one or two extreme cases, the rope, and by November 1813 Wellington was describing his army as 'the most complete machine for its numbers now existing in Europe.'

General Clausel came up to Vitoria two days after the battle but, hearing of Joseph's defeat, made a precipitate retreat to France through Saragossa and the Somport pass while General Foy, on the Biscay coast, rounded up all the scattered garrisons and retreated into France by Hendaye. This left the well-defended port of San Sebastián and the city of Pamplona at the southern end of the Roncesvalles pass as the last French bastions in Spain.

17

The Battle for the Pyrenees:
1813–1814

> Your task, as Lieutenant of the Emperor, is to re-establish
> my business in Spain and to relieve Pamplona and San
> Sebastián.
>
> > Napoleon to Marshal Soult: July 1813

THE NEWS OF Vitoria reached Napoleon on 1 July 1813 at Dresden, where he was resting his army after a hard-fought series of engagements against the Russians and Prussians. The shaky alliance with his father-in-law the Emperor of Austria still held, to the extent that the Austrians were not in the field, but this defeat at Vitoria might tilt the scales against him. Furious with Joseph, Napoleon's first concern was to retrieve the French position, for the British army was now on the southern frontier of France, poised to advance across the Pyrenees.

To his dismay, Marshal Soult was sent from Dresden to Bayonne to form an Army of Spain from the troops which had crossed the Pyrenees. With him went money, a warrant for the arrest of King Joseph (which Soult declined to use), and instructions to renew the war immediately and drive the British back from the frontier. Napoleon then went to Prague in an attempt to come to terms with Russia and Prussia. Moves towards peace were resisted by Britain for it was felt there that the war with France must now be fought to a conclusion. If Prussia and Russia agreed to an armistice, Austria would remain neutral and Napoleon would be able to turn his might against Wellington's army in the Pyrenees.

Wellington meanwhile adopted a defensive position, for supply, as so often before, was proving a problem. American warships and privateers were now attacking British shipping in the Bay of Biscay, and roads from Corunna to Pamplona had deteriorated under the heavy traffic of waggons and mule trains. Wellington now needed a depot close to the French frontier and the obvious choice was San Sebastián. This need coincided with his determination not to make any advances while San Sebastián and Pamplona lay untaken at his rear. General Sir Thomas Graham's corps was sent with a battering train to San Sebastián, while the rest of the army blockaded Pamplona and held the Spanish frontier against incursion by Soult. All these arrangements were in place by early July 1813.

Soult arrived at Bayonne on 12 July and immediately set to work to reorganize and revitalize the shattered elements of the three armies that had escaped into France after Vitoria. He knew about fighting in Spain and, thanks to his pursuit of Sir John Moore to Corunna in 1808/9, something about fighting the British. When all the troops had been gathered in, Soult found himself with about 80,000 men, including perhaps 7,000 poorly-mounted cavalry. He was very short of artillery, but since infantry would be the decisive arm in the mountainous terrain of the Pyrenees, this was not necessarily significant. Equipment and morale were what mattered. Soult fed and reclothed his men, rebuilt them into an army by means of regular drills and parades and within weeks had a fighting force. The Army of Spain was organized into three corps, under d'Erlon, Clausel and Reille; each corps contained three divisions, and there was a 17,000-strong Reserve Division.

Meanwhile, Soult and his staff considered how to implement the second part of Napoleon's orders: 'to re-establish my position in Spain, and relieve Pamplona and San Sebastián'. The Pyrenees, even without an entrenched and efficient opponent, present a formidable barrier to any invader. Soult had three choices: he could advance along the coast and across the Bidassoa; he could move inland and push through the Maya pass; or he could move still further inland and up the Val Carlos from St Jean-Pied-du-Port to the pass at Roncesvalles. Since San Sebastián, supplied nightly by coastal vessels from Bayonne, was as yet in no real difficulty, Soult decided to initiate his campaign by lifting the blockade of Pamplona with a two-pronged thrust through Maya and Roncesvalles. These were defended by two British divisions, Rowland Hill at Maya and Lowry Cole at Roncesvalles. General d'Erlon's corps was to advance through the Maya pass and attack Wellington's left, while Clausel and Rielle, advancing from St Jean-Pied-du-Port through Roncesvalles, descended upon Pamplona from the right, brushing aside Lowry Cole's division. Clausel's corps was then to make a frontal assault on the British defences, around Pamplona while Reille's corps scrambled up the pilgrim route further east and attempted to outflank the British position at the Lindus plateau on the crest of the mountains. Meanwhile, the British forces on the Bidassoa front would be held in place by feints from the Reserve Division.

Both attacks, on 25 July 1813, took Wellington by surprise. He had been convinced that the French would advance on the Bidassoa front, to lift the siege of San Sebastián. An assault on the city by Graham's corps on the 25th failed, for San Sebastián was a strong fortress, stoutly defended. Wellington rode the twenty miles from his headquarters at Lesaca to confer with Graham, and while he was away news arrived from the north of a sizeable French advance through the Maya pass. The Quartermaster-General, Sir George Murray, took charge, warning the 7th and the Light Divisions of this attack and putting them on the alert.

Wellington's return to Lesaca at nine that night coincided with an urgent message from Lowry Cole, in the Roncesvalles pass with his own 4th Division, a brigade from the 2nd Division under Major-General Byng, and Morillo's Spanish Division. The despatch, sent at 1 o'clock that afternoon, informed Wellington that a large French force had attacked Byng's brigade in the pass, but that Cole was confident of holding his own. The despatch was eight hours old and in the meantime Cole had withdrawn from Roncesvalles.

Wellington, still convinced that Soult's object was San Sebastián, decided to wait until Soult's intentions became clear, but nevertheless took certain precautions. Graham was instructed to embark his battering train onto the ships lying off San Sebastián and hold his troops ready to move, and one division from the forces around Pamplona was directed to move north to support Cole south of Roncesvalles.

The Field Marshal then retired for the night – only to be roused again at three in the morning. Fresh despatches received from Hill contained news of the previous day's events at the Maya pass. Hill, having held on through heavy fighting during the day, had since thought it advisable to withdraw from the pass and take up a fresh defensive position by the village of Elizondo. General Hill was not easily dismayed and coming from him, this was grave news indeed.

Nothing more had been heard from Lowry Cole's force around Roncesvalles, but a major threat was clearly developing. Reinforcements were ordered up from the left flank to support Hill, and the task of defending the Bidassoa section of the front was deputed to the Spanish. Then Wellington rode over to Elizondo where Hill was holding his ground and had seen no sign of the French since falling back from the Maya pass the previous evening. He had lost more than 1,500 killed or wounded on the 25th, and the situation had only been saved by the sudden arrival of two battalions of infantry from the 7th Division which made a spirited charge against the flank of the advancing French. However, when it was known that Cole had fallen back on Sir Thomas Picton's 3rd Division, some miles to the south of Roncesvalles, Hill had no option but to fall back as well, so this check to the French was no help. Lowry Cole was a confident general when under Wellington's immediate command, but on his own became beset by uncertainties. On the 25th he had beaten off the French attacks with very little loss, but feeling unsure of his flanks had ordered his division to fall back from the pass to link up with Sir Thomas Picton's 3rd Division, much closer to Pamplona. Since Sir Thomas Picton was senior to him, Cole was thereby relieved of unwanted responsibility. But the passes through the Pyrenees were now wide open to a French advance. Wellington spent 26 July riding along his front line, adjusting the disposition of various regiments and divisions in anticipation of renewed fighting when the French came through.

Fortunately, Soult was already in difficulties. His plan had been based on a rapid advance through these rugged mountains to the fertile plains of Spanish Navarre, for with little transport available his men had only what food they could carry. The delay enforced by Byng's brigade at Roncesvalles on the 25th had upset his timetable. His men were now very short of food, and must make every effort to punch through to Pamplona before their supplies ran out.

At dawn on the 26th Soult discovered that the Roncesvalles pass was open. He sent Clausel's corps up the main road towards the Col d'Ibaneta and Rielle's up the pilgrim track, the two to meet at the top. Then the weather intervened. A thick mist settled on the mountains, and the corps on the pilgrim track became hopelessly lost. Reille was eventually obliged to return to the main road and follow Clausel's divisions to the top. Elements of Cole's rearguard still held Ibaneta, and the two French corps were detained there until the evening.

At the Maya pass, on the right wing of the French advance, d'Erlon's corps, which should have been pressing on towards Pamplona, spent most of the 26th bickering with Hill's outposts round Elizondo. Wellington was by now fully aware of Soult's intentions, and these delays gave him the time he needed. As the French advance seemed to be aimed at Pamplona, Soult must be kept off and the siege lines maintained against any attempted sallies by the Pamplona garrison. Picton's 3rd and Cole's 4th Divisions were established on a ridge near the village of Sorauren, three miles north-east of Pamplona.

Wellington, having surveyed the position at Sorauren and discussed the situation with Cole and Picton, was writing out his orders on the parapet of the bridge over the Ulzana river when Soult's troops appeared in the hills ahead and a French cavalry patrol came clattering into the village. There was just time for Wellington to thrust the orders at his ADC, Lord Fitzroy Somerset, before both men had to mount and gallop to safety. The orders, to Sir George Murray, were for the 6th, 7th and 2nd Divisions to come up on Picton's flanks with all despatch, while Wellington joined Picton and Cole to await the French attack.

Wellington's arrival at the front line on the ridge above Sorauren was greeted with cheers and shouts of 'Douro! Douro!' from the delighted Portuguese. Picked up by the British infantry, it spread from battalion to battalion as he cantered his horse along the line to Picton's headquarters. Picton's defensive position, on a steep ridge east of the village, was now occupied by his own 3rd and Cole's 4th Divisions, two Spanish divisions, a brigade of Portuguese infantry, and two independent Spanish battalions.

Soult did not attack that afternoon. Those cheers and shouts had informed him of Wellington's presence − at which he always became indecisive − and Clausel's division was still coming down from Roncesvalles. While Soult took a siesta, the 6th Division came up on Picton's left, and when the 2nd and 7th had arrived on his northern flank, the British position looked secure.

After a thunderstorm on 27 July, the French finally came forward on the 28th, and were repulsed at every point. Marching up to the crest of the ridge above the village, they were greeted at the top by long ranks of British, Portuguese and Spanish infantry who blasted their columns away with volleys of musketry. Although they captured the village of Sorauren, the French were forced to a halt and made no further moves towards Pamplona. Soult was in a quandary. His army had run out of food, and his troops would starve if he attempted to stay where he was: there were thin pickings for foragers in the foothills of the Pyrenees. He could not make another advance on Pamplona as long as the British stood in his way, while a retreat would not only invite an attack on his rear, but almost certainly enrage the Emperor. Soult therefore decided to wheel his army north across Wellington's front and march on San Sebastián, a move ordered on the 29th and begun on the morning of 30 July.

When he saw the French move off, Wellington ordered his army to advance. Soult's right-hand formation, d'Erlon's advance guard, escaped from an encounter with Hill's corps, but Clausel's troops, intercepted on the road to Ostiz north of Pamplona, were brought to battle by the 7th Division and severely mauled before they got away. The two French divisions holding the village of Sorauren were quickly overwhelmed, and their rearguard was savaged trying to hold off the 3rd and 4th Divisions which Picton had sent forward as soon as the French began to move.

Soult now abandoned his attempt to march on San Sebastián and ordered a retreat to the Bidassoa and France. Wellington assumed that Soult would withdraw through the Maya pass and sent the bulk of the British army to block it. In fact Soult chose the Echelar pass, but even so, with the Light Division coming up to reinforce the 4th, he was driven over the pass in great confusion.

For the second time in six weeks the French had been driven out of Spain, but Soult resolutely tried again, attempting to relieve San Sebastián on 31 August. Heavy mist in the Bidassoa valley cloaked the advance of Rielle's corps until it collided with Bernado Friere's Spanish troops on the heights at San Marçial, above the Bidassoa. The Spanish, fighting with great skill and determination, had repulsed two French assaults before Friere asked Wellington for reinforcements. These Wellington declined to supply, telling Friere: 'If I send you the English troops you ask for, they will win the battle; but as the French are already in retreat, you may as well win it for yourselves.'

Three French divisions under General Clausel made their way back over the Bidassoa, but when a great rainstorm broke along the frontier and the river rose, four brigades were cut off on the south bank. Trying to fight their way back across the river over the bridge at Vera, they were opposed by a single company of the 95th Rifles under Lieutenant Cadeaux who held the bridge like a latter-day Horatius, from three in the morning until daybreak, when he and sixty of his men were killed.

While this series of combats were being fought along the Bidassoa, Graham stormed San Sebastián again on the morning of 31 August. The assult force from the 5th Division was brought to a halt in the breach, and another storming party drawn from elements of all the other divisions went to their assistance, supported by artillery fire. San Sebastián fell in the middle of the afternoon, and, as had happened at Badajoz, its taking was followed by a collapse of discipline, and another night of drunkenness, looting and riot.

18

The Battle for Germany:
1813

How could poor conscripts, so young they had no
moustache, so thin their ribs were like lanterns, how, I ask,
could poor creatures like this endure such misery.
                    Joseph Bertha, a conscript of 1813

WITH THE BRITISH army hovering on the southern frontier of France, it is time to go back and examine the state of affairs in the heart of Europe. After Napoleon's failure in Russia and the ruin of the *Grande Armée*, it was clear that the next phase of his struggle for mastery would take place between the Elbe and the Oder, for even before the Russians crossed the Nieman and pushed on across the frontiers of the Grand Duchy of Warsaw, there was evidence that his allies would no longer support Napoleon's cause.

General Yorck's defection in December 1812 was the first sign that Prussia was faltering in her allegiance. Only the Austrian Emperor's innate caution and his apprehension lest the defeat of France should lead to domination by Russia or Prussia kept the Austrians from immediately throwing their armies against Napoleon's depleted forces.

Resilience in adversity has always been the hallmark of a great leader, and on his return to Paris in mid December 1812 Napoleon bent his still considerable energies to the rebuilding of his military machine. The arsenals of his Empire would, in time, produce the *matériel* for a fresh struggle – the cannon and muskets, powder and shot – but he needed men, and he needed horses.

From the Russian campaign some 70,000 troops survived, mostly those who, returning to France before the occupation of Moscow, had been spared the horrors of the retreat. Several tens of thousands more were recalled from garrisons east of the Rhine. The Class of 1813, called up in September 1812, meant 140,000 conscripts would be emerging from the depots, and 80,000 men of the National Guard were transferred into the regulars. The remaining Imperial Guards and several picked corps of cavalry and artillery were recalled from Spain. A brigade of cavalry was found by transferring 3,000 mounted *gendarmes* to military service, and 12,000 gunners from the port-bound French navy, plus 20,000 fit and disciplined but underemployed *matelots*, found themselves drafted into the army.

The numbers available were scarcely adequate to face the Russians and guard the frontiers of France. Levies were made upon the states of the Confederation of the Rhine, and Italy was called upon for more men. The Class of 1814 was called to the depots in February 1813, and the Class lists from 1808 onwards were trawled for evaders. On paper these conscriptions produced impressive numbers, but the conscripts were mostly youths, lacking the stamina of grown men. They were not of the calibre of the victors of Austerlitz or Wagram, Marengo or Castiglione. They were the barrel-scrapings, the best that could be found, the under- or over-aged, the sick, lame or lazy, the reluctant-to-serve. Nor were their officers of the quality of old. Leading as they did from the front, from marshal to *sous-lieutenant*, French officers were killed in quantity in any engagement. Losses which could not be made good, for the new men lacked fire and leadership qualities. Nevertheless, by the late spring of 1813 Napoleon commanded half a million men.

The shortage of horses was acutely felt. Remounts were needed for the cavalry, and draught horses for the guns and for transport. Cavalry was essential for scouting and reconnaissance, and to exploit any victory with rapid pursuit, while to compensate for its inferior quality Napoleon had the intention of providing every infantry battalion with artillery support but horses for the guns were simply not available. Not only had a quarter of a million horses been lost in Russia, so had French control over vast horse-breeding tracts of Eastern Europe. This deficiency of cavalry and draught horses was to plague Napoleon in the months to come.

Meanwhile, war continued in the east, where Murat and Prince Eugène were trying to buy time by delaying the advance of the Russians and their allies, whose forces were constantly pushing forward and steadily increasing. By mid January 1813 the Russian army was over the Vistula. On 7 February they occupied Warsaw. French detachments totalling more than 40,000 were left to garrison Danzig and Thorn as Prince Eugène took over the command from Murat and fell back to Frankfurt on the Oder. There he was reinforced by a corps of 30,000 men under Marshal St Cyr but the frozen rivers providing no obstacle to the advancing Russians and their swarming Cossacks, the French defensive positions were swiftly outflanked. On 6 March Eugène fell back again, to Wittenberg on the Elbe, while the Russians marched on to enter Berlin and link up with the Prussians. On 12 March 1813 the French hold on the Elbe became increasingly fragile when the French commander there evacuated Hamburg and marched his troops to Wittenberg.

The Prussians now openly allied themselves with Russia. Under pressure from his ministers, his people and, most of all, his wife, Frederick-Wilhelm finally abandoned the French alliance, and on 13 March Prussia declared war on France. Within days the Prussians had taken the field with an army of 80,000, a force of some quality, and twice as large as Napoleon had expected.

From 1807 the Prussian Army had been restricted by the terms of the Treaty of Tilsit to just 40,000 men but annually for the past four years half had been 'retired' while another 20,000 recruits were called up. By this means a large reserve of trained soldiers was established, enabling the Prussian army to mushroom when the Reservists were recalled. By June the Prussians had assembled more than a quarter of a million men, including 30,000 cavalry, and 400 guns; among their leaders were three very competent generals: Yorck, now publicly restored to favour, who had learned his trade under Napoleon; von Bülow; and, most formidable of all, the aged but aggressive Marshal Blücher. Blücher's first task was to occupy the strategically important city of Dresden.

That former Marshal of France, Crown Prince Bernadotte of Sweden, then brought his small but well-trained army of 30,000 into the field and with spring approaching, these allied armies advanced on France.

The year 1813 saw a series of confrontations, combats and battles which, for the sake of clarity, it is both convenient and accurate to divide into two phases, separated by a brief truce. During the first phase, from early April until June, Napoleon fought and defeated the Allies at Lützen and Bautzen. There followed a two-month pause, ostensibly while the Austrian Foreign Minister, Prince Metternich, attempted to negotiate a peace, but actually to give the Allies time to rebuild their armies, while Austria prepared to mobilize and join them. Fighting was renewed in August, when Austria entered the war, and following an indecisive battle at Dresden, Napoleon was heavily defeated at the so-called 'Battle of the Nations', at Leipzig. The outcome of the 1813 campaigns was the dissolution of the Confederation of the Rhine and the advance of the Allied armies to the eastern frontiers of France. With Wellington defeating the French at Vitoria and along the Franco-Spanish frontier and poised by the end of the year to cross into France, a military vice was slowly closing on the French Emperor.

The French and Allied armies began to deploy at the end of March 1813. Napoleon, determined to strike first, assembled his forces at Mainz on the Rhine, south-west of Frankfurt. From there he would march on Berlin with his Army of the Main while Davout, with the Army of the Elbe, diverted Allied attention by threatening Dresden and the south. Sweeping round the Hartz Mountains and throwing Prussia into turmoil, the Emperor would appear on the north flank of the advancing Russian army, eventually arriving at the Oder – a thrust which would also retrieve the 40 to 50,000 veteran French troops now besieged in garrisons stretching back to Poland.

This classic of Napoleonic strategy had to be abandoned, for the Emperor did not have enough men to ensure the success of such a manoeuvre. Those he had lacked the strength to march so hard and so far, and the shortage of horses meant difficulties with scouting and hauling the guns. Moreover, the Confederation of the Rhine was unravelling as Prince Metternich intrigued with Bavaria, Saxony and Würtemberg.

Abandoning his plan of encirclement, at least for the moment, Napoleon decided instead to deal with the Russians and Prussians. By mid April the Russo-Prussian forces to the east of Jena numbered 110,000 including 25,000 cavalry, and when Napoleon joined his army at Mainz on 18 April 1813 he had some 200,000 men with which to oppose them. By 25 April he was at Erfurt, with his army deployed along the upper Saale, and during the next few days they were set in motion towards Leipzig. Meanwhile, Kutusov having died on 25 March, the Czar had given the Allied Command to General Wittgenstein, despite protests at this appointment from other Russian generals. The Russians and Prussians had concentrated and were moving in a line roughly parallel with the French but slightly further south.

On 1 May there were a number of encounters between French and Allied formations, some of which developed into heavy infantry attacks and cannonades, and during one of these, near Weissenfels, Marshal Bessières was killed. His death was a blow to Napoleon, for they had soldiered together since 1796, and Bessières had commanded the Guard Cavalry since 1809. 'Bessières lived like Bayard, and died like Turenne,' the Emperor said. Bessières had also possessed one quality lacking in most of the other marshals: he knew how to obey orders.

The IIIrd Corps under Marshal Ney occupied Lützen late on the evening of 1 May and the Army of the Elbe, advancing from the south, prepared for a more serious encounter on the following day, while the Army of the Main closed up from the north. Ney's instructions were to hold Lützen and occupy the villages in his line of advance, while the other corps of the Army of the Elbe hooked round to attack the Russian left. Ney kept three divisions in Lützen and sent two south to Kaja, on the Flossgarten river south of Leipzig.

Allied cavalry and Cossack patrols had been probing about the flanks of the Army of the Elbe for the last two days. On 1 May they detected a French infantry brigade out on its own near Kaja, and Wittgenstein decided to begin his main advance by wiping out this force. However, the Prussian cavalry sent in to the attack at noon on 2 May found the position occupied, not by a single infantry brigade, but by Ney's two advance divisions. These swiftly beat off the Prussian cavalry, then Blücher brought up his artillery and sent in infantry. A general action spread along the front, Ney came up from Lützen with the three other divisions of his corps, and heavy fighting continued, as more and more troops were committed.

The sound of cannon-fire alerted the Emperor to the fact that the main Allied army was on his front. Marmont's VIth Corps was ordered to support Ney's Corps, while Bertrand threatened the Allied left and Macdonald took his IXth Corps against the Russians' right. The Prussians were already evacuating Leipzig and, with his dispositions made, Napoleon rode back to Lützen to rally Ney's battered corps; their shouts of '*Vive l'Empereur!*' alerted the Russians and Prussians to his presence. His ability to inspire his soldiers remained unimpaired, and he was everywhere on the field, encouraging and compelling his conscripts – even, so legend has it, with the Imperial boot. Whatever the persuasion employed, the young soldiers of Ney's IIIrd Corps managed to hold on until Bertrand and Macdonald began to put pressure on the Allied flanks.

On the Allied side, Blücher had been wounded and General Yorck, who then took command of the Prussians, failed to get a grip on the battle. The Czar's continual interference with Wittgenstein's decisions, not least by refusing him permission to commit the grenadier divisions, meant that Wittgenstein found himself without sufficient reserves just as Marmont and Bertrand began to close in on his flanks.

The crux of the battle came at about 3 p.m., when with the available Russian reserves already fully committed, Wittgenstein ordered Yorck's Prussians to advance into Kaja. There they were immediately repulsed by the Young Guard and a charge from Ney's resurgent IIIrd Corps.

By early evening Bertrand's and Macdonald's troops were finally in position and, with his concentration complete, Napoleon ordered a general advance on the Allied line. This classic Napoleonic assault began with a point-blank cannonade of the Allied line. The Russian and Prussian forces which had thrust themselves forward into the trap between Bertrand and Macdonald were quickly overwhelmed, the village of Gross-Görschen was retaken and the Allied line fell back in disorder. Nightfall and Napoleon's shortage of cavalry prevented what would have been a total Allied defeat and a decisive French victory.

Casualties were high on both sides – about 20,000 – and while the reputation severely diminished by his failure in Russia had been re-established, Napoleon had lost Bessières and more men than he could afford. He was also unpleasantly surprised by the skill and tenacity displayed by the Allied troops, in particular the Prussians who, well handled by their generals, had fought stubbornly.

Wittgenstein realized that the hoped-for collapse of the French Empire was not going to happen at once and the Allies therefore withdrew to the east, through Dresden. They fell back on Bauzen, on the River Spree, to join a division of 13,000 troops under the Russian general Barclay de Tolly, which had been engaged in preparing a defensive position there. Wittgenstein elected to make a stand on this line against the advancing French.

To exploit his success at Lützen, Napoleon sent half the Army of the Elbe, under Ney, north to Wittenberg to absorb the currently neutral Army of Saxony, which became his VIIth Corps. This corps, advancing north to threaten Berlin would dismay the Prussians and perhaps lead to a split with Russia. The rest of Ney's forces would move east, following Wittgenstein, and the Vth Corps, under General Lauriston, would link these two wings together.

By 11 May 1813, 70,000 French troops under Napoleon's personal command had crossed the Elbe and were close to Dresden, while Ney had another 50,000 men at Torgau, further north. The Emperor then merged the Army of the Main with the Army of the Elbe, and detached Prince Eugène to take command of all French forces in Italy where, with this 'Army of Observation', he was to threaten the Austrian frontier and thus concentrate Austrian attention in the south at this critical time.

The new Army of the Elbe was divided into two wings. The Northern wing, 85,000 men under Ney, comprised five infantry corps, the IInd Cavalry Corps, and a division of hussars. The Southern, under Napoleon, comprised the Imperial Guard, the Ist Cavalry Corps and four infantry corps, some 122,000 men. The link between the two wings, as between the former Armies, was Lauriston's Vth Corps, detached from Ney's command.

As well as making these military preparations, Napoleon was active on the diplomatic front, sending Caulaincourt to the Czar to suggest a cessation of the current hostilities and a peace conference to be held in Prague. Prince Metternich had already proposed such a conference, but Napoleon had no intention of letting the Austrians put themselves forward as mediators. As far as he was concerned the Austrians were his allies, not neutrals. If there was no peace, he intended to deal first with Russia, and then, as necessary, with the Prussians. The Austrians must not interfere militarily or politically until the issue of peace or war had been decided.

While Caulaincourt was talking to the Czar, Ney prepared to advance on Berlin and Napoleon moved east to re-establish contact with the Allied army at Bauzen on the River Spree. Adhering to his well-tested tactics, he planned a frontal attack to fix the enemy in position, then an encirclement to take them in the flank and rear. At Bautzen his own wing would attack directly across the Spree while part of Ney's force, diverted from the advance on Berlin, came in on the Allied right flank from the north. At the same time, Ney was to mask Berlin with two full corps.

Ney seldom seemed able to carry out orders to the letter. Here he omitted to mask Berlin and came south with his entire force. He then failed to grasp the importance of the Emperor's next command, which was to wheel to the east of Bauzen to cut Wittgenstein's line of retreat, bringing Lauriston's Vth Corps with him as he came, and the Allied escape route was thus left wide open.

The Allied army was deployed along a series of low hills and ridges behind the Spree with the town of Bautzen, on the east bank of the river, slightly south of centre. The French line was shorter than the Allied line, but Ney and Lauriston to the north overlapped the Allied right though neither side was aware of this tactical advantage.

The Emperor engaged the Allied army on 20 May 1813, beginning with a frontal assault across the river by three full corps, after which Ney was to fall on their right flank. This suited the Czar and Wittgenstein who intended to employ exactly the same tactics, holding Napoleon's advance on their front and then attacking his left. The

Czar believed, however, that the 'hook' part of Napoleon's 'hold-and-hook' tactic would come in on the Allied left (southern) flank, not from the north. The Allies therefore placed the bulk of their army and reserves on their left flank, to resist and to counter-attack when the French assault faltered.

The French began the battle of Bautzen about noon with the usual furious cannonade. French sappers then bridged the Spree for the infantry regiments to surge across, and by evening the Allied army had been driven out of their entrenchments around Bautzen and their front line had been pushed back from the river. Oudinot's corps created havoc on the Allied left, where the Russians were under the Czar's personal direction, and confirmed the Czar and Wittgenstein in their belief that the flank attack would come in there.

Ney's forces were already coming down from the north, and when darkness fell Napoleon seemed poised for a decisive victory. On the 21st, Ney and Lauriston assaulted the Allied right while Victor and Reynier hooked around the Allied flank. At the same time Oudinot, Macdonald and Marmont recommenced battering the Allied left flank, while Napoleon and Soult mustered their central forces on the east bank of the Spree, north of Bautzen, waiting until the time was right for a general assault. The 'pinning' manoeuvre in this battle was on the wings, not the centre.

Oudinot and his colleagues met stiff resistance to their attack in the south, where the Allies had the bulk of their troops and, aware of the shape the battle was now taking, were desperate to prevent a further erosion of their position. Although by shortly after noon Oudinot had been driven from the ground he had won on the 20th, this served Napoleon's purpose, since the Allies began to leave their second-line defences in order to follow up his retreat, thus thinning their centre and expanding to the flank. With Ney now heavily engaged on the northern flank and Oudinot putting up a stiff fight to the south, by mid afternoon on 21 May the moment had arrived for a major strike in the centre.

At two o'clock some 20,000 infantry quietly moved across the river by Napoleon in the morning began a violent assault on the Allied centre. Following an hour-long cannonade from 80 guns, the infantry went in, Soult's IVth Corps rapidly gaining possession of Blücher's position. The Prussian infantry, fighting with skill and tenacity, inflicted heavy casualties on the French troops and the IVth Corps' attack petered out. This was partly because artillery support could not come forward, and partly because Blücher, anticipating Ney's and Lauriston's move around his flank, had pulled his forces back to avoid encirclement. Napoleon was now pressing the Allied line in the centre with every man and gun he could find, but the Russian line held. Oudinot in the south was now in serious difficulties, facing the bulk of the Allied forces while trying to shore up the flank of the French centre, and try as they would the French could not prise the Allied troops loose.

All now depended on Ney. Unfortunately Ney, having advanced with uncharacteristic lethargy, became obsessed with capturing the village of Preititz, on the Prussians' northern flank, battering away there instead of pushing on to the Allied rear, as ordered. Having taken Preititz, he then assaulted Blücher's position directly, instead of manoeuvring behind it and thereby forcing Blücher to withdraw. Fighting as they were, on the defensive and in prepared positions, the Prussians were still holding Ney on the right when the Russian position in the centre finally began to crumble.

The Russians had been fighting for hours and were tired and low on ammunition. Oudinot in the south and Napoleon's divisions in the centre, including the Imperial Guard, now began to advance steadily to deliver the *coup-de-grâce*. Blücher, however, was able to extricate his Prussians. On Ney's appearance the Allies had made preparations to break off the engagement and at about 4 o'clock the Czar ordered a general withdrawal.

This was an ordered retreat, not a rout. The Prussians moved north-east to Weissenberg, the Russians, with all their guns, back to Löbau. The French were too exhausted and too short of cavalry to mount any pursuit and their losses were serious, a further 20,000 in addition to the 20,000 lost at Lützen three weeks earlier.

The Allied losses of about 20,000 men could be replaced; far more serious was the loss of confidence among their commanders. Six months earlier both the French army and Napoleon's military reputation had been in ruins. Now they had risen, Phoenix-like, to win two battles inside a month, battles which might, but for the French shortage of cavalry, have been decisive defeats for the Prussian and Russian armies. Wittgenstein, for one, was never again sure of himself when Napoleon was in the field against him.

The Allied commanders fell to quarrelling and apportioning blame. Wittgenstein resigned and was replaced by Barclay de Tolly. Then the Russians fell out with the Prussians and Barclay de Tolly, although he prepared for a withdrawal into Poland, eventually drew back only as far as Silesia. Napoleon was able to exploit this dissension to the extent of sending Davout to retake Hamburg, which he entered on 1 June, and despatching Oudinot towards Berlin; but he could do no more. His advance was constantly hampered by Cossacks which he did not have the cavalry to repel, and this was Napoleon's problem. Even if he were able to force a victory in the field, he had not the strength in cavalry to exploit it.

It therefore suited both sides to accede to the mediation of Prince Metternich. A cease-fire was arranged for 2 June, and at Pläswitz on the 4th a suspension of hostilities was agreed upon until 20 July, during which time terms for a general peace were to be sought. Both sides thereupon began to re-arm, recruit and train with the greatest possible alacrity. Peace may have been possible after Bautzen but nobody really wanted it.

19

'The Battle of Nations':

Leipzig, 1813

> You will see by the news that an Armistice is being
> negotiated. This Armistice will interrupt the course of my
> victories.
> Emperor Napoleon: 2 June 1813

IN JUNE 1813, the 'wild card' in European politics was the Empire of
Austria. Napoleon knew that if he were to retrieve his position in
Europe, Austria must be kept neutral. His marriage to the Austrian
Emperor's daughter Marie-Louise, though it had proved happy and
productive, was essentially a diplomatic move and short of surrender-
ing previously annexed Austrian territory, Napoleon had spared no
effort to conciliate and placate his Imperial father-in-law. The results
had been disappointing: the Austrians had provided one corps for the
Russian campaign, but made no effort to help in Napoleon's present
confrontation with Russia and Prussia. Yet nor had they taken the
field against him; if he could not enlist their active support, Napoleon
intended at least to keep the Austrians neutral.

It was known that the Austrians were expanding their army. The
Austrian Emperor, or at least Metternich, claimed this growing power
would enable Austria to arbitrate from strength between the warring
powers and, by threatening to put that strength behind the more
conciliatory party, enforce a general peace. Metternich did not go
into details; he knew precisely what he wanted in return for his
efforts, and a general peace was not his first priority.

Metternich first proposed an armistice between France and the
Allies. He then insisted that, to enable him to demonstrate Austrian
impartiality, Napoleon must release Austria from any political or

military obligations. This Napoleon did. Metternich then persuaded Prussia and Russia to agree that they would negotiate only through him, and would not conclude a separate peace with Napoleon. Thus equipped with full powers to negotiate on behalf of the Allies, Metternich met Napoleon in Dresden on 26 June 1813.

In the map room of the Mercolini Palace, Metternich presented the demands of Russia, Prussia, and Austria in return for peace. As he did so, Napoleon's fury grew. Each nation had separate demands, and all were unacceptable. The Russians required the dissolution of the Grand Duchy of Warsaw; the Prussians required the break-up of the Confederation of the Rhine; Austria required the return of Illyria and all her former Italian provinces. When Metternich had finished Napoleon, erupting, threw his hat across the room, pointing out that Metternich's 'impartial' mediation seemed to require the liquidation of the French Empire. He also reminded Metternich that the French had recently fought and beaten the Prussians and Russians twice in three weeks. Why should he make such concessions?

'For peace,' replied Metternich, blandly.

Metternich had seen the French army in Dresden. He had noted their fatigue, and the large number of young faces in the ranks. He had spies in Paris and knew, not least from Talleyrand, that the nation was in desperate need of peace. The implication that a rejection of the terms would result in Austria joining Russia and Prussia, adding another 200,000 men to the Allied armies, was not less clear for remaining unstated. Furthermore, Britain was subsidizing the Allies, and Metternich knew that Crown Prince Bernadotte was about to bring Sweden formally into the Alliance. With fresh supplies of men and money, and two more allies waiting in the wings, Metternich held all the cards.

Napoleon was aware of these facts. He calmed down, and attempted to negotiate. He offered Austria the return of Illyria – not out of fear, but in return for her help in 1812. He also offered to placate Russia with the return of land in eastern Poland, but beyond that he would not budge. He would not betray the Poles; he would concede nothing to Prussia; and he regarded French regency over the Confederation of the Rhine as vital to French security. Metternich flatly rejected these concessions and the talks broke down. On the following day, 27 June, Austria signed an alliance with Russia and Prussia, the Treaty of Reichenbach, after which the Austrians gave Napoleon until 10 August to comply with Metternich's terms, and on 12 August 1813 the Emperor Francis abandoned his son-in-law and declared war on France.

The considerable forces arrayed against Napoleon from August 1813 were divided into three main armies. Crown Prince Bernadotte was placed in command of the Army of the North, consisting of 110,000 Swedes and Prussians based around Berlin, Blücher had 95,000 men in the Army of Silesia, which was forming at Breslau to the south-east; and Prince Schwarzenberg had 230,000 Austrians, Russians and Prussians in the Army of Bohemia on the upper Elbe. Apart from these the Russian Army of Poland, with 60,000 men under Baron Bennigsen, was forming near Warsaw. The total of the Allied armies – Russians, Prussians, Swedes and Austrians – exceeded half a million men in the front line, with perhaps 300,000 in reserve. The Czar insisted that the Austrian Prince Schwarzenberg should be Commander-in-Chief, knowing that he could overawe Schwarzenberg more easily than he could the other obvious candidate, the Prussian Marshal Blücher.

Napoleon was not idle during the summer truce. He drained France of men on this occasion, rather than attempting to rely on foreign levies, and by August 1813 he had gathered about 400,000 men in Germany, with 280,000 under Prince Eugène in Italy, or in reserve. Although in terms of numbers the two sides were evenly matched, the quality of the French army was now at its lowest ebb, with ill-trained cavalry and too many raw recruits among the infantry, but his officers were experienced, and, for the first time since the earliest days of the Empire, he had the advantage of a more homogeneous, mostly-French force. These young men – the 'Marie-Louises' as they came to be called – were to perform wonders in the weeks ahead, despite the dampening effect of news from Spain of the defeat at Vitoria.

Napoleon, making Dresden the centre for his campaign, spared no effort to have depots built there and filled with munitions and stores. His army was again divided into two main 'wings'. The larger, commanded by himself, based on Dresden and consisting of 250,000 men in seven corps, would defend Dresden against any Allied assaults in that vicinity. The second wing, 120,000 men in four infantry corps under Marshal Oudinot, was to advance on Berlin, dealing with Bernadotte's Army of the North on the way. The final formation, Davout's XIIIth Corps, was charged with the defence of Hamburg and the Lower Elbe.

These arrangements were a departure from Napoleon's usual well-tried practice of concentrating all his forces before battle. Now, faced with an enemy superior in numbers, he was dividing his army into three separate groups and his marshals disapproved. Marmont put his doubts into words: 'I greatly fear that on the day we gain a great victory, the Emperor may learn he has lost two.'

The opening moves of this campaign were marked by indecision. On 17 August Napoleon, advancing with his wing to the old battle-ground at Bautzen, learned that strong Russian reinforcements were moving across his front to join Blücher's Army of Silesia at Breslau – whereupon he decided to march hard to the east and hit Blücher before these reinforcements could arrive. On the following day he changed his mind: he would instead attack the Russian corps of 40,000 men under General Wittgenstein. On 21 August he changed his mind again, and decided after all to attack Blücher near Breslau, but as he approached, Blücher withdrew out of reach.

This withdrawal was in compliance with a plan agreed upon by the Allied commanders: they would not fight Napoleon. He was yet to be beaten in the field, and considerable awe was felt of his prowess as a commander. The Allied commanders would fight his marshals if the opportunity arose, but the Emperor they would wear down, by constantly retreating while other armies advanced on his rear and on his lines of communication, until, under this constant but elusive pressure, he must finally fall back. Great though he was, even Napoleon could be in only one place at a time. As the Russians had during the 1812 campaign, the Allies were relying on time and space to operate in their favour.

This policy was soon in action. While Napoleon was chasing Blücher in the east, Schwarzenberg's Army of Bohemia advanced from Prague to threaten Dresden. Leaving Marshal Macdonald to pursue Blücher, Napoleon hastened back to Bautzen, unknown to the advancing Austrians. Calling up three infantry corps and the Imperial Guard from Dresden, he made ready to fall on Schwarzenberg's right flank but before he could do so, he learned that Oudinot had been checked and then repulsed during his advance on Berlin. Then he heard from Dresden that St Cyr could not hope to hold out for long in the face of the Allied forces massing from the south. With its storehouses full of arms, food and ammunition, Dresden was vital. Sending Vandamme with a strong corps to embarrass any retreat of Schwarzenberg towards Prague, Napoleon led the rest of his troops in a breakneck march across country to the defence of Dresden, covering 90 miles in 72 hours. They arrived on 26 August 1813, in time to deal with Wittgenstein's Russians, who had already reached the city suburbs. The Emperor was displeased with his marshals and their inability to counter the Allied armies without his assistance.

Napoleon had resisted the attractions of a completely entrenched camp at Dresden, satisfying himself with a strong bridgehead on the right bank and a line of trenches and cannon-filled redoubts. St Cyr had positioned his 20,000 troops in the suburbs around the old city, the Altstadt, south of the Elbe, connected by two bridges to the Neustadt, on the north bank. Given more men, he should have been able to hold Dresden unassisted.

Schwarzenberg, arriving before Dresden with the rest of the Army of Bohemia on 25 August, was doubtful of his prospects of success when Napoleon's arrival became known early on the 26th, but he was in an invidious position. The Czar, the Austrian Emperor and the King of Prussia were all present offering advice and eager to share the glory and no one wished to suggest a withdrawal.

Schwarzenberg launched six heavy attacks against the suburbs of Dresden at about 6 p.m. on 26 August. A cannonade from three hundred French guns greeted this advance, and by nightfall the French remained unshaken, nothing had been achieved, and Schwarzenberg withdrew his forces to the heights south of the city. A heavy rainstorm during the night seriously affected the movement of troops on the 27th, but Napoleon's lighter artillery was still able to manoeuvre, while the Allies' heavier guns were stuck in the mud.

Having decided that the French centre could hold its own, Napoleon planned – as at Bautzen – to attack both flanks of his enemy, rather than hurling his might at their centre. Victor's infantry and Murat's cavalry struck hard at the Austrian left while Ney, with the remaining cavalry and the Young Guard, attacked Wittgenstein's Russians on the Prague road. The Allies resisted strenuously on their flanks. Their centre remained inactive all day, cannonaded by the Dresden redoubts.

From a hill near Rächnitz, due south of the city, the Czar, the King of Prussia, Schwarzenberg and a large Headquarters staff observed the fighting until late in the day a shot from a French gun at 2,000 yards' range killed General Moreau, standing next to the Czar. During the Council of War which followed the Czar pressed to continue the fight, but Prince Schwarzenberg's announcement that he was withdrawing his Austrians led the Allies to decide upon a retreat, and by dawn on 28 August, the French were left in possession of the field.

In two days of fighting the Allied armies had lost nearly 40,000 men while French losses barely exceeded 10,000, but French jubilation was short-lived. On 28 August news arrived that Marshal Oudinot, having let his army scatter during the advance on Berlin, had been forced by the Prussians under von Bülow to retreat to Wittenberg; and that, in the east, Macdonald had been attacked by Blücher on the 26th and lost 15,000 killed, wounded or taken prisoner, together with 100 cannon. Marmont's forecast at the start of the campaign proved only too accurate. These two defeats destroyed any political or military advantages of Napoleon's victory at Dresden, and confirmed the Allies in their decision to attack his marshals at every opportunity while avoiding battle with the Emperor himself. The wisdom of this policy was further illustrated on 30 August when General Vandamme and his Ist Corps, falling unsupported upon the retreating Allied flank, were overwhelmed at Toplitz by a combined Russian and Prussian force under General Ostermann and General Kleist. Vandamme and 13,000 of his men were taken prisoner and his corps was almost wiped out. Taken with the French reverses near Berlin and Breslau, the Allies' victory at Toplitz marked a turning-point in their hope and confidence.

Napoleon's strategy for the campaign was falling apart. The Army of Bohemia had retreated from Dresden and refused to engage and he therefore elected for a decisive stroke in the north. Marshal Ney, who had replaced Oudinot in command of that wing, would march on Berlin, while three other corps, under Murat, Marmont and St Cyr, held Dresden and the vital depots.

The plan did not last even a day. Macdonald was falling back on Dresden with Blücher and his victorious Army of Silesia in hot pursuit, and the Allied scheme to avoid the Emperor but attack his marshals was seen to be paying dividends. Over the next few days the same tale came in from every section of the front. When the Emperor went to help Macdonald, Blücher promptly fell back, while Schwarzenberg moved in against St Cyr's positions at Dresden. Napoleon therefore rushed back to Dresden. While he was there, Ney, who was marching on Berlin, became involved in a confused battle with Bernadotte's Army of the North and swiftly lost 10,000 men. The Emperor was even less pleased with this defeat when he heard that Ney had given up all attempts to command the army and simply plunged into the battle, sword in hand. Napoleon therefore decided to join Ney's advance on Berlin, but while he was moving north, news caught up with him that Schwarzenberg was again threatening Dresden, Bernadotte was on the Elbe at Rosslau, further to the north, while Macdonald was still retreating before Blücher's Army of Silesia. So it went on for three whole weeks, while the Emperor and his forces wore themselves out, marching to and fro, from one sector of the front to another, achieving nothing.

On 5 October Napoleon moved against Blücher, who fell back to combine with Bernadotte and his Army of the North. Bernadotte, ever-cautious, wished to fall back behind the Saar, while Blücher was anxious to move closer to Schwarzenberg's Austrians near Leipzig, and risk a battle.

Napoleon could neither attack the Allied armies one by one, nor prevent them combining. Eventually he was compelled to concentrate his forces to the east of Leipzig on 14 October, by which time, thanks to Blücher, the three Allied armies were near enough together to plan a combined attack – encouraged by news of disaffection among the Confederation of the Rhine. This proved true when on 13 October the Bavarians concluded a treaty with Austria.

Napoleon massed his troops south-east of Leipzig, preparing to fling the bulk of his force upon Schwarzenberg. Although his numbers were inferior – 200,000 against the Allies' 260,000 – he had no intention of fighting a defensive battle. Having pinned down Schwarzenberg's army in the Allied centre, Augerau's IXth Corps and the cavalry would envelope their right wing, make a massive flanking attack and overwhelm the Allies.

The 'Battle of the Nations' began at 6.30 on the morning of 16 October 1813 and rapidly developed into a battle of attrition. The main Austrian attack was made by four corps, which went in separately, without co-ordination, and the various units failed to support each other. The French defence also fell into confusion, and the chance to split and destroy the attacking Austrians was swiftly lost. The latter continued to press their attacks home on the French lines for several hours, suffering great losses from the 700 well-sited guns of the French artillery.

By mid morning the Allied offensive against the French centre was petering out, but Napoleon delayed the flanking movement by the 62,000-strong IXth Corps from a reluctance to advance in the centre while Blücher was still threatening Marmont on the north. When it became clear that Wittgenstein's forces in the centre were played out, the Emperor judged it time to smash through the Allied line and brought 150 guns into action. After an hour-long cannonade the French centre went forward, led by Murat at the head of 10,000 cavalry. By four in the afternoon the French had pushed the Allies back, but the Austrians in the centre, battered as they were, had still not broken and when night fell on the 16th it was clear that the battle was far from over.

The French had lost 25,000 men to the Allies' 30,000, but Napoleon had only one possible reinforcement on hand, a division of 14,000 men under General Reynier, while the Allies were expecting

Bernadotte's Army of the North and Bennigsen's Russians, a rein-forcement of 140,000 men.

Preparations to renew the fighting went on all night, but there was little action on 17 October. Napoleon might have moved again against Schwarzenberg, before the arrival of Bernadotte and Bennigsen could give the Allies a crushing superiority, but he fell again into lassitude, 'A carelessness', wrote Marmont, 'which it is impossible to explain.' He even sent a message to his father-in-law, the Austrian Emperor, offering an armistice but there was no answer. Even with Reynier's corps, the advent of Bernadotte and Bennigsen meant that the French were outnumbered two to one. Mortier was sent to guard the passages of the Elster, and on the night of 17/18 October Napoleon began to pull his men back, the sight and sound of his withdrawal being masked by darkness and torrential rain. The Allied pickets awoke next morning to find the French two miles further back all along the front. When the armies made contact, in mid afternoon, the resulting battle grew in fury as more and more divisions and brigades became engaged. The withdrawal had weakened the cohesion of Napoleon's army, and in the late afternoon two brigades of Saxons and some Würtembergers from Reynier's newly-arrived VIIth Corps deserted, leaving a gap in the French line. Just before dusk the combined forces of Bernadotte and Bennigsen drove Marmont's men out of their po-sitions and forced Reynier's depleted corps to fall back.

With ammunition now perilously low, Napoleon ordered a full re-treat through Leipzig. The artillery and the cavalry began to file back through the city and early on the 19th the infantry began to pull out. Oudinot was detailed to hold the town, street by street, with 30,000 men, while the rest of the army crossed the Elster river causeway to Lindenau. The withdrawal was covered by the Polish general, Ponia-towski, who had received his marshal's baton in recognition of his services in the previous day's battle.

Napoleon's intention, having evacuated his men across the Elster, was to blow up the causeway in the face of his pursuers. Having prepared the charges, the officer in command left the ignition of the fuses to a corporal, who fired the charges too soon when the causeway was still crowded with French troops, and most of the rearguard was still in the city. In the explosion and the rout which followed, thou-sands were killed, and thousands more were captured in the streets of Leipzig, including Reynier and Lauriston. Oudinot managed to es-cape by swimming across the swollen Elster, but as he made a similar attempt, Poniatowski's horse lost its footing and the gallant Pole was drowned.

Napoleon got what was left of his army away to the Rhine, but there could be no doubt that the outcome of the Battle of the Nations at Leipzig was a defeat for the French. They lost nearly 70,000 men, killed, wounded or taken prisoner, as against Allied losses of 54,000. The fighting during 1813 had cost the French about 400,000 men, a tragedy to equal that of 1812. Napoleon's prestige was fatally damaged and within days his allies began to fall away. Würtemberg soon followed Bavaria in leaving the Confederation of the Rhine, and the King of Saxony, captured at Leipzig, readily entered into an alliance with the Allies. The Allied army followed on Napoleon's heels towards the Rhine, already laying plans to invade France and march on Paris, but first there was some mopping-up to be done. Marshal St Cyr surrendered Dresden on 11 November and the garrisons of Danzig and Torgau capitulated shortly afterwards.

By Christmas the Allies were on the east bank of the Rhine: but France had already been invaded. On 7 October 1813 Field Marshal Lord Wellington had taken his Peninsular Army storming across the Bidassoa river to stand at last on the soil of France.

20

The March on Toulouse:

France, 1813–1814

It was a most wonderful march, the Army in great fighting
order and every man in better wind than a trained pugilist.
Captain Harry Smith: 1813

METTERNICH'S TEN-WEEK TRUCE between June and mid August
1813 enforced a delay on Wellington, poised with his army on the
southern threshold of France. He was not disposed to invade France
while there was a prospect of peace in eastern Europe, since this
would free Napoleon to fall upon him with vigour, but the delay
wasted good campaigning weather, and gave Marshal Soult time to
regroup his forces and prepare defences against the attack that was
surely coming.

It was not until the first week of September that Wellington heard
of the breakdown of discussions between the Allies and Napoleon,
and Austria's declaration of war on France. Although this was
welcome news, Wellington was reluctant to make a major advance
across the frontier for of the various problems which beset him, the
possibility of Napoleon's personal intervention was not the greatest.

A major difficulty was that his superiority in numbers over Marshal
Soult depended on the 25,000 Spanish troops which now made up a
third of his army. Properly led, they had shown outstanding qualities
in the field, but the Spanish government refused to pay or feed them,
and since Wellington's own scanty resources were fully extended
by the needs of his British, Portuguese and Hanoverian soldiers, the
Spanish troops had either to plunder or to starve. While this was just
tolerable within Spain, any Spanish plundering in France, or attempts
at reprisal for Spanish treatment at French hands over the last six

years, might rouse the countryside against him. Wellington had seen what an infuriated peasantry was capable of in Spain, and had no wish to confront such enmity in France.

Then there was the matter of Marshal Suchet, still commanding an army of 60,000 in Aragon and Catalonia; he had proved more than capable of dealing with guerrilla incursions, and his forces represented a permanent threat to Wellington's flanks and communications. Attempts to distract him by landing troops from Sicily in Catalonia having failed, his intervention remained a possibility. Rumours of Napoleon's victory at Dresden did nothing to increase Wellington's confidence in the advisability of taking the war onto French soil, but he decided on a strictly limited advance, with the aim of establishing a shallow bridgehead beyond the tidal waters of the Bidassoa, on the Franco-Spanish frontier. The French occupied a strong natural position on the heights above the north bank and for the past month Soult, ignoring Napoleon's instructions to advance into Spain, had been preparing a line of redoubts between the Bidassoa and Bayonne, thirty miles further north. He was determined to fight the British in his own country and from prepared and well-defended positions.

The first of these defence lines followed the course of the Bidassoa along the frontier into the hill mass of La Rhune, and then along the French side of the Pyrenees to St Jean-Pied-de-Port. The second rested on the sea at St Jean-de-Luz eight miles to the north of the Bidassoa and followed the course of the Nivelle east to the village of Ascain and then south-east along the Col de St Ignace into the hills of the Mondarrain. The third and final line of fortification followed another river, the Nive, and defended the southern approaches to Bayonne.

All these lines were well-entrenched and had redoubts equipped with cannon. Believing the lower tidal reaches of the Bidassoa to be impassable, and that Wellington would therefore favour an enveloping drive from Roncesvalles, Soult had concentrated the bulk of his forces along the central and eastern sections of his line. Wellington, however, had information that the estuary was fordable at the time of the lowest (spring) tides each month, and unobtrusively moved unit after unit to his seaward flank until he had more than 25,000 men assembled there. He planned to feint at Soult's left and centre, where he was expected, with the Light Division and the Spaniards. The attack was planned for 17 September, but negligence among his engineers meant that the necessary bridging train was not brought forward from Vitoria in time. The tides would be suitable again on 7 October, and meanwhile Wellington mounted a series of wholly successful manoeuvres against the French left, designed to reinforce the assumption that he would attack there.

At dawn on 7 October 1813, the light companies of Major-General Hay's 5th Division emerged from their concealed positions on the southern bank to cross the Bidassoa. The water was armpit-deep and mud sucked at their feet but they easily took Hendaye, sending the French outposts fleeing to the rear. A mile further upstream, Lieutenant-General Sir John Hope's 1st Division and two Spanish divisions attacked from San Marçial, crossed the river, and engaged in a skirmish around the village of Biriatou, where they encountered a brief stand by a single French battalion on the Croix de Bouquets. Within the hour Wellington's troops had pushed through the French defences and were swarming forward on a wide front to probe the outer defences of St Jean-de-Luz. Having taken all the high ground between St Jean-de-Luz and the Bidassoa with the loss of just 400 men, Wellington halted his advance.

The taking of the complex series of French redoubts and entrenchments on the La Rhune massif proved less straightforward over particularly difficult terrain, but the Light Division and Longa's Spaniards, a small division made up of former *guerrilleros*, worked their way steadily forwards, the French positions falling one after another. They failed to take the La Rhune massif that day, but the French commander abandoned it the following day and, having penetrated the French line in the centre, Wellington again called a halt. He had so far met with complete success, and the commanding view over the French second line from the summit of the La Rhune massif enabled him to plan his next attack in detail.

No further move was made for a month. Wellington's fears of provoking a guerrilla resistance gradually abated. The British were ordered to pay for whatever they needed, and soon the local people were setting up stalls and markets, happy to profit from these foreign soldiers who were so much less destructive than their own. As to the unpaid, underfed, ill-disciplined and vengeful Spaniards in his army, Wellington eventually decided that he would retain only the cream of them, such as Morillo's division and Longa's useful ex-guerrillas, which he would feed and pay himself and thereby be able to restrain their worst excesses. The rest were sent south to strengthen the siege of Pamplona, which finally fell on 31 October 1813.

Soult remained undaunted, and devoted his considerable energies to improving the fortifications around St Jean-de-Luz and along the Nivelle, convinced now that Wellington's next attack would come in, as at the Bidassoa, against the French right wing. His defences around St Jean-de-Luz were strong, his right flank secured against attack by the Atlantic and by a fortified position, the Camp de Bourdegain. Inland from St Jean his line lay along the Nivelle to Ascain, with the fortified village of Urrugne and a chapel on the hill of Socorri as forward outposts. Ascain, a small town on the south bank of the Nivelle, had been fortified, and the village of Sarre on the north bank of the river provided another strong position. After Ascain the line left the river to pass southwards through difficult country into the Petite Rhune, overlooked by the British observation point on the Grande Rhune but fortified and equipped with several redoubts. A further line of redoubts stretched from the Petite Rhune back towards the Nivelle, west of the fortified village of Sarre, and then continued eastwards across the Nivelle, onto the Mondarrain massif, and yet further eastwards again to the Nive, and the walled town of St Jean-Pied-de-Port at the northern foot of the Roncesvalles pass. Soult had some reason to believe in the impregnability of this line, yet with only about 52,000 men he could not hold the entire line in strength, and with no strategic reserve could only reinforce one position by withdrawing men from somewhere else. He trusted to the natural difficulties of the terrain and the garrisons of the redoubts to buy him time, but that same terrain then worked against him, making it impossible for him to switch men rapidly from point to point. Much would therefore depend upon the accuracy of Soult's assessment of where Wellington's main blow would fall. Soult predicted an attack along the coast and placed 25,000 men between Ascain and the sea, while General Clausel with 16,000 men in three weak divisions was to hold the front between the Petite Rhune and the Nivelle and General d'Erlon with 11,000 held the defences between the Nivelle and the Nive.

With the fall of Pamplona at the end of October and the news of Napoleon's defeat at Leipzig, Wellington felt ready to move forward again. His commanders may have been concerned about the strength of the French lines and the fact that Soult continued to increase his army by conscript drafts, but Wellington was not. He had a fine and flexible army capable of performing any task he set it, he held the initiative – and he had the advantage of an excellent observation post on the Grande Rhune, from which he was able to examine Soult's entire line. At the end of the first week in November he was observing Soult's dispositions through his telescope, as was his habit, when he found what he was looking for – a loophole to the east. In less than an hour he had dictated his orders for the assault and when Sir

George Murray read them back, Wellington nodded with satisfaction. 'Ah, Murray,' he said, 'this will put us in possession of the fellow's lines.'

The plan exhibited the usual Wellingtonian virtues of surprise and simplicity. The main attack under Sir William Beresford would go in between Sarre and the Nivelle, where Clausel's men were thinly spread over a three-mile front, and the 20,000 men of the 3rd, 4th and 7th Divisions would punch a hole right through the French line. Meanwhile, General Giron's 6,000 Andalucian infantry were to skirmish forward on their left, round the eastern slopes of the Grande Rhune and along the Col de St Ignace. To their left again, the Light Division would seize the Petite Rhune and swing to the right against any French troops coming east to stem Beresford's advance. Once this gap had been opened, the rest of the army would pour through to the north, and Soult's line would be outflanked. Finally, in a sweep north along the right bank of the Nivelle 20,000 British troops – three divisions, the 2nd, 6th, and a Portuguese division, under Sir Rowland Hill – were to strike at d'Erlon's men, spread out between the Nivelle and the Nive, thus prising the entire French line out of its prepared positions.

As always, some distractions were arranged. Since Soult clearly expected an attack on his coastal sector, Wellington would oblige him by directing the navy to bombard the St Jean-de-Luz defences, and on the morning of the main assault the 1st and 4th Divisions, under General Hope, would feint against the Camp de Bourdegain. These two actions should engage the bulk of the French army in the west, enabling Wellington to fling nearly twice Soult's numbers against his thinly-spread centre and right defences. The order to advance was signalled at daybreak on 10 November 1813 by the firing of a gun from the summit of the Grande Rhune.

The first task was the capture of three vital strongpoints, the summit of the Petite Rhune and two redoubts lying between the British positions and the village of Sarre. The two brigades of the Light Division moved out under cover of darkness. General Kempt's brigade had to fight its way up the rugged Petite Rhune from rock to rock, taking each redoubt (or 'castle') as they came on it. Colbourne's brigade, meanwhile, had circled round to take another Petite Rhune redoubt, and by nine in the morning the entire position was in British hands. The Light Division then regrouped to be ready for action again when Beresford's troops had taken Sarre.

Beresford's attack had been held up by stout resistance in the first

redoubt before Sarre, but the second fell within fifteen minutes to
cannon fire and an infantry assault urged on by Wellington himself.
Advancing rapidly, Beresford's men had taken Sarre by eight in the
morning. The 'start-line' for the general advance through the French
positions having been secured, the attack began at 9 o'clock. The 3rd
Division cleared the way for their Portuguese brigade to cross the
Nivelle at Amotz and come in on the flank of the French engaged
with Hill's troops on the right bank of the river. There was some
resistance east of Amotz, but the Light Division swiftly drove out the
French troops and pushing on north-westwards got as far as the
Signal Redoubt, well behind the main French line. The colonel of the
defenders surrendered personally to Brigadier Colbourne following an
assault by the 52nd Foot.

By the early afternoon of 10 November the French line was coming
apart. On the right bank of the Nivelle, Hill's corps had completely
overrun d'Erlon's defences, and Clausel's men in the centre were in
full retreat with the Light Division and the Portuguese *caçadores* hard
on their heels. By 4 o'clock Beresford's 3rd and 7th Divisions had
advanced five miles and were ready to cross the Nivelle by the bridges
near St Pée, so outflanking the entire French line. The heights
beyond the Nivelle were in British hands by nightfall. Soult's second
line had gone the way of the first, crumbling before another totally
unexpected assault. Those who could escape the rout fell back to the
third line and into St Jean-de-Luz, and that night Soult abandoned
the Camp de Bourdegain and withdrew to the defences around
Bayonne. He had lost more than 4,000 men in one day of scrambled
fighting.

In the month following this action French morale remained low,
even though Wellington was unable to exploit his success. On 11
November the weather broke, and sweeping rains soon turned the
Pyrenean foothills and the open plains to the north into a maze of
marshland seamed by boggy roads, rushing rivers and swollen streams.
Notwithstanding protests from London, Wellington was adamant:
'There are some things which cannot be done,' he wrote, 'and one of
them is to move troops through this country in pouring rain.' The
campaign of 1813 in Southern France ground to a standstill.

Marshal Soult used this breathing space to reorganize both his
army and his strategy. Since Wellington seemed able to penetrate his
defence lines, he decided to concentrate his forces to the north of the
Nive, leaving strong patrols of *voltigeurs* to watch the river crossings
and give warning of any British incursions – which might be expected
when the weather improved.

Wellington had problems of his own. On 10 November 1813, the night after the Nivelle battles, his Spanish troops pillaged the town of Ascain, looting and raping and setting fire to houses. Although the Spaniards had become increasingly useful and their departure would cost him his numerical superiority over Soult, Wellington decided that they must be returned to Spain. Retaining only Pablo Morillo's small division of 4,500 men, he sent the rest back across the Pyrenees. With them went a letter to the Spanish government in which he concluded a list of his complaints with the tart comment: 'I am not invading France to plunder. Thousands of men have not been killed and wounded in order that the survivors may rob the French.'

His army, if now reduced to some 63,000 men, was nevertheless of excellent quality. On 9 December, the weather having cleared, he sent five divisions across the Nive at Cambo and Ustaritz where they encountered slight opposition, the *voltigeurs* falling back as the British advanced. On the 10th Soult sent his entire army against the Anglo-Portuguese divisions between the Nive and Bayonne, but the French troops came on without enthusiasm and were soon thrown back by the Light Division. Their attack on the two divisions at Barrouillet was initially more successful, as Sir John Hope had maintained only a thin skirmish line, but when British reinforcements fell on their flank the French attack petered out. British losses of some 2,000 against French of about 1,000 were counterbalanced during the night when three German battalions deserted and crossed the lines to the British camp.

On 13 December 1813 Soult struck again, this time with six divisions against Hill's isolated corps at St Pierre d'Irube, on the right bank of the Nive. Hill had just 14,000 men, and was not helped by the cowardice of two of his colonels, one of whom abandoned his battalion and fled while the other marched his men to the rear, leaving a large gap in Hill's thinly-stretched defences. Matters were not improved by the loss of the temporary bridge at Villefranque, which prevented Wellington sending Hill any assistance. 'Daddy' Hill, however, was a fighting general, and was able to first blunt and then beat off the French attack, at the cost of some 1,700 men.

Soult had attempted a right and then a left hook at Wellington's line without success, and he had lost more than 6,000 men. The weather was wet and the nights freezing and with winter gripping the Pyrenees, the New Year arrived without further action.

Peace reigned on the southern front until mid February, 1814 and Soult's position had worsened. Napoleon, back in France after his defeat at Leipzig and scraping together another army, ordered him to send two infantry divisions, a cavalry division and five artillery batteries to Paris. Soult's Italian brigade, his only reserve, was to be sent to Italy against the Austrians, and the only Spanish brigade still serving with him had to be disbanded as unreliable. Soult was left with fewer than 40,000 men, while Wellington was able to muster at least 60,000 first-class British, Hanoverian and Portuguese troops, plus (supposing he could feed, pay and, not least, control them) unlimited numbers of Spaniards. By the middle of January it was known that the Austrians, Prussians and Russians had invaded France, and after a week of sunshine had dried the roads Wellington resumed his offensive on 13 February 1814.

Wellington sent Beresford eastwards against Bordeaux with five divisions and reluctantly, to boost his numbers, he recalled Freyre's Spanish infantry brigades. General Hill, with his own 2nd and the Portuguese Division, plus Morillo's Spaniards, hooked round the southern flank of Soult's army as it fell back along the foothills of the Pyrenees, attempting to take up defensive positions along the various rivers. Bayonne, now held by a single French division, was attacked by General Hope on 23 February, but the garrison held out until the war ended. With the six remaining divisions of his army Soult attempted to halt Wellington's advance at Orthez on 27 February, but Hill's corps, crossing the Gave de Pau, again outflanked Soult, who fell back towards Toulouse.

The gradual collapse of all French resistance in the south continued into March. On the 12th the citizens of Bordeaux rose against Napoleon's troops and opened the gates to Beresford's 7th Division. On 24 March Soult abandoned field operations and concentrated his army inside the walls of Toulouse and on 27 March the Peninsular Army began an investment of the city.

The old city of Toulouse was surrounded by a high, brick, medieval wall, with the wide Garonne on the west and the Canal du Midi to the north and east. An assault across the Garonne through the suburb of St Cyprian, the most straightforward course, was rendered impossible by the discovery that Wellington's bridging train was too short to span the river, which left the alternative of crossing the Garonne at some undefended point and capturing the ridge known as Mont Rave which overlooked the city.

Wellington had no intention of attempting to storm a strongly fortified city holding an army of 42,000 plus its garrison and a quantity of artillery, but he felt he could manoeuvre Soult into a withdrawal. General Hill was to lead his 2nd and Portuguese Divisions against St

Cyprian, from which the main bridge into Toulouse crossed from the right bank of the Garonne. On the north side, Picton's 3rd and the Light Division were to feint towards the bridges over the Canal du Midi. Finally, four divisions under Beresford were to attack the Mont Rave position in two phases, the Spanish divisions the north end, the other two the centre and southern end where the Mont Rave (or Calvinet Heights) terminated in a strong redoubt. On 10 April 1814 the Spaniards began their assault, attacking up the slope at the double. They drove in the French outposts on the Mont Rave but a counter-attack sent them down again in complete disorder and they fell back through the lines of the Light Division, waiting to assault the bridges over the canal. Picton's all-out attack on the bridges was met with a storm of musketry and cannon fire which cost him 400 casualties before he, too, fell back. The Spanish, having regrouped, assaulted Mont Rave again and were again beaten off.

All now depended upon Beresford's assault in the south and centre of the Mont Rave. His divisions drove the French from the southern end and fought their way along the crest, clearing the Calvinet positions as they advanced, so that when the Spaniards came in for the third time, they found Beresford's infantry in possession of the lines. Once the Calvinet Heights had been taken, the French fell back within the city walls.

Wellington had his artillery brought up but before he could order the bombardment of the town, Soult withdrew down the Carcassonne road to join forces with Suchet, who had finally abandoned Catalonia. Toulouse declared for the Bourbons and on 12 April Wellington entered the city at the head of his army, and as he was changing for dinner that night, Colonel Frederick Ponsonby galloped in from Bordeaux with news of Napoleon's abdication, six days before. Although hundreds had died needlessly along the Calvinet Heights and on the Garonne bridges, it seemed that, after twenty-five years of war and Revolution, the struggle for Europe was over.

21

The Battle for France:

1814

We had nothing left but Courage: Power and force were in
the enemy's camp. Discouragement was universal, not on
account of the daily risks we took, but because we saw no
end to them.

Armand de Caulaincourt: 1814

THE END OF 1813 found the French nation exhausted. For a quarter
of a century she had been at war. Millions of soldiers had been killed
or had vanished into captivity, the towns and villages were full of men
mutilated on battlefields as far apart as the Pyramids and Borodino,
the Treasury was empty, the economy was in ruins, the enemy was at
or through the gates. When Blücher crossed the Rhine on New Year's
Day 1814, everyone except Napoleon realized that the end could not
be long in coming, that his dream of Empire was finally over. Napoleon however, was not like other men.

Immediately upon his return to Paris, three weeks after the disaster
at Leipzig, Napoleon set about raising another army. The French
people would – *must* – brace themselves for one final and successful
effort but such an effort was beyond them. The nation was now
motivated by fear – of the advancing enemy – of the Cossacks – of
the loss to returning Royalist *émigrés* of their lands and their hard-won
liberties should Napoloen be overthrown.

The odds against the French were now enormous. The armies of
Prussia, Russia, Austria and Sweden now drumming their way towards the Rhine could muster more than 300,000, a number increasing daily as victory brought ever more allies into the fight. Against
them could be ranged no more than about 80,000 sick or exhausted

survivors of the battles of 1813. Nor could reinforcements be drawn from Napoleon's allies and subject states – all were falling away rapidly to grasp neutrality or seek some accommodation with the victors. The Princes of the Confederation of the Rhine – Baden, Berg, Würtemberg and Westphalia – all deserted the Emperor. Amsterdam rose against its French garrison and within weeks all the Low Countries had declared their allegiance to the House of Orange, whose young Prince was even now serving with the Duke of Wellington.

Even ever-faithful Prince Eugène could not spare men from Italy where he was fending off a superior Austrian army along the Adige and worrying about the loyalty of Joachim Murat, the King of Naples. In the Pyrenees Soult was attempting to counter the strong pressure being exerted by Wellington, whose army would doubtless spill into France when the snows melted. By any military criteria, Napoleon had nothing left to fight with.

Yet again the weary people of France were called upon for men, and yet again they responded – after a fashion. In 1813 the best of the National Guard had been enrolled as regular troops to serve in Germany. Now the remainder were transferred *en bloc* into the army. The Class of 1815 was called up a year early, bringing a nominal 150,000 into the ranks. Edicts enlisting every man in government service fit enough to carry a musket should have brought in gendarmes and foresters, the ancient survivors of the Revolutionary battles, and many more who had slipped through the Class call-ups of previous years, on paper nearly a million men – but, as in 1813, thousands slipped away, to hide in the forests or flee across the frontiers. Even so, tens of thousands did, slowly, answer the call of patriotism, for the enemy was now at the gates. Most of them, again, were mere boys who had to be trained and equipped, but time was slipping away. The Pope, released from captivity, was sent to the Vatican with a request that he arbitrate between the warring Powers. The almost-forgotten Prince Ferdinand was released from Valençay and offered the Spanish throne in return for a cessation of hostilities, but although the Supreme Junta was prepared to abandon the English and Portuguese allies in return for their Prince, this was a weak card. Wellington was already over the French frontier and had little further need for Spanish armies.

By the Treaty of Reichenbach Austria had recovered her previous territories in Italy, which counterbalanced the loss of her possessions in the Low Countries. She had thus no particular interest in a continuation of the struggle against Napoleon, which would entail further sacrifices of men and money and, indeed, the overthrow of Napoleon would be likely to result in an accession of power to Russia and Prussia. Both countries, and in particular Russia, were likely to lay extensive claims to Polish territory, in which Austria also had an interest. The Prussian generals Blücher and Gneisenau were in favour of an energetic offensive, but King Frederick-Wilhelm's main aim was the preservation of his army. Many of the Russian diplomats and generals were wary of continuing to fight so far from their frontiers, but Czar Alexander was eager to press forward, longing to offset Napoleon's entry into Moscow by his own entry into Paris. Russian activity in the field would also add weight to the extensive claims over Polish territory which the Czar was keen to pursue, another point of difference between Russia, Austria and Prussia.

In November 1813, therefore, the Allies offered France her 'natural frontiers' of the Rhine, the Alps, the Pyrenees. Napoleon, still cherishing his dream of universal empire, at first temporized, then accepted those terms, but it was then too late.

The British, so long the paymasters in the struggle against Napoleon, refused to countenance any compromise now. Castlereagh was informing the Austrians as early as November 1813 of Britain's insistence that France should relinquish all claims in Germany, Italy and Spain, that Holland should become an independent kingdom with sufficient territory to secure her from France, and that Antwerp should be in friendly hands. This, together with Napoleon's refusal of the terms already offered and news of Wellington's successes in the Peninsula, stiffened the Allied resolve. On 18 December 1813 the Austrians marched into Switzerland and the Prussian General Wrede crossed the Rhine at Hünigen. On 29 December Blücher began to cross the Rhine, and on the 30th Prince Schwarzenberg moved his forces to Colmar in Alsace-Lorraine.

The previous weeks had been spent reorganizing the Allied armies and deciding upon a plan of campaign. One part of Bernadotte's Army of the North, under von Bülow, was to invade Holland and occupy Antwerp. It would be joined there by a British force under Wellington's former second-in-command, General Sir Thomas Graham. This army would then sweep south through a Belgium more than ready to rebel against French domination, and open the gates to northern France. The other half of the Army of the North, under Crown Prince Bernadotte and two Russian generals, Bennigsen and Winzingerode, would pen up Davout in Hamburg and along the Lower Elbe, put pressure on the Danes, who still stood by Napoleon, and continue the siege of the French garrison at Magdeburg.

Meanwhile Blücher, with the 100,000 men of the Army of Silesia, would fix Napoleon's attention on the central front along the Rhine while the Commander-in-Chief of the Allied armies, Prince Schwarzenberg, with the 200,000-strong Army of Bohemia, the Czar, the King of Prussia, the Emperor of Austria and a host of German princelings, would enter France from the direction of Basel and concentrate at Langres, north-west of the Jura massif, to press upon Napoleon's right flank and eventually link up with Wellington marching north from Toulouse.

By January 1814 the French forces available to oppose these overwhelming numbers were too few, largely untrained, and distributed in penny packets. Fewer than 70,000 were available to defend the north and east of France. In Belgium, only 15,000 troops were to face von Bülow and control a restive population. South of Strasbourg, Marmont, Ney and Victor had no more than 30,000 men in their three 'corps'. Reserves were non-existent. Of the 900,000 or so called to the colours in October 1813, fewer than 120,000 had actually appeared at the depot gates. There was a shortage of cavalry horses and cavalrymen, trained officers, and experienced NCOs.

Nor could Napoleon expect anything from Italy or Spain. The Spanish rejection of his terms for the return of Prince Ferdinand left Wellington free to advance into Gascony and denied the Emperor reinforcements from Suchet or Soult. A more personal blow was the defection of his brother-in-law and old comrade, Joachim Murat, who sent his Neapolitan army to fight with the Austrians against Prince Eugene. And, finally, on 14 January 1814 the King of Denmark signed a non-aggression pact with the Allies, thus freeing more troops for the invasion.

Murat was motivated by self-interest, hoping to secure his position in Naples. Nor was he alone in his perception that Napoleon's star was fading. Many people in Paris, even in Court circles, notably Fouché and Talleyrand, were already in secret communication with the Allies or with the Bourbon exiles. Napoleon could depend only upon himself, upon those of his marshals who remained loyal, and upon what troops he could muster.

By 17 January 1814, three weeks after crossing the Rhine, Blücher's advance had driven Ney, Marmont and Victor back behind the Meuse, which the Army of Silesia crossed in the face of slight opposition on 18 January. By 23 January the advance-guard was seventy miles into France and had established a bridgehead over the Marne at Joinville. Meanwhile Prince Schwarzenberg, moving the main army up from Basel, reached the Langres plateau on 14 January. Marshal Mortier had been sent to support Victor against Schwarzenberg, but the people of the area largely ignored orders to form defensive militias or mount guerrilla attacks on the invaders in the Spanish style.

Prince Schwarzenberg found that the fortress of Langres was unoccupied, Mortier having retired beyond Chaumont. Further operations were delayed while the rest of Schwarzenberg's army came up, and while the Austrians considered the proposals of Napoleon's Foreign Minister, Caulaincourt, for negotiations. It was agreed that a Congress of plenipotentiaries should meet at Châtillon-sur-Seine, and meanwhile the army moved cautiously forward. On 24 January the vanguard encountered Mortier at Bar-sur-Aube, which Mortier skilfully abandoned after a bloody but indecisive battle. He retired, feebly pursued by the Allies, upon Troyes. With Blücher's crossing of the Marne at Joinville and the Army of Bohemia's advance to Bar-sur-Aube, the junction between the Armies of Silesia and Bohemia was almost effected.

On 25 January Napoleon left Paris, reaching his headquarters at Châlons-sur-Marne the next day to assume personal command. His forces at Châlons comprised the Young Guard under Ney and part of the Guard's cavalry. To the north, Macdonald was back on the Meuse; to the east Marmont had retreated to Bar-le-Duc, while Allied forces had penetrated as far as Sens and Auxerre. The ring was closing about the Emperor.

Napoleon, rising to a challenge, could usually discover something to his advantage in the most difficult situation and in this case his advantage lay in the possession of interior lines. The junction of the Allied armies was as yet somewhat tentative, and the roads in this part of France were the finest in Europe. Furthermore, the pressure of events lifted Napoleon to one final flowering of his military genius, and the young conscripts, the 'Marie-Louises', gave him all the support any commander could wish for. It could not last, but while it did, it was glorious.

Napoleon's defence of Paris began with a strike against Blücher's scattered forces, which had become widely dispersed during their rapid advance from the Rhine. Blücher's headquarters were at St Dizier and he had no more than 20,000 to 25,000 men at his immediate disposal, as General Yorck's divisions were well to the rear. Napoleon, with 35,000 men, aimed to hold Blücher while Marshal Marmont moved to attack his rear at Bar-le-Duc, but the plan succeeded only in part. As Blücher himself was now moving from Vitry-le-Français on Brienne, that town where the young Napoleon had gone to school long ago, Napoleon's blow struck thin air, although he took St Dizier, a number of Prussian prisoners, and a few guns. Leaving Marmont to hold off Yorck, Napoleon then set out towards Brienne, hoping to overwhelm Blücher before he could fall back on Schwarzenberg.

On 29 January Blücher was turning his men about to take up a defensive position near Brienne when General Grouchy fell on his outposts with a force of cavalry and horse artillery. Ney's and Victor's infantry then came up and by mid afternoon on a dark, chill winter's day the French and Prussians were fully engaged. The young conscripts stood up well to their first experience of battle and Blücher eventually withdrew southwards to La Rothière to join Prince Schwarzenberg. In heavy snowstorms, Napoleon followed Blücher to La Rothière where the Allies had about 110,000 men with 25,000 Bavarians under General Wrede available to operate against the French left, and 33,000 Russians in reserve under Barclay de Tolly. On 1 February 1814, this force bumped into Marshal Victor's vanguard.

Having lost contact with Blücher, the Emperor had halted and deployed his troops in the fields around La Rothière and they were still moving into position when Blücher's attack came in the early afternoon. The French cavalry were able to cut down Blücher's Russian gunners and were in their turn beaten off by the Russian cavalry, who captured twenty-four guns from the horse artillery of the Imperial Guard, but the French infantry held La Rothière for the rest of the day.

The battle at La Rothière, fought with driving snow soaking the ammunition and rendering whole battalions unrecognizable, was a soldiers' battle, fought at close quarters. When Wrede's Bavarians came up on the left to outflank Marmont, the French finally fell back, hurried on their way by Barclay de Tolly's reserve. Napoleon counterattacked at La Rothière that evening and retook the village, but the Allied pressure was now such that it was clear he would have to withdraw. It was well after dark before he was able to disengage and pull back towards Troyes, where Mortier waited with the Old Guard. More troops were lost during this withdrawal, and the citizens of Troyes gave a welcome as cold as the weather to the exhausted and bedraggled French army.

The events of the past few days had not enhanced the Emperor's reputation, and he had lost more guns and men than he could spare. However, he had also gained an insight into the Allies' tactics for this campaign. With Caulaincourt discussing terms for peace at

Châtillon-sur-Seine with Castlereagh and representatives of the other powers, the Allies were under the impression that, with their un- doubted superiority of numbers, they had only to follow up their present advantage with a leisurely advance on Paris. Napoleon, on the other hand, was convinced they could only overwhelm him if he permitted the various Allied armies to combine. He must therefore impose upon the campaign a kind of guerrilla warfare – hit the enemy hard, then pull back to regroup and hit again, and again slip away, before they were able to combine against him. This was not at all in Napoleon's usual style, but he was given unlooked-for assistance by the Allied commanders, for in electing to advance towards Paris the Allied commanders made the mistake of dividing their forces.

Blücher was to advance by way of the Marne, while Schwarzenberg proceeded along the Seine. Inevitably, their armies began to drift apart, thus presenting Napoleon with ideal targets. On 3 February Marmont, left in the rear, saw off Wrede's Bavarians at Arcis- sur-Aube. That same day Grouchy, with the Guards cavalry, fought a successful action against the Russian cavalry near Troyes. The French towns along the Yonne were well garrisoned and the troops were easily able to drive off the advancing Allied divisions. Schwar- zenberg began to edge away southwards, while Blücher pushed stead- ily on towards Paris.

However, if Schwarzenberg was faltering in the east, the Allies were continuing to press forward in other parts of the country. In the north, Antwerp and Brussels had fallen to the troops of von Bülow and with Blücher at Meaux, just 25 miles from the capital, the citizens of Paris were beginning to panic. On 6 February Napoleon had confirmation of Murat's desertion and received news from Châtillon- sur-Seine, where the foreign ministers of Europe were talking peace even while the armies fought, that the Allies were only prepared to offer France her pre-Revolutionary frontiers of 1792. This meant los- ing Belgium, which had been a part of France since 1795, and this proposal was promptly rejected by the Emperor.

There was no hope of a diplomatic solution. The end was clearly coming and nothing the Emperor could do would prevent it; he might shuffle and re-shuffle his shrinking forces but with every despatch came the news that the ring of Allied armies around Paris was getting tighter, and when Paris fell, his Empire would go with it.

The situation became clear during the first days of February, as the Emperor fought one battle after another, pushing back the tightening ring of foes. On 9 February, Marmont reported from Champaubert in Champagne that one of Blücher's commanders, General Sacken, was at Montmirail, thirty miles east of Meaux, with a corps of some 15,000 men. Napoleon marched his forces for Champaubert with 30,000 men under command, while Marshal Blücher, with Yorck and Sacken, mustered some 45,000. These were small armies compared with the forces deployed for battle in 1812 and 1813, but they were far more suitable for the command and communication capabilities of the day.

The battle at Champaubert began on the morning of 10 February 1814, when Marmont and Ney engaged an isolated Russian division under General Olssufiev, who had elected to stand and fight and was therefore swiftly overwhelmed. The Russian general was taken prisoner while four-fifths of his men were killed, wounded or captured. This successful action placed the Emperor's men right in the middle of Blücher's, Yorck's and Sacken's widely dispersed forces, and Napoleon was delighted with this victory.

That evening he wrote to his Empress:

My Dearest Louise – Victory! I have shattered twelve Russian regiments, taken 6,000 prisoners, 40 guns, captured the Commander-in-Chief, and all for the loss of 200 men. Have salutes fired at Les Invalides . . . I march on Montmirail.

The letter was for the most part pure fantasy, or exaggeration, or propaganda, but Blücher was temporarily impressed by Napoleon's success. On Blücher's orders Sacken and Yorck attempted to concentrate again at Montmirail, but Yorck's orders arrived too late for him to get there before Napoleon had met and defeated Sacken on 11 February.

Initially the Emperor's forces were inferior in number to Sacken's, which forced him onto the defensive, but his infantry and artillery were able to hold the Russians until Mortier could come up with the Old Guard. He was then able to break through between the Russians and the scanty two brigades sent by Yorck, roll up Sacken's line and force the Russians into retreat. Under the stimulus of this success, Napoleon became his old self again – alert, vigorous, totally in command, master of the battlefield. In an unhesitating pursuit he attacked Yorck at Château-Thierry on 12 February and the Allies had to fight a severe rearguard action before they were able to escape over the Marne, heading north towards Soissons.

Blücher, meanwhile, had remained on the road between Montmirail and Vertus, unaware of these defeats until he received news of Yorck's retreat on the evening of 12 February. On the 13th he advanced to Yorck's relief and repulsed a French division at Étoges. Moving swiftly to confront Blücher, Napoleon concentrated his forces between Montmirail and Vauchamps; Blücher's vanguard, advancing too far, was driven out of Vauchamps back on the main body. Recognizing the strength of the French forces and learning that Napoleon was commanding them, Blücher at once retreated. Hard-pressed by Napoleon's cavalry, the Prussians and Russians lost 6,000 men in rearguard fighting, against French losses of no more than 600. Threatening news from the Seine halted Napoleon's pursuit of the Army of Silesia, however, and Blücher was able to gather his scattered forces and regroup at Châlons.

This last exhibition of Napoleon's military prowess is known in the annals of the Napoleonic Wars as the 'Six Days' Campaign of 1814', and was outstanding in terms of how much he achieved with so little. With an inexperienced army of 30,000 men, and everything under his personal hand and eye, the Emperor was seen again at his brilliant best. But it was too late for these successes to make a difference. However many battles he might win or the generals he might defeat the Allies would not treat with him, and five days after their defeat at Vauchamps, they began to advance again on Paris. The end was coming.

Soult was engaged against Wellington south of Pau and the best soldier of them all, Marshal Davout, was defending the port of Hamburg. Napoleon had at his side the last and the best of his marshals, Berthier (who was seriously ill), Ney, Oudinot, Marmont, Mortier, Macdonald, Victor, and that brilliant young cavalry commander, General Grouchy, who continued to work military wonders around Paris as the battle for France entered the last weeks of February and the early weeks of March 1814.

Leaving Marmont and Mortier at Vauchamps Napoleon turned south-east to attack Schwarzenberg, whose cavalry had ranged as far towards Paris as Fontainebleau and Melun. On 17 February at Mormant, 18 February at Montereau and 21 February at Méry-sur-Seine, he inflicted such heavy punishment that news of Augereau's advance up the Saône caused Schwarzenberg to retire with the Army of Bohemia on Troyes.

The discussions between the Powers at Châtillon, following their suspension between 9 and 17 February, was not such as to encourage Schwarzenberg to make a stand. Napoleon, flushed by his successes, refused to parley except on the basis of the 'natural frontiers' of France, and rejected Allied suggestions for an armistice. At a council of war between Blücher and Schwarzenberg at Troyes on 22 February, it was arranged that Blücher should retire northwards towards the Marne to combine with von Bülow and divert Napoleon's attention. Before this movement could be effected Napoleon stormed Troyes and caused Schwarzenberg to retire beyond Bar-sur-Aube. On 25 February it was decided that Blücher should act independently while Schwarzenberg continued to withdraw with the main army by way of Chaumont to Langres.

The wheel had now turned full circle. After their successes in January, the end of February saw the Allies either clinging grimly onto their positions, or in full retreat. Napoleon had some 75,000 troops under his personal command on 24 February when he entered Troyes, but his overall military position was not improving. No recruits were coming forward, and his existing troops were nearing exhaustion. Worst of all, there was no national enthusiasm for the war, despite these various successes and the publication of enthusiastic bulletins which made his victories seem more decisive than they were.

Following a skirmish at Méry, Blücher attacked and defeated Marmont at Sézanne. As he hoped, this led Napoleon, anxious about Paris, to abandon his position in front of Schwarzenberg and march northwards, with a large part of his army. As he approached, Blücher withdrew.

Austria had for long been the most hesitant partner in the coalition, but Napoleon's rejection of an armistice so disgusted the Emperor Francis that a closer bond between the four Powers now took shape in the Treaty of Chaumont. By this Treaty, dated 1 March 1814 but not actually signed until 9 March, they pledged themselves to continue the war until France should be reduced to her pre-Revolutionary limits, and bound themselves not to negotiate separately with Napoleon. The forces that each was to maintain were defined, and Britain promised large subsidies totalling £5,000,000. Napoleon was given until 11 March to accept a settlement based on the French frontiers of 1792.

Directing Marmont and Mortier to block Blücher's advance on Paris, Napoleon moved from Troyes, intending to take Blücher in the rear. Oudinot, Macdonald, Gérard and Kellermann were left to counter Schwarzenberg, and to take advantage of the latter's notorious lack of confidence when in proximity to Napoleon, the French pickets were ordered to shout '*Vive l'Empereur!*' in earshot of the Austrian sentries. Nevertheless, Schwarzenberg ordered a general advance on 27 February. After a brave resistance Oudinot was completely defeated at Bar-sur-Aube and the whole French force was driven back beyond the Seine. On 7 March, in an uncharacteristic burst of confidence, Schwarzenberg drew up a memorandum designating Paris as the goal of all operations.

Hard-pressed by Marmont and Mortier, and with Napoleon threatening his rear, Blücher swung north and crossed the Aisne at Soissons to meet the forces coming south from Belgium under von Bülow. Exhaustion sent Blücher to bed, which temporarily halted the advance, but it was decided that the 100,000 or so Prussians and Russians under his command should concentrate at Laon. As Napoleon approached, Blücher occupied the plateau of Craonne with 25,000 Russians, where he was attacked on 7 March by 40,000 French. The Russians held out for a whole day, inflicting heavy losses before being driven back on Laon, and both Grouchy and Victor were wounded.

His crippling lack of cavalry for reconnaissance purposes led Napoleon to suppose that at Craonne he had clashed with the rearguard of a Blücher who had now abandoned the advance on Paris and was retreating north into Belgium. He therefore followed him towards Laon, where the concentration of the Allies had been completed on 8 March. On 9 March Napoleon advanced to the attack from the south. A thick mist had enabled the French to deploy unseen, but even when it cleared to reveal the weakness of their forces the Prussians remained on the defensive. A struggle at the foot of the hill on which the town stands went first one way, then the other, flickering up on the arrival of Victor's corps in the afternoon, continuing until dark without result.

Marmont, attacking from the east, encountered superior numbers so strongly posted that he made less headway even than the Emperor. After nightfall Yorck surprised Marmont in a counter-attack which put his corps to flight with a loss of 4,000 men. An energetic pursuit combined with a turning movement would probably have destroyed Napoleon, but at this inopportune moment Blücher was again confined to his sick-bed, and his second-in-command, Gneisenau, dared not risk a decisive encounter. Napoleon held his ground at Laon and attempted to retrieve the situation at first light on the 10th when, seeing that victory was out of the question, he withdrew across the Aisne.

The Emperor's situation was now desperate. Wellington was marching on Toulouse with 90,000 men, driving Soult before him, while two Allied armies, each at least 100,000-strong, were converging on Paris from the south and east. Napoleon had about 75,000 men under arms and Caulaincourt had obtained an extension of the time allowed by the Allies for Napoleon to respond to their terms, hoping to persuade his master to see reason, but on 17 March Napoleon dictated his own proposals, containing concessions so minor that they would not have been accepted even had the Allied generals permitted the French envoy to cross their lines.

In the face of Blücher's strength Napoleon decided to fling himself against the main army under Schwarzenberg. Cossack patrols informed the Prince of Napoleon's presence on his right flank and, guessing that Napoleon intended to cross the river at Arcis-sur-Aube, Schwarzenberg deployed his troops accordingly. Napoleon had not been able to concentrate as many troops as he would have wished, since Blücher had begun to advance again and had defeated Marmont. He came first upon Wrede's Bavarian Corps – not the full six corps of the main army – and forced them to fall back after a hard fight. It might have been his last: a shell exploded directly under the Emperor's horse, and following his Abdication he cursed the fate which spared his life that day.

The following day Schwarzenberg had concentrated his forces but then displaying his usual lack of determination, he hesitated. The Emperor therefore led his troops boldly forwards, but perceiving the enemy's strength he then beat a hasty retreat though his rearguard was caught by the Allies and driven from Arcis-sur-Aube.

French resistance was finally at an end. For three months, ever since Blücher had crossed the Rhine, the French army had marched and fought and beaten off attack after attack from every quarter, but once the political will to continue the war against Napoleon was established, the outcome was never in serious doubt. Leaving Arcis, he retired eastwards to St Dizier, intending to rally what garrisons he could find, attack the Allies' communications, and raise the country against the invaders – but his plans fell into Allied hands before he could execute them. The Czar and the other commanders decided that they should now disregard Napoleon and march directly on Paris.

Marmont and Mortier retreated to Paris, and took up defensive positions on Montmartre, Marmont on the right wing, Mortier at the foot of the hill, and the last battle was fought here on 30 March. The Empress and the King of Rome had fled from Paris the previous day, Napoleon's brothers Jerome and King Joseph watched the battle from the heights of Montmartre while Talleyrand, Fouché and various other functionaries remained in the city to greet the Allies.

The French defence was courageous and the Allies advanced slowly and with great loss. In the early afternoon, however, Marmont was driven to the edge of the plateau north-east of Montmartre, and despatched an officer to negotiate while Blücher's Army of Silesia

engaged Mortier, who had initially repulsed the Prussians but was
unable to withstand a second attack.

When they saw that all was lost, Jerome and Joseph directed the
marshals to treat with the enemy, and rode away towards the Loire.
An armistice was negotiated, by the terms of which Paris was to be
evacuated and Talleyrand declared the Emperor Napoleon to have
been effectively deposed. White cockades appeared on hats, and cries
of '*Vive le Roi!*' replaced those of '*Vive l'Empereur!*'.

Napoleon was at Vitry when he heard of the threat to Paris. Hurrying
towards the capital, he reached Fontainebleau in advance of his army
and there he was joined on 30 March by Marmont's cavalry. He was
pressing on towards Paris when he learned that it had capitulated. In
despair he returned to Fontainebleau where more troops joined him
and by 2 April he had managed to muster 60,000 men. As always, as
his forces grew, so his spirits revived, but although the troops were
willing to fight, his marshals were not.

Everyone but Napoleon had had enough of this endless, pointless
war. The marshals were adamant that it was all over and that peace
must be made, and they urged Napoleon to accept the inevitable with
what grace he could. When their appeals failed, the final sanction was
applied by Marshal Ney. His courage in battle, against all odds, could
never be doubted – but even Ney knew that it was over.

'The Army will not march,' he told the Emperor flatly.

'The Army will obey me,' replied Napoleon.

Ney shook his head. 'The Army will obey its generals.'

'What do you want me to do?' asked Napoleon, finally.

'Abdicate,' said the Marshals, 'in favour of your son.'

'Very good,' said the Emperor. 'Since it must be so, I will abdicate.
Will you accept the King of Rome as my successor and the Empress
as Regent?'

On 4 April 1814 Napoleon I, Emperor of the French, drew up an
Act of Abdication in favour of his young son, the King of Rome, with
his wife Marie-Louise as Regent.

With that Act the Napoleonic Wars, which had ravaged Continental Europe since 1796, were finally over . . . or so it seemed.

22

Elba and Vienna:

1814–1815

We who were lately masters of Europe, to what servitude are
we reduced? Oh, Napoleon, où est tu?

General Foy: 1813

IT FELL TO THE Czar Alexander, in the absence of the Emperor of
Austria the 'senior' monarch, to determine the future Government of
France. Napoleon must be eliminated, but then what? The Bourbons
might be restored, but his opinion of them was not high, and during
the months of campaigning there had been no sign of Bourbon fervour in eastern France; furthermore, the nation would surely not
accept a return to the ways of the *ancien régime*. Perhaps the country
would be better pleased with a Republic? Talleyrand was clear that,
once it was certain that no peace or truce was possible with Napoleon, his own legislative Council would invite the return of the Bourbons. The Czar, the King of Prussia and Prince Schwarzenberg then
drew up a proclamation pledging the Powers not to treat with Napoleon or any member of his family. Alexander was equally clear in his
mind that nothing lasting could be achieved without the support of
the French army. Approaches were made to Marmont, a brilliant
soldier who owed everything to Napoleon but felt that he had been
unjustly castigated after his defeat at Laon and was, moreover, only
too conscious that his surrender of Paris had ruined Napoleon's chan-
ces. Marmont was disillusioned, weary of war and promised to move
his troops to Versailles from the Emperor's position at Essones during
the night of 4/5 April.

Having reached a preliminary agreement in their deliberations, the
Powers were thrown into some confusion when the Emperor's Act of

Abdication was brought to them on 4 April by Caulaincourt, Ney and Macdonald, who brought Marmont with them. The deliberations, with and without the Emperor's envoys, went on far into the night. At dawn the matter had been resolved, for General Souham, without waiting for Marmont's orders, had brought his corps to join the Allied camp at Versailles. The army, now divided against itself, could no longer dictate events.

More defections followed. The aged Marshal Augereau gave up his march on Lyon. Couriers from the south said that Marshal Soult must either surrender to Wellington or be overwhelmed in Toulouse. The Allied sovereigns now felt able to dictate their terms. They knew that if they accepted Napoleon's terms for abdication, he would continue to rule through his wife and son. Their demand therefore was for the restoration of the Bourbons. Shocked by Marmont's defection, Napoleon issued a fresh declaration from Fontainebleau on 6 April 1814:

> The Allied Powers having proclaimed that the Emperor Napoleon is the only obstacle to the re-establishment of peace in Europe, the Emperor Napoleon, faithful to his oath, declares that he renounces, for himself and his heirs, the thrones of France and Italy, and that there is no personal sacrifice, not even of life itself, that he is unwilling to make in the interests of France.

On 12 April Napoleon refused to ratify the Treaty of Fontainebleau and talked of suicide; in the night he took the poison he had carried with him during the Russian campaign. Perhaps it had lost its potency – or perhaps, as he thought, his survival indicated that he was still destined for great things. He ratified the Treaty on 13 April 1814.

By the terms of this Treaty Napoleon retained his title of Emperor, and full sovereignty over the ninety-square-mile island of Elba, south of Sardinia. He was to receive an annual revenue of two million francs, and a force of 600 soldiers (later increased to 1,000) drawn from the Imperial Guard was allotted to him. The Empress was given full sovereignty over the duchy of Parma, with succession to her son and descendants, and the Emperor's family were to be given substantial pensions from the French Exchequer.

On 20 April the Imperial Guard paraded in that courtyard of the palace of Fontainebleau which is still called the Cours des Adieux. There the Emperor said goodbye to his personal bodyguard, the *grognards* – the old 'Moustaches' – selecting the 1,000 volunteers for Elba as he passed along their ranks. On 28 April, after an unpleasant journey to the south of France, with people turning out to jeer and stone his coach as it passed, he embarked on a British brig and sailed into exile.

On 30 April 1814 the Allied Powers reached a formal agreement with the Bourbon heir, Louis XVIII. By the terms of the Treaty of Paris, Louis XVIII was restored to his kingdom – not the vast empire of Napoleon, not the France of the 'natural frontiers', but the country of his ancestors, the pre-Revolutionary France of 1792. The future shape of Europe was to be settled by the Allied Powers at a special conference, the Congress of Vienna, which was to meet for the first time in September 1814.

Although he worked for their cause, 'The Bourbons', said Talleyrand, 'had learned nothing and forgotten nothing', during their two decades in exile. Louis XVIII returned to a country which had all but forgotten him. Although the gouty and corpulent Louis chose to maintain that he had been ruler of France for the past nineteen years, he was more liberal in outlook than the despot he replaced. Censorship was to be lifted, conscription abolished, the more liberal elements of the Civil Code – no longer the 'Code Napoléon' – retained or restored to the statutes. Louis XVIII may have had scant regard for British notions of constitutional sovereignty, but he intended to avoid the mistakes of his ancestors, and play the part of a liberal monarch. Unfortunately for these good intentions, he was burdened with obligations from the past, and encountered considerable if silent hostility from Napoleon's former subjects.

To the people of France Louis was a stranger who had spent the last twenty years as the ally of their enemy, Great Britain. His Bourbon Charter might guarantee liberalism, but few French people, in particular the peasants, had faith in this document. The general fear was that their land and their liberties would fall victim to the hordes of *émigré* aristocrats in the king's train. The returning *aristos* did indeed regard such restitution as their right, and were loud in demands for immediate satisfaction. There was unease and dissatisfaction among extreme Royalists and Bonapartists alike, an indication of trouble to come.

Another source of potential trouble lay in the former soldiers of the Imperial Army. With the ending of the war, the Thames-side hulks and the prison gates released vast numbers to return to France and add to the recently discharged, unemployed and impoverished soldiers of Napoleon's armies. After decades of war there was no work for them as civilians, and little money for their meagre pensions. They were neither well treated, nor respected. Their efforts for France were not recognized, their Colours were dishonoured, the white Bourbon cockade replacing the treasured *tricolor*. Many old heroes and general officers were forced into half-pay or penury while men of no experience received high rank and comfortable sinecures in the new Royal Army. The Imperial Guard was replaced with a 6,000-strong Royal *Garde du Corps* of fops and *émigré* noblemen; hundreds of new generals were appointed, men who had never commanded so much as a platoon. Peasants and old soldiers grumbled together, recalling times not long past when the French were respected and the army was a 'career open to talent'. News of this discontent soon reached Elba and perhaps the Emperor smiled.

The British soldiers of Wellington's Peninsular Army were scarcely more fortunate. Having been appointed Ambassador to France on 21 April, and travelled to Paris for the 'triumphal entry' of Louis XVIII, Field Marshal Lord Wellington left France on 23 June 1814 to face a tumultuous welcome in London, where wealth and honours were heaped on his head. His soldiers received his warmest thanks, and very little else. Those who were not discharged were sent to North America where the war against the United States continued. One distinguished Peninsular general, Wellington's respected and beloved brother-in-law, Sir Edward Pakenham, eventually met his death at the Battle of New Orleans in January 1815.

In London, Wellington was the man of the hour, a national hero. He took his seat in the House of Lords on 28 July 1814 and heard his Patents of Nobility as Viscount, Earl, Marquess and Duke read out to the assembled peers and Parliament voted him £500,000 for the purchase of an estate. He travelled to Paris in August to take up his appointment, and remained there until January 1815, when he took Lord Castlereagh's place at the Congress of Vienna.

In Vienna the sovereigns of Europe, their numerous advisers, diplomats, ambassadors and courtiers, were attempting to get to grips with the problems of peace. While it was said that they all spent as much time at routs and balls and in the beds of their mistresses as they did at the conference table, possibly this was no bad thing. Despite the need to maintain a united front against Napoleon, the Powers were finding it only too easy to fall out and there were moments when war between the victors did not seem inconceivable.

A major problem was Poland – the Grand Duchy of Warsaw, and the Poles. The Czar had always regarded the Poles and 'Polish' territory as falling within the Russian sphere of influence, as a buffer zone between Holy Russia and the west; if Poland were to exist at all, it should be as a Russian satrapy, completely subordinate to his will and to Russian interests. In this he had the support, if perhaps only temporarily, of the Prussian King Frederick-Wilhelm.

Frederick was prepared to support Alexander over Poland if Alexander would support his claims over the small and scattered states of the recently disbanded Confederation of the Rhine, in particular Saxony, but these interests were at odds with those of Britain and Austria – a situation which brought into play the Powers' recent adversary, France.

The King of France, 'first victim of the Revolution', had insisted on being represented at the Congress of Vienna and had, inevitably, chosen Talleyrand as his representative. Talleyrand maintained that while Napoleonic France had been Europe's enemy, Bourbon France was an ally whose voice should be heard. To achieve his ends, Talleyrand engineered a secret Triple Alliance between Great Britain, Austria and France, which might have plunged Europe again into a general war. Fortunately, its terms were so unrealistic that all parties began to draw back almost as soon as it was discussed. Talleyrand had, however, ended France's isolation and earned himself a place at the conference table.

Happily for the peace of Europe, discussions between the Powers were not broken off, and on 11 February arrangements for the redistribution of territories were approved by the Powers. Poland was partitioned, with Austria recovering all and Prussia most of their former possessions there. Russia gained the remainder, while Prussia gained about two-fifths of Saxony. The Congress continued its discussion of other matters in a more relaxed and sensible atmosphere . . . until 7 March 1815, when information was received at Vienna that Napoleon had left Elba with 1,000 men on 26 February and was at large somewhere in the Mediterranean.

It was never likely that Napoleon would settle for peaceful retirement on Elba. He was just forty-six, and if his energies were at a low ebb at the time of his abdication, a few months of rest restored him to his former mental vigour, a vigour which a tiny island 19 miles long and 61 wide could hardly hope to contain. He busied himself with improvements. The streets of Portoferraio, his tiny capital, were cleaned up and street lighting put in. A theatre and an opera house were built. He designed a new national flag. Thousands of trees were planted by his order, and he instigated improvements in farming designed to make the island self-sufficient in food. The islanders were at first exhilarated, then exhausted by the whirlwind in their midst, but for Napoleon there was never enough work to fill the day. Nor was he free of personal or financial problems.

The Bourbon government showed no intention of honouring the financial terms of the Treaty of Fontainebleau, and Napoleon was hard-pressed to maintain his court. His funds were being so rapidly depleted that his beloved mother had to sell her jewels to pay the small army. It became increasingly clear that the Empress, having succeeded in reaching her father in Austria despite the efforts of Joseph and Jerome Bonaparte to thwart her, had no intention of joining him in exile. Gradually she ceased even to communicate with Napoleon. Her last letter arrived in September 1814, and her alienation from him was completed when he threatened her with abduction. Other correspondents were not slow to inform the Emperor of her relationship with her aide-de-camp, Count von Neipperg, a creature of Prince Metternich.

Nor was this all. The Emperor had his informants everywhere, even at Vienna. From them he learned of the doubts expressed as to whether the crowned heads of Europe could ever sleep quietly while the 'Corsican Ogre' lay within a day or two's sail of the south coast of France; Talleyrand did not think so, and brought forward the idea of some more remote exile – the Azores, the island of St Lucia in the West Indies, even St Helena. Privately, other voices expressed the thought that an assassin's blade or bullet might serve the purpose better.

From his informants Napoleon learned, too, of the rising tide of discontent in France. The failure of the other parties to it to keep their side of the Treaty agreed at Fontainebleau, his wife's defection, his fears of further exile or assassination, the belief that he alone could solve the problems of peace as he had those of war, coupled with that restlessness that was so much a part of his nature, all provided him with motive, but the growing public discontent in France gave him his opportunity. When his English guardian, Sir Neil Campbell, went to the mainland for some leave, Napoleon sailed from Elba on the night of 26 February 1815 with his small army of 1,000 men, including 100 Polish Lancers who had their saddles but no horses, plus 300 local volunteers. The expedition landed at Golfe-Juan on the morning of 1 March 1815, and the scene was set for Napoleon's last great adventure.

In Vienna, Wellington and Metternich agreed that if Napoleon were to land in France he would march directly on Paris. In this assumption they were proved correct. The Emperor spent the night in the small fishing port of Cannes, but did not linger there. His one chance was, as he himself put it, 'To march ahead of the news of our arrival', overwhelming all opposition by the shock of his return and the speed of his advance.

On the first day, pushing on at all speed, commandeering horses and mules where they could, the party covered sixty miles. Day after day they pressed on northwards, through Grasse and Sisteron, picking up old soldiers here and there, hard fighting men who dug out their uniforms, took a musket from the waggons and fell in behind. The first real test came on 8 March at Laffrey near Grenoble, when their path was barred by a 700-strong battalion from the 5th Ligne. Napoleon had enough men to brush this force aside, but he had given strict commands that not a shot was to be fired or a musket presented during this march on Paris. Instead, he ordered that the *Marseillaise* be played and the tricolor displayed, both potent symbols, Imperial and Revolutionary, which had been forbidden by the Bourbons. Walking up to the levelled muskets of the 5th Napoleon flung open his coat: 'If you want to shoot your Emperor, here I am.'

Napoleon had always known the way to the hearts of his soldiers. With a cry of '*Vive l'Empereur!*' the men of the 5th put up their weapons and joined the Emperor. They were followed later that day by the 7th Ligne, and that night the people of Grenoble opened their gates as the troops of the garrison donned the tricolor cockade. So it went, as the Emperor pressed on through Lyon and north to Paris.

The former marshals of the Empire heard of Napoleon's return with mixed emotions. Most were appalled, a few were delighted. Some retired to their estates to await developments, some fled abroad. Some looked out their swords and prepared to rejoin their Emperor, and some were dead, like General Junot, who committed suicide, or were soon to die, like the invaluable Berthier, who fell (or jumped) to his death from a window. The one who mattered was Ney.

Ney was now a Marshal of the Royal Army. Ever emotional, he declared his loyalty to the Bourbons and left Paris with a detachment of troops, promising to return with the Emperor in an iron cage, but this fervour did not last. At Auxerre his men deserted, Ney himself went over to Napoleon, and the Bourbon position in France began to collapse.

On 16 March, the day after Ney's defection, Louis XVIII issued a proclamation releasing his officers from their oaths of loyalty. On 19 March he heaved himself into his carriage and fled north to Belgium. Twenty-four hours later, on 20 March 1815, Napoleon entered Paris and a crowd of cheering Parisians carried him in triumph to the Tuileries. By 10 April Napoleon was again the master of France.

At Vienna, the news of Napoleon's departure from Elba, the rapidity of his advance through France, and his popularity with the French, put the delegates in a quandary. The people of France clearly preferred him to Louis, and since the latter had abandoned his throne with such celerity, was it reasonable to go to war to restore to the French people a monarch they had so emphatically rejected? For a brief moment there was doubt. On 13 March 1814 the plenipotentiaries declared themselves bound to aid Louis XVIII and declared Napoleon an outlaw. Four days later Britain, Austria, Prussia and Russia pledged themselves each to put 150,000 men in the field, and to keep them there until 'Bonaparte should have been rendered absolutely incapable of stirring up further troubles'.

Napoleon addressed pacific overtures to Great Britain and Austria, declaring his adherence to the terms of the Treaty of Paris and his wish for peace, but Metternich returned a blank refusal to his agent, and the Prince Regent sent his letter back unopened. War it must be and even while extending his olive-branches, Napoleon had been making military preparations.

Raising an army to overawe and, if necessary, defeat the Allied Powers presented a political as well as a military problem. Napoleon was reluctant to reimpose conscription – its abolition had been one of Louis' few popular actions. The Royal Army of 200,000 came over to him *en masse*, and another 50,000 retired veterans and men on leave were called back to their standards in April and May. There was also the 'Class of 1815', totalling about 150,000 men. On paper at least this Class had been called up before Napoleon's abdication, and could therefore be recalled to the depots without the need for a fresh and provocative proclamation. By these means some 300,000 men were in the ranks of the French army by the end of April 1815. The Emperor would need every one of them.

The Allies also recalled their forces to the field. Their intention, as in 1813/14, was to engulf Napoleon and disperse his strength over five separate fronts. Barclay de Tolly was to muster 150,000 Russians in Germany. Prince Schwarzenberg, who hoped to have seen the last of Napoleon, was gathering 200,000 Austrians to swamp Alsace and Lorraine by way of the Black Forest. Another 75,000 Austrians were to advance along the Riviera and up the Rhône towards Lyon but to assemble these large armies would take time. Meanwhile, the main effort must come from the Duke of Wellington, who by the end of June had under him 110,000 British, Dutch and Hanoverian troops around Brussels. On his left, mustering at Liège for an advance along the Meuse to Namur, was Marshal Blücher with 117,000 Prussians.

While these armies were being hurriedly collected, Whig voices in the British House of Commons raised a protest: 'The Bourbons have lost the Throne again through their own mistakes,' declared one MP. 'It would be monstrous to declare war on France in order to impose on a people a Government they do not want.' Only 72 votes were given in favour of these sentiments, while 273 voted against.

While such ideas were being openly expressed, Napoleon could turn them to his advantage, either by achieving a settlement, or by raising the cost of intervention by demonstrating his ability to wage another war. The inevitable delay while the Allied forces were assembling gave him his opportunity, but it was necessary for him to judge his timing. If he waited, he could expect to raise and train more men but, after a few weeks at best, the Allied forces mustering against him would outnumber him more with every day that passed. What he needed, as in 1813/14, was a striking victory to force the Allies to accept his offer of peace and set him securely on the throne. The sooner he could force a decisive engagement, the better it would be for his prospects.

Wellington and Blücher were the obvious targets. Rumour had it that there were disagreements over strategy between the two commanders, and that their armies were not under any united command. With the British concentrated on Brussels and the Prussians on Liège, further east, Napoleon might hope to interpose his army between them, and smash each in detail. Leaving his generals to secure his flanks and maintain the security of France against revolt, he marched his main army north and by the time he had concentrated his forces just south of the Belgian frontier on 14 July [June] 1815, they numbered 90,000 infantry, 22,000 cavalry and 366 guns.

The British or Anglo-Dutch Army, under Wellington, consisted of 79,000 infantry and 14,000 cavalry, with 196 guns. Only about a third were British and few were veterans. Most of the magnificent Peninsular Army had not yet returned from the United States. One corps was commanded by the young Prince of Orange, who had been on Wellington's staff in the Peninsula for three years, and the 2nd Corps was under the veteran Sir Rowland Hill. Picton, Kempt and Colbourne were there, and the cavalry and horse artillery were commanded by Lord Uxbridge, so it would do, at a pinch.

However, Wellington had convinced himself that any attack from Napoleon would involve a sweep through Mons, to the south-west of Brussels, around the Anglo-Dutch right flank, to cut them off from the sea. When the campaign began, Wellington had to revise that opinion when it was nearly too late.

23

Ligny and Quatre Bras:

1815

Though hostilities will soon commence, yet no one might
suppose it judging by the Duke of Wellington. He gives a
ball every week, attends every party, partakes of any
amusement that offers . . . Bonaparte is said to be at
Maubeuge, thirty or forty miles away.

Revd Spencer Madan
13 June 1815

THE BATTLE OF Waterloo, fought on 18 June 1815, should be considered, not as one decisive encounter, but as the final act in a three-
day drama which began with the actions at Quatre Bras and Ligny
on 16 June. What happened in these prior engagements, and how the
contending armies were prepared for the battle, are crucial parts of
the Waterloo story.

On 15 June, the day Napoleon crossed the Belgian frontier, Wellington's army was assembled south and south-west of Brussels, with
Blücher's forces in an arc between Charleroi and Liège. Although
there was some suspicion and mistrust between the Prussian government and Great Britain, Blücher and Wellington got on well personally, and it was agreed between them that if one was attacked, the
other would immediately move to his assistance. This was a sensible
decision, but one which would take, they calculated, three days to
implement. Napoleon had come to the same conclusion and in that
time gap he saw his opportunity.

Wellington's army was gathering west of Brussels for Wellington
believed that if Napoleon struck north he would advance through
Mons. Why Wellington came to this conclusion is still unclear. Had

Napoleon attacked Wellington's right flank, this would only have pushed Wellington's forces over to the east, thus causing that concentration of the British and Prussian armies that Napoleon must have been anxious to avoid. The Emperor had assembled his army south of the border by 10 June, but such was the secrecy surrounding their arrival and intentions that the Allied commanders were still not fully aware of the situation when the French army came flooding across the frontier a week later, marching for the town of Charleroi.

Napoleon began to draw his forces together on 6 June, and by 14 June he had 124,000 men concentrated in three columns, around Beaumont and Philippeville. He left Paris on 12 June reaching his advance Headquarters at Beaumont on the 14th and with the Emperor in personal command, the campaign could now begin. Soon after dawn on the following day, French cavalry trotted across the frontier towards Charleroi. No one in that glorious veteran host could have imagined that the Empire of Napoleon Bonaparte had but three days left to live.

The advancing army was divided into two wings and a reserve. The left wing, under Reille and d'Erlon, would push up towards Wellington and the right, under Gerard, against Blücher. The central mass, under Napoleon's own command and comprising Vandamme and Lobain's corps, the Guard and the cavalry reserve, would strike to either side as soon as any enemy force worth destroying had been found and pinned down.

There were delays, and it was afternoon before the Sambre was crossed by the Charleroi bridge. Napoleon at once began to advance up the Fleurus and Quatre Bras roads. At 3 p.m. Marshal Ney joined the army, and was given the command of the left wing, with instructions to secure Quatre Bras. The Emperor then proceeded to reconnoitre the Prussian position at Gilly and, handing over the command of the right wing to Grouchy, returned to Charleroi.

A glance at the map will reveal the importance of Quatre Bras for it commanded a north–south/east–west road junction. Whoever held Quatre Bras could march at will in any direction.

The Allies were taken completely by surprise. It was not until 3 p.m. on 15 June that the Duke received news that the Prussian 1st Corps had been attacked near Thuin and their outposts driven in. This was not enough to convince him of the direction of Napoleon's attack, even when the Prince of Orange came with the information that the Prussians had been pushed out of Birche, and that he himself had heard gunfire around Charleroi. Wellington ordered his army to collect at their divisional headquarters and to be ready to march at a moment's advice, but there remained the possibility that Napoleon might be moving against Mons and merely feinting against Charleroi and until he was more certain, Wellington would not commit his troops in any one direction. Meanwhile, the many British civilians in Brussels must not be alarmed. The Allied officers in Brussels would go, as planned, to the Duchess of Richmond's ball.

Wellington did have the advantage that his troops were clustered around Brussels, beyond the Emperor's immediate reach. Blücher, however, had assembled his army just north of the Franco-Belgian frontier and Napoleon intended to fall upon the Prussians like a thunderbolt, smash them swiftly and then march on Brussels. Had he done so, all might have gone well with him, but he entrusted the vital task of seizing Quatre Bras to that most gallant but erratic of generals, Marshal Michel Ney.

Napoleon's orders to Ney had been quite specific. He was to advance northwards at his best speed up the Charleroi–Brussels road, sweeping aside any enemy in his path to seize and hold the crossroads at Quatre Bras. Meanwhile, Marshal Grouchy was to push the Prussians back along the Fleurus road towards Sombreffe, five miles east of Quatre Bras, where Blücher was attempting to concentrate the widely scattered corps of his army.

The gallant Ney was not the man he had been in Russia. His conscience was torn between his loyalty to the Emperor and his oath of fidelity to Louis XVIII and, perhaps on this account, he failed to act with his former verve and decisiveness. A similar curious lethargy seemed to envelop all the commanders. Grouchy and Vandamme advanced so slowly that they only moved the Prussian 1st Corps back to Fleurus, three miles south of Sombreffe, before halting for the night, and Ney made the mistake of halting at Frasnes, three miles south of Quatre Bras. As he did so, a Dutch brigade of 4,500 infantry and six guns under Prince Bernhard of Saxe-Weimar occupied the crossroads. They easily drove off the skirmishing force Ney sent forward, and when Ney himself came up to reconnoitre, fields of shoulder-high rye concealed their true weakness from him. As Ney had only joined the army the previous afternoon, it may be supposed that he was still getting his bearings. Whatever the cause, he missed the opportunity of seizing that crucial crossroads. He halted, and reported back to Napoleon.

Despite the delays and lethargy of his commanders, Napoleon held a dominant strategic position on the night of 15 June. His *Armée du Nord* lay concentrated between the two Allied armies, and could swing against either with ease. Only one of Blücher's corps was in position, although two others were at hand, and it was not until midnight that the Duke of Wellington received the confirmation of the direction of Napoleon's movements. This prompted him to issue fresh orders – his troops were now to concentrate between Nivelles and Quatre Bras, thus closing up the gap between his forces and Blücher's.

At the Duchess of Richmond's supper table, the Prince of Orange appeared at Wellington's side and whispered in his ear. The Duke finished his supper and, as he was saying good night to the Duke of Richmond, asked for a map. Looking at it, he exclaimed to the Duke: 'Napoleon has humbugged me, by God! He has gained twenty-four hours on me. I have ordered the Army to concentrate at Quatre Bras, but we shall not stop him there, so I must fight him here . . .', his thumb-nail scoring a line on the map along the Mont-St Jean ridge, south of the village of Waterloo.

Napoleon was still in Charleroi on the evening of 15 June. He slept for a few hours but was in the saddle again by dawn on the 16th, having decided to press on directly to Brussels and fight Wellington wherever he found him. This would give him both a victory in the field and the propaganda coup of capturing another capital. Then Ney arrived at his bedside at two o'clock in the morning and the Emperor learned that Quatre Bras had not been taken. His reaction is not recorded but the Emperor stressed yet again the vital importance of seizing Quatre Bras. In addition, to protect his flanks from Blücher while he advanced on Brussels, it would be necessary to drive the Prussians well away to the east. Orders went out to Grouchy detailing the plan for the next stage of the campaign. Grouchy was to march north-east through Sombreffe and drive the Prussians before him back to Gembloux, while the Emperor forged north.

Ney was to do at once what he should have done the day before; take Quatre Bras. When both marshals had done as ordered, the Emperor could bring his corps forward to join Ney at Quatre Bras for the march on Brussels.

Napoleon's plan for 16 June assumed that the Allies, in their surprise and confusion at his sudden appearance, would not risk a forward concentration. Grouchy having reported that Prussian forces were massing at Sombreffe, Napoleon's orders directed Ney, when he had driven away whatever was in front of him at Quatre Bras, to swing to his right and fall upon the Prussian flank at Ligny, which an advance guard under Grouchy would have driven up the Fleurus road. As the day wore on, however, Napoleon discovered that the Prussian forces were stronger than the single corps he had estimated, and decided to defer his attack until his right wing had come up. Ney was similarly reticent, and delayed his attack on Quatre Bras until he had Reille's infantry corps under his command.

Communication of the Emperor's orders proved a difficulty. Marshal Soult, as Chief-of-Staff, was no replacement for the peerless Berthier, and one of his more serious shortcomings is demonstrated by the following extract from the orders to Ney transmitted to him by Soult:

The Emperor is going to the mill of Brye, where the highway from Namur to Quatre Bras passes. This makes it impossible that the English Army should act in front of you. In the latter event, the Emperor would march directly on it by the Quatre Bras road, while you would attack it from the front, and this army would be destroyed in an instant. Therefore keep His Majesty informed of whatever takes place in front of you. . . . His Majesty's wishes are that you should take up your position at Quatre Bras; but if this is impossible, and cannot be accomplished, send information immediately with full details, and the Emperor will act there as I have told you. If, on the contrary, there is only a rearguard, attack it and seize the position. Today it is absolutely necessary to end this operation, and complete the military stores, to rally scattered soldiers and summon back all detachments.

Small wonder, perhaps, that Ney had still not advanced and instead of being concentrated around Quatre Bras, his divisions remained scattered back along the road from Charleroi.

There is something unreal about the fog of indecision surrounding the events of 15/16 June 1815. Only Blücher's forces seemed to display any sense of purpose. Wellington's earlier orders were still being put into effect when they were countermanded by those to concentrate at Quatre Bras, and Napoleon appeared to change his mind even as he issued his orders.

When Wellington and his Staff arrived at Quatre Bras just after ten o'clock on June 16th all was still quiet. There was no sign of Ney's forces, and the troops from Brussels would soon be coming up, so Wellington decided to ride eight miles across to Bussy for a conference with Blücher. From a windmill on the hill there, the two generals could see the French and Prussian armies deployed to the south and more troops from Gérard's corps coming to join the Emperor's forces. Wellington doubtfully observed the Prussian regiments, deployed on forward slopes behind the River Ligne. 'If they fight here, they will be damnably mauled,' he remarked. Blücher's only comment was that his men '. . . liked to see the enemy', even if this meant being exposed to cannon fire. Wellington promised to send reinforcements, if he was not himself attacked and by 3 o'clock he was back at Quatre Bras, where the situation had deteriorated rapidly in last few hours.

General Reille, ordered to sweep the enemy out of the Bussy Wood and take the crossing, had fought Wellington in Spain. Convinced that more troops were concealed about the crossroads than was immediately apparent, he advanced slowly and cautiously, and his attack took time to develop. This was fortunate for Wellington, as fewer than 10,000 of his troops had yet come in. Wellington's troops began to arrive only during the early afternoon and many, as a result of orders and counter-orders, were weary and disorganized. Fortunately, advised by Reille, Ney too held back and failed even to scout the Allied line, and with every hour that passed, more British regiments came up, and the Allied position grew steadily stronger.

Nevertheless, when the French advanced in force at 2 o'clock, they soon discovered the weakness of the Anglo-Dutch line. Cannon were brought forward, and the line was on the point of giving way when Picton's division, supported by a brigade of cavalry, arrived from Brussels. The late afternoon saw heavy fighting in the woods and fields around Quatre Bras, but the Allied line held. At Ligny, the Prussians were in a far more difficult position.

Blücher's forces occupied a string of hamlets on the north bank of the River Ligne. This, though not deep, was about twenty feet wide and would at least hinder attacking infantry and cavalry. Napoleon's plan was to threaten Blücher's left with Grouchy's corps then hurl the bulk of his force directly at the Prussian centre, fully engaging Blücher's attention until Ney came over from Quatre Bras to fall on his right. Once the Prussians had been driven from the field, the French would wheel left on Wellington at Quatre Bras and roll his forces up as well.

As usual the French attack opened with a cannonade which, and as Wellington had predicted, wrought havoc among the exposed Prussian infantry. Within half an hour the Prussians were under pressure all along their front and had already lost the village of St Amand. Now was the time for Ney to appear behind the Prussian right wing.

Ney, however, had his hands full at Quatre Bras, where he was now outnumbered by Wellington's ever-expanding forces. D'Erlon, the commander of Ney's reserve, was just approaching Quatre Bras to reinforce him when an order arrived from Napoleon that he should march towards Ligny and fall on the Prussian flank and rear. D'Erlon, though confused, duly complied. However, when a copy of the Emperor's order reached Ney he sent another despatch ordering d'Erlon to return to Quatre Bras.

Poor d'Erlon. As always, order and counter-order inevitably lead to disorder. Though d'Erlon's intervention could have proved beneficial on either battlefield, he and his men spent the afternoon marching to and fro about the countryside between Ligny and Quatre Bras, achieving nothing.

At Quatre Bras, Ney was losing control of both himself and the battle. It was his clear duty to hold Wellington at Quatre Bras, at whatever cost to himself, thus enabling Napoleon to win a decisive victory at Ligny, yet the Emperor's summons to d'Erlon had reduced Ney to fury. He ordered Kellermann's cuirassiers to sweep the British and Dutch infantry from his path. Kellerman, though a gallant cavalryman who would charge anything that moved, was understandably reluctant to charge 25,000 infantry with his unsupported cavalry. The two argued and Kellermann, also losing his temper, led his men at the gallop against the British line.

The cuirassiers broke through one British brigade and had reached the crossroads at Quatre Bras before the British infantry collected their wits, formed square and began to shoot them down. Kellermann's horse was shot from under him and although he managed to scramble away, great damage was inflicted on the rest of his cavalry. Ney then led an infantry assault on the Anglo-Dutch line, but Wellington's ranks were being constantly reinforced, and when the Foot Guards came up in the early evening he was able to attack all along the French line. Fighting fiercely, the French were forced back on their original positions. Ney had lost more than 4,000 men and most of his cavalry while the Anglo-Dutch losses were higher, at about 4,700 men. Ney had achieved nothing but he had, up to a point, served Napoleon's strategic purpose, since he had prevented Wellington from sending a single man to Blücher's aid – and Blücher was now falling back.

Napoleon's battle with Blücher was a long and obstinate struggle not the swift victory he had hoped for. D'Erlon's appearance on the French flank had caused Vandamme, not knowing who it was, to begin to evacuate his position, convinced his men were about to be attacked front and rear. This enabled Blücher to put in a heavy counter-attack in the centre which was only stopped by the bayonets of the Imperial Guard, but this was Blücher's last throw. He charged at the head of his last cavalry reserves, was thrown from his horse, and nearly taken prisoner. His army had indeed been 'damnably mauled', and the Prussian centre, which had held all day, finally collapsed as evening fell, the troops forming square as they withdrew, to fight off the roving regiments of French cavalry. Prussian losses at Ligny were about 16,000 men while the French had lost about 12,000. Napoleon might claim a victory but Blücher's Prussians were able to collect themselves at dawn and fall back unmolested towards Wavre, north-east of Ligny.

There was now a pause. On the 17th, Napoleon took his time preparing for the next phase of the campaign. His information was that the Prussians were now in full retreat towards Liège and Namur, marching away from Wellington's army in some disarray, and weakened by desertions. This was incorrect though Blücher, thrown and ridden over by cavalry, was 'lost' to his army for some hours, and the command passed to General Gneisenau, whose long-standing and unfounded suspicions of Wellington's good faith were heightened now by a feeling that the Prussians had been deserted by Wellington. The withdrawal towards Wavre was dictated more by a desire to re-establish his line of communications than with any thought of a future combination with the Anglo-Dutch, and he was remiss in not informing Wellington of this vital move as it left the Anglo-Dutch left flank completely exposed. Happily, Blücher soon recovered sufficiently to resume command.

That recurring lassitude which of late years seemed to bedevil Napoleon at inopportune moments descended upon him again. It has been said that he was ill with bladder problems and a heavy cold, but whatever the reason, to delay issuing orders for the rest of the campaign until noon or later on 17 June was to lose a large amount of the precious time he had gained by his rapid concentration. It was not until early afternoon that Grouchy's cavalry moved, with orders to discover where the Prussians were, and whether they showed any signs of combining with Wellington. Heavy rain through the afternoon and evening slowed him down, and though by nightfall Grouchy was aware that some Prussians were making for Wavre, the desertion of some 8,000 towards Liège the day before made him uncertain of the direction of the main body.

At dawn on the 17th, Wellington was still in position behind Quatre Bras where by 7.30 he had the news of the Prussians' defeat. 'Blücher has had a damned good licking and gone back to Wavre,' he said. 'As he has gone back, we must go too. I suppose in England they will say we have been licked. I can't help it; as they are gone back, we must go too.'

The Prussian army was largely intact and on the point of being reinforced by von Bülow's corps, which had at last made its way up from Liège. Orders went out for the Allied troops at Quatre Bras to fall back towards Waterloo, and those still *en route* for Quatre Bras to head there instead. By mid morning the withdrawal had begun and here Napoleon missed another opportunity. Had he been able to catch Wellington on the move, he might have hustled him back to Brussels and beyond. Instead, it was noon before he took himself to Quatre Bras and by then the British infantry were well on their way to the Mont-St Jean ridge south of Waterloo.

The Emperor and Ney had failed to exploit a promising situation. Had Ney attacked Wellington again on 17 June and held him at Quatre Bras, Napoleon might have moved around the exposed flank of the Anglo-Dutch left and dealt it a death-blow, before Blücher could reappear. Although Napoleon shed his lassitude on arriving at Quatre Bras and initiated an energetic pursuit of Wellington's rearguard cavalry screen, he failed to entangle them deeply enough to compel the Duke to return to their aid. Grouchy was also culpable for following his Emperor's somewhat sketchy orders to the letter and quite exceptionally slowly, rather than applying intelligence and initiative to the situation. The Prussians played their part in the French downfall, in re-forming and being ready to take the field again at least 24 hours before Napoleon thought they could possibly do so.

After twenty years of warfare the outcome hung on this next encounter. As the armies, French, Prussian, English, Hanoverian and Dutch, began to march, the skies opened. The rain came sheeting down, drenching the fields and flooding the roads, but still the armies marched. By nightfall the Prussians were at Wavre. Grouchy, supposedly in hot pursuit, had got no further than Gembloux, twelve miles to the south. Wellington's troops were soaked to the skin and out of food, finding what shelter they could in the hedges behind the Mont-St Jean ridge, while a mile to the south the Emperor Napoleon found shelter for the night at the inn beside the road called La Belle Alliance. He and Wellington had been at war for years without meeting in battle. Tomorrow the matter of their generalship would be put to the ultimate test.

24

Waterloo

Your Lordship will observe that such a desperate action
could not be fought or such advantages gained without great
loss: and I am sorry to say that ours have been immense. It
gives me great satisfaction to assure your Lordship that the
Army never, upon any occasion, conducted itself better . . .
Field Marshal Wellington
Despatch from Waterloo: 19 June 1815

DAWN ON SUNDAY, 18 June 1815 gave promise of a thoroughly
miserable day. It had rained all night and the troops mustering for
the battle were soaked to the skin, plastered with mud, hungry, dirty,
and suffering from lack of sleep.

The battlefield at Waterloo is quite small. It is best imagined from
the south, where the road running north from Quatre Bras towards
Brussels passes the inn of La Belle Alliance and slopes into a wide but
shallow valley. A few hundred yards to the left lies the 'château' of
Hougoumont, in reality a large farmhouse set among orchards. After
La Belle Alliance the road runs past the farm of La Haye Sainte, and
less than 200 yards further north is a crossroad, with a minor road
leading left and right along the ridge of Mont St-Jean. This marks the
main position of the Allied army, which was deployed along the ridge,
facing south towards Hougoumont and La Belle Alliance.

North of the ridge the main road enters the Forêt de Soignes and
runs through the village of Waterloo and thence to Brussels. The
French took up a position astride the lower ridge to the south-east of
La Belle Alliance. The ground of the battlefield is rolling and uneven
and although the ridges are not very high – no more than 120 or 150

feet above the valley floor – their slopes are quite steep. With the château at Hougoumont surrounded by walls and hedges, the farm at La Haye Sainte and two small farms away to the east, La Haye and Papelotte, occupied as forward outposts, the British had made the Mont-St Jean ridge into a formidable defensive position, well suited to Wellington's battlefield tactics.

Wellington arranged his troops along the ridge as they came up on the evening of 17 June. Most of Napoleon's infantry did not reach the front until after midnight and at least one division only on the morning of the 18th, and the two armies lay not quite a mile apart, facing each other across the valley. Napoleon had already decided to employ his traditional attack, a frontal infantry assault preceded by a prolonged cannonade and supported by cavalry. This decision was opposed by Marshal Soult and General Reille. Having fought Wellington in the Peninsula, both had decided reservations about the merits of a frontal attack on a British line.

'Well posted, as Wellington knows how to post them, and attacked from the front, the English infantry are unshakable,' said Reille. 'But the English army is less agile and supple than ours, and if we cannot beat it by direct assault, we may do so by manoeuvring.' Napoleon would not listen. He told Soult and Reille that because Wellington had beaten them, they thought he was a great general. 'In fact,' said he, 'Wellington is a poor general and his troops are of poor quality . . .' as he intended to demonstrate.

It was necessary for Napoleon to rest his weary army, and wait for the ground to dry out a little before the artillery could be moved, but the bulk of the French army was in position by 10 o'clock. After the initial heavy artillery bombardment, Napoleon intended that Marshal Ney, the Field Commander, should send d'Erlon's corps against the centre of Wellington's line, while Reille's corps fell on Wellington's right. This somewhat primitive tactic matched the fabled French *élan* against British stubbornness, column against line, as at Maida nine years earlier and Napoleon had no doubt which would prevail.

Wellington was also relying on well-tried tactics, taking full advantage of the terrain to mask his intentions and enhance the strength of his defensive position. As usual he hid the bulk of his troops on the reverse slope behind the ridge, just out of cannon-range. Strong forces held the two isolated points – a picked detachment of the King's German Legion at La Haye Sainte, a battalion of the Foot Guards at Hougoumont. There was no reason for Wellington to assume any subtlety in the forthcoming French attack, with Napoleon's forces deployed as they were in plain sight around La Belle Alliance.

To defend his position Wellington had 67,000 men and 156 guns, as against Napoleon's 71,000 men and 246 guns. On the face of it the opponents were fairly evenly matched, but while the French troops were largely veterans, Wellington's were not. Only about a third of his troops were British and many were untried, except for the Peninsular veterans of the King's German Legion and the Light Division. Of the rest, Hanoverians, Belgians and Dutch, many were recruits, going into action for the first time, while some of the Dutch and Belgians had been serving Napoleon only the year before. 'It was', he said later, 'an infamous Army' – but it was all he had, and in the event it did all he could have hoped for.

By midnight on 17 June Wellington had Blücher's promise that von Bülow's corps would be despatched to Waterloo at daybreak on the 18th. The Prussians set off as planned, but delay followed upon delay, and they were still not in sight by mid morning, when Napoleon's cannon opened the battle.

The battle of Waterloo began at 11.35 on 18 June when the artillery of General Jerome Bonaparte, now part of Reille's corps, opened a heavy fire on the British position at Hougoumont. This was followed by an assault on the château and the woods which surrounded it by four regiments of infantry. This attack was a feint, for Napoleon intended the real attack to take place against Wellington's left-centre, half a mile further to the east. The copse and orchard were soon cleared by the French, but in the buildings and the garden the Guards beat off attack after attack. Jerome might have manhandled his cannon forward to blast breaches in the walls of the château, but instead he continued to sacrifice his infantry. The light companies of the Scots and Coldstream Guards, commanded by Colonel James Macdonell, kept up a steady fire and did not hesitate to rush out on their attackers with the bayonet, and Hougoumont held.

It was not until around 1.30 that Ney opened the next phase of the battle, cannonading Wellington's centre with a battery of eighty guns at La Belle Alliance. By this time von Bülow's Fourth Prussian Corps was in sight, about six miles away to the north-east at Chapelle St Lambert. Napoleon, having received information from Grouchy that the Prussians were massing at Wavre, deduced that what he saw was part of the Prussian army; but he brushed aside any thought that the odds against him had lengthened. The Prussians were still far away with Grouchy in pursuit of them. Napoleon could win this battle before the Prussians were able to intervene.

Grouchy was in fact at Walhain, nine miles south of Wavre, and on the horns of a dilemma. At 10 o'clock that morning Napoleon had sent him a despatch: 'You will direct your movements on Wavre so as to approach us, act in concert with us, driving before you the Prussian Army which has taken that route and which may have halted at Wavre, where you must arrive as soon as possible.' Soult's fell hand can be detected in the confused wording of this despatch. Napoleon intended that Grouchy should place himself on Blücher's flank and hold him off from Waterloo – but, as Ney had done before him, Grouchy misinterpreted his orders. By the time the despatch reached him, the Prussians were already marching to Wellington's assistance. Critics have maintained that Grouchy, hearing the opening cannonade from the direction of Waterloo, should have heeded the urging of his generals and marched towards it – but that was not what he had been ordered to do.

On identifying the approaching force as Prussian, Napoleon sent Lobau's VIth Corps with two brigades of reserve cavalry to stem von Bülow's advance, then opened the first major assault on the centre of Wellington's line with a massive bombardment from the eighty guns now massed to the right of La Belle Alliance. Wellington's line vanished under a haze of flying earth and metal, but apart from Bylandt's Dutch brigade on the forward slope of the ridge, the bulk of the British forces were lying down on the reverse slope and most of the balls skipped over their heads. The bombardment continued for a half-hour before Marshal Ney and General d'Erlon led four full divisions, totalling 18,000 men, against the centre of Wellington's line astride the road to Brussels. The French came on in four great columns, each a phalanx containing eight battalions – a wonderful target for the Anglo-Dutch artillery, a most unwieldy formation to command, quite unsupported by either cavalry or horse artillery. Nevertheless, in many a fight troops had broken up in panic at the mere approach of such a multitude and Bylandt's troops fled to the rear in disorder. One French brigade diverged to storm La Haye Sainte, the rest continued to advance against Wellington's left-centre, subjected to a blast of musketry as the British infantry rose from behind the ridge and came forward to meet them. The French infantry reeled back and while they were still confused and encumbered with their dead and wounded, General Sir Thomas Picton ordered his men to charge, then fell from his horse, a musket ball in his brain. While d'Erlon's infantry were engaged in this murderous contest with Picton's men, General Lord Uxbridge brought two brigades of heavy cavalry, Ponsonby's Union Brigade and Somerset's Horse Guards and Life Guards into the fray. An avalanche of British horsemen came cascading down the slope and charged into the thick of the French columns. These broke and were hurled down the slope and chased off, losing two Eagles, 3,000 prisoners and several thousands wounded or killed. The cavalry, as so often before, losing all control, rode into the French lines sabring the fugitives and their exhausted horses foundering in the boggy ground, the men fell easy prey to the cavalry and lancers Napoleon flung upon them from left and right. General Ponsonby was killed after he had been taken prisoner, and his brigade was all but wiped out. Of the 2,500 who charged, a full thousand were left dead or disabled. The British line held and Napoleon had achieved nothing.

It was now 3 o'clock in the afternoon. The fight was still raging about Hougoumont and the Prussians were by this time in plain sight advancing slowly towards the French right flank. There was no sign of Marshal Grouchy, and it was vital that Napoleon should defeat Wellington quickly before the Prussians arrived. In the centre, the King's German Legion still held out at La Haye Sainte and the regiments of d'Erlon's corps marched against them again and a fresh brigade of Reille's corps reinforced the assailants of Hougoumont, but little headway was made by the French against either position. The Anglo-Dutch line withdrew slightly to gain more cover from the ridge and Ney then decided that since his infantry could not carry the Mont-St Jean ridge, the cavalry must atempt it. He ordered up two divisions of *cuirassiers*, 5,000-strong, which were sent in an unsupported charge against the British line. These divisions were followed by Lefebvre-Desnoëtte's division, which attacked without orders, and the entire French cavalry force then rode to destruction. They were greeted by British and Brunswick infantry formed in square and supported by British horse artillery firing case-shot. One of the artillery batteries thus engaged was commanded by Captain, later General, Cavalie Mercer who described the scene in his memoirs.

Our first gun had scarcely gained the interval between their squares, when I saw through the smoke the leading squadrons of the advancing column coming on at a brisk trot, and already not more than one hundred yards distant, if so much, for I don't think we could have seen so far. I immediately ordered the line to be formed for action – case-shot! and the leading gun was unlimbered and commenced firing almost as soon as the word was given; for activity and intelligence our men were unrivalled. The very first round I saw brought down several men and horses. They continued, however, to advance. I glanced at the Brunswickers, and that glance told me it would not do; they had opened a fire from their front faces, but in both squares appeared too unsteady, and I resolved to say nothing about the Duke's order [to take shelter with the infantry squares when the cavalry attacked] and take our chance – a resolve that was strengthened by the effect of the remaining guns as they rapidly succeeded in coming into action, making terrible slaughter, in an instant covering the ground with men and horses. Still they persevered in approaching us (the first round had brought them to a walk), though slowly, and it did seem they would ride over us. We were a little below the level of the ground on which they moved – having in front of us a bank of about a foot and a half or two feet high, along the top of which ran a narrow road – and this gave more effect to our case-shot, all of which almost must have taken effect, for the carnage was frightful.

Frightful indeed. The British and Allied infantry came to welcome the presence of the French cavalry, which did them comparatively little harm and caused the French artillery to cease firing on the squares until the cavalry cleared away. Wellington now ordered his own cavalry reserves to advance and the French troopers were driven from the plateau, but their attack was renewed again and again, until the slope of the ridge and the ground around the squares was carpeted with dead and wounded men and horses.

Having failed to break a single British square, Ney called up the rest of the reserve cavalry from the second line, Kellermann's two divisions of cuirassiers and the heavy squadrons of the Guard, and the scattered brigades reformed and fell in as supports to the fresh squadrons. Had they been supported by infantry, they must have won the day but they were not, and soon became hopelessly entangled among the infantry squares, which they could not break. Wellington gradually pushed forward all his infantry reserve to reinforce those squares of British and German infantry. He used up all his cavalry reserves except those on the extreme left, and at last the French cavalry were driven down the face of the ridge.

Wellington had expected Blücher's forces to arrive before noon. At 1.30 von Bülow's leading division arrived at Chapelle St Lambert and attracted Napoleon's attention but at 3.30 a despatch from Grouchy brought the information that he was proceeding to Wavre and clearly would take no part in the battle at Waterloo. About 4 p.m. von Bülow's corps reached the woods, about two miles from the French right flank, and encountered the vedettes of Lobau's VIth Corps, sent to contain them. This they did so skilfully that they delayed three times their number around the village of Placenoit for two hours. Eventually the Prussians drove them off, but Napoleon then despatched four regiments of the Young Guard, and these fresh troops cleared the village. Von Bülow's last reserves had been used up and the only effect he had had on the battle was that he had compelled Napoleon to divert against him some 14,000 men, who might otherwise have been used against Wellington.

As his cavalry attacks had been repulsed and the British line remained unbroken Napoleon ordered Ney to carry La Haye Sainte with his infantry.

An hour after Grouchy's message reached the Emperor, the first effects of this failure were felt on the right flank of the French Army. Bulow's corps, the advance guard of the Prussian Army, opened fire on the French cavalry and the infantry of Lobau's VIth Corps, sent by the Emperor to delay them near the village of Placenoit on the right flank of the French position. The Prussians drove the French back out of Placenoit and pressed on, undeterred by the news that Grouchy's corps was attacking their rearguard, which was commanded by General Thielmann, and just leaving Wavre.

'It matters little if Thielmann is crushed at Wavre, provided we can gain the victory here,' said Gneisenau, the Prussian Chief-of-Staff. It was now all a matter of time. If Wellington could hold until the Prussian arrived, the Allies would win the battle. If Napoleon could beat a path through the British line within the next hour, the day would be his. The Emperor had been in the field since dawn but the command of the battle had so far been directed by Marshal Ney. Now the Emperor finally took a hand, directing that La Haye Sainte must be taken at all costs and without delay.

This was a task to Ney's liking and Ney went in against La Haye Sainte with three battalions of infantry and some engineers. The doors of the farm were battered in, the defenders were out of ammunition, and this time La Haye Sainte fell; less than 50 of the 900 gallant defenders of La Haye Sainte escaped up the road to the Allied line.

Wellington's centre was now Ney's to command. He filled the farm with sharpshooters and rushed an artillery battery up to within 300 yards of Wellington's line. The troops on either side of the breach were utterly exhausted and Ney sensed that the Allied line was crumbling. What remained of Reille's and d'Erlon's corps were equally at the end of their strength, so he appealed to the Emperor for fresh troops. It was not a good moment. Napoleon had in reserve only the fifteen battalions of his Old and Middle Guard, and when Ney's request reached him he was watching the development of a new and dangerous attack by the Prussians at Placenoit, where Pirch's corps had now reinforced von Bülow.

'Troops?' cried Napoleon. 'Where does he expect me to find them . . . does he expect me to make them?'

Instead of sending all his remaining forces forward to punch their way through Wellington's front, he sent two battalions of the Old Guard to his right flank, where they swept into Placenoit, and drove the Prussians back nearly half a mile.

Wellington used this pause to adjust his line and strengthen his centre. General Zieten's corps had now come up on his left, which enabled him to draw his last two brigades of British cavalry into the centre, concentrate his troops there and call up other regiments from the right. Zeiten had almost failed to arrive. One of his officers, confused by the smoke and the crowds of dead and wounded along the ridge, assured him that Wellington's men were in full retreat and Zieten was about to withdraw when General Müffling, the Prussian liaison officer on Wellington's Staff, rode up to plead with him. 'The battle is lost if the 1st Corps does not march to the Duke's rescue,' he cried. Zieten hesitated, then marched again for the ridge.

It was not until after 7 that Napoleon made up his mind to deliver his last blow, and send his precious Imperial Guard into the battle.

There remains to this day a doubt as to how many battalions of the Imperial Guard were sent in on that last desperate charge. Some accounts say eight, some four, but the majority agree that Napoleon himself led six battalions of the Guard up towards La Haye Sainte, where he handed them over to Marshal Ney. The battle had been raging for almost nine hours when the troops of the battered French regiments on the slopes beyond La Belle Alliance saw the battalions of the Imperial Guard marching in solid columns towards the front line. Spirits revived, bands struck up, hats were raised on bayonets, even the wounded propped themselves on their elbows, cheering the veterans of the Imperial Guard marching to their last great fight.

The Guard came on in review order, in columns of battalions, the ranks seventy to eighty men wide, led by their officers. Marshal Ney was riding beside the front rank when, for the fifth time that day, his horse was shot from under him. Undeterred, the Marshal drew his sword and joined the front rank of the Guard, the drums throbbing out the *pas de charge*.

Under fire from British and King's German Legion guns between Hougoumont and La Haye Sainte which cut swathes in the densely-packed columns, the Guard closed ranks and came on, a great blue wave tipped with burnished steel.

The Guard overran the Brunswick Brigade on the forward slope. Then they captured two British artillery batteries which had just been firing into their ranks. Then they attacked the left-hand square of Halkett's Brigade, formed from the 30th and 73rd Foot, and drove it back in confusion. The Belgian General Chassé, who until the Abdication had been one of Napoleon's generals, then brought a battery of horse artillery onto the ridge to fire grapeshot into their ranks. Still the Guard marched on until the grape-shot was followed by a bayonet charge from a Belgian infantry brigade. This drove back one battalion of the Guard but the Grenadiers of the Guard were now engaged with Wellington's old regiment, the 33rd Foot, and the 69th Foot, also of Halkett's Brigade. These battalions were only prevented from retreating by the Colonel of the 33rd, who took the Regimental Colour and ordered his men to stand fast and use their bayonets.

Close behind the 33rd Foot their old Colonel from India days, Field Marshal Lord Wellington, sat his horse, and just behind Wellington the 1st Foot Guards were lying down behind the crest. Two battalions from the Chasseurs appeared out of the smoke and were within fifty yards of the crest when the Duke gave the command. 'Up Guards . . . Ready!' The British Foot Guards rose up and came forward to the crest.

It may have been the sudden appearance of that wall of red-coated infantry, which seemed to spring out of the ground to their front. More likely it was the smashing volley that the Guards poured into their ranks, but for whatever reason, as Captain Powell of the Foot Guards wrote later, 'The Imperial Guard, which had never before faltered in the attack, suddenly stopped.'

While the Guard hesitated, the 1st Foot Guards – later the Grenadier Guards – poured in two more volleys, carpeting the ground with French dead. Then the Chasseurs made the fatal mistake of attempting to deploy, under fire. Within minutes their ranks had fallen into total confusion. Wellington ordered the Foot Guards to advance with the bayonet and this they did, bayoneting and firing on the Imperial Guard as they reeled back down the slope towards Hougoumont. There they met the last of the Guard still advancing, the 4th Chasseurs, and the remnants of the 4th Grenadiers.

The 1st Foot Guards returned to the top of the ridge with the Imperial Guard hot on their heels. The Guard topped the rise yet again and at once attacked the Guards and the remnants of Halkett's Brigade. They might have done more but then the 52nd Foot, now commanded by that redoubtable and experienced Peninsular veteran, Sir John Colbourne, came forward over the crest of the ridge on the left flank of the Imperial Guard and began to fire volleys into the flank of the 4th Chasseurs. The Chasseurs wavered in their turn and the 52nd charged home with the bayonet, driving them back. This was a sight that had not been seen before, and a great cry of horror, '*La Garde recule!*' went up from the ranks of the Emperor's watching soldiers.

The infantry regiments coming forward in support halted as the Guard came running back. This retreat of the Guard spread, morale collapsed and the retreat swiftly developed into a rout. The panic was spread by the advance of the Prussian corps which was now putting troops in against the French left. Within ten minutes of the Guard's retreat Lord Wellington rode up onto the crest of the Mont-St Jean ridge into plain sight of his troops. There he halted, waved his hat above his head to attract attention and pointed south, the signal for a general advance. Every man and gun that could still move then flooded down the slope of the Mont-St Jean ridge and fell like a torrent on the Emperor's army.

Napoleon was well forward, close to La Haye Sainte, when he saw his front collapse. He ordered his last battalions of the Old Guard to form square across the main road, hoping to rally the troops behind them, but the fleeing troops swept on southwards. Raked by musket fire and artillery, three battalions of the Old Guard battalions fell back to La Belle Alliance where their commander, General Cambronne, called upon to surrender, added to the legends of the Napoleonic wars with the brief reply, '*Merde!*'

Chaos reigned over the battlefield. Most of the French were in full retreat, but others still stood and fought against the flood of Allied troops cutting into their disintegrating ranks. As night wore on, the pursuit rolled over the more than 40,000 dead and wounded on the battlefield. Shooting, stabbing, bayoneting, plying sword and sabre, the entire, intermingled mass of French and Allied troops fell back towards Quatre Bras. Lobau's men held Placenoit until nightfall, keeping the Charleroi road free, otherwise the Prussians might have cut off the whole army and Napoleon's retreat.

Napoleon, riding back behind La Belle Alliance, took shelter inside a square formed by the 1st Grenadiers of the Imperial Guard, and this fell back in good order. After a mile or so he left the square to gallop south to Genappe, to see if it might be possible to make a stand behind the river there but panic gripped the French army. '*Sauve qui peut*' was the only cry anyone would listen to and so the retreat went on, a mob of men and horses fleeing across the fields, the Prussian cavalry on hard on their heels.

At nine o'clock that evening, Wellington and Blücher met at La Belle Alliance. There, surrounded by cheering soldiers throwing their hats in the air while the bands played 'God Save the King' and 'Nun danket Alle Gott', each greeted the other as the victor. After a brief conference it was agreed that the Prussian army, being less exhausted than the Anglo-Dutch, should continue the pursuit. There was no stand at Genappe, or at Quatre Bras, or at Charleroi, or anywhere else. The Prussian cavalry chased the French through the night, cutting down any they encountered and by dawn the Prussians were in France.

Epilogue

THE DEFEAT AT Waterloo marked the end of Napoleon Bonaparte and of his Empire, but not the end of the Napoleonic ideal. That continued to flourish, and the *Code Napoléon* remains to this day the basis for law and society in many European countries. Waterloo, however, was the Emperor's last chance and the defeat sealed his fate.

French losses in the battle exceeded 26,000 men. A further 8,000 were taken prisoner, and all the French artillery and other military equipment was lost. The Allies lost more than 25,000 men, about two-thirds of them British; more than half the British officers in Wellington's army were killed or wounded. The total casualties in the three days of fighting from 16 to 18 June were more than 60,000 French and 55,000 Allies. It took days to clear the wounded off the battlefield. Their sufferings were terrible, many being murdered or abused by looters. The Prussians suffered 9,500 casualties but were able to maintain their pursuit throughout the night of the 18th and during the following day.

By the evening of 20 June, Napoleon was already back in Paris and talking of a new army. Davout, his Minister of War, was willing to continue the fight and there were some 117,000 troops available about the country in various states of training to provide the nucleus for another army but the political will was missing. Allied forces were already spilling into France along the Rhine and across the Alps, and the French people wanted only peace.

Talleyrand and Fouché were already in touch with the Allied commanders, the Senate and the Chamber of Deputies were hostile to any continuance of the Emperor's rule, and Napoleon himself was unwilling to see street fighting in Paris. On 22 June he signed a Declaration of Abdication in favour of his son and on 25 June retired to Malmaison. On 29 June the heads of the Prussian columns appeared on the heights to the north of Paris, with Wellington's army but a day behind them, and with that the Bonapartists lost heart. A Convention was signed on 3 July by which the French army was to retire to the Loire. The Provisional Government again recognized Louis XVIII, and Louis returned to his capital on 8 July, the day after the Allies made a triumphal entry.

Blücher had sent a flying column to seize Napoleon but the Prussian cavalry reached Malmaison some hours after Napoleon had driven off to the south. He disappeared for ten days and his whereabouts were only discovered when he appealed to Captain Maitland, commanding the blockading squadron off Rochfort, for permission to to sail for America. He then wrote to the Prince Regent, requesting asylum in England: 'I come like Themistocles, to set myself at the hearth of the British people. I put myself under the protection of the laws which I claim from Your Royal Highness as those of the most constant, the most powerful and the most generous of my enemies.'

The idea of Napoleon Bonaparte as an English squire is intriguing, but it was not to be. His appeal was ignored, and on 15 July Napoleon went on board HMS *Bellerophon* and surrendered himself to her Captain. Within days he was on his way to St Helena, where he spent the last six years of his life in lonely exile, writing the history of his Empire and his wars. He died of cancer in 1821, and now lies buried in Les Invalides, in the heart of Paris.

Blücher died in September 1819, aged 77, worn out at last by his exertions. Wellington continued to serve his country for another thirty-seven years though like Blücher and Napoleon he never fought another battle. A few weeks afterwards, he said to Lady Shelley, 'I hope to God that I have fought my last battle' and in this, as in most other things, he got his way.

Honours poured upon him. He added the title of Duke and Prince of Waterloo to the collection already bestowed on him by Portugal, Spain and Great Britain. He became Commander-in-Chief of the British Army, Master-General of the Ordnance. He re-entered politics and became a Cabinet Minister, Home Secretary, and eventually Prime Minister. As Lord Warden of the Cinque Ports he retired to Walmer Castle, where he died in September 1852, aged eighty-three. He was buried with great pomp in the crypt of St Paul's, and is still recognized as the grea test general his country has ever produced.

The fates of the other main participants in this story may be briefly noted. Napoleon's stepson, Eugène de Beauharnais, had declined to rejoin him for the Hundred Days, retiring instead to Munich with his beloved wife, the Princess Auguste-Amelie of Bavaria, with whom he lived happily until his death in 1824. His mother, the loyal Empress

Josephine had died in May 1814, deeply mourned by her son and by Napoleon.

Bernadotte became King Charles XIV of Sweden in 1818 and ruled well until his death in 1844; his descendants reign in Sweden to this day. Jerome Bonaparte, Napoleon's youngest brother, and erstwhile King of Westphalia, returned to France in 1847 and became a Marshal of France and President of the French Senate before his death in 1860. Napoleon's eldest brother, Joseph, had no wish for kingship after the torments of Spain. After Waterloo he fled to America, where he lived until 1832 when he came back to Europe. He died in Florence in 1844.

Talleyrand became Prime Minister after the second Restoration and removed his rival Fouché, having him appointed Ambassador to the United States – a fate worse than death to an active politician of that era. Talleyrand was unpopular with Louis XVIII, who dismissed him from office while compensating him with the post of Grand Chamberlain and a salary of 100,000 francs a year to supplement his already large fortune. Under Louis-Philippe he was in 1830 appointed Ambassador to the Court of St James's where his old friend the Duke of Wellington greeted him on his arrival. Louis XVIII died in 1824 and Talleyrand, who had attended the coronation of Louis XVI in 1775, attended that of Charles X almost fifty years later having survived the Revolution, the Empire and the Restoration. He died in 1838.

The fortunes of Napoleon's marshals were mixed. Davout held high military commands under Louis XVIII but died in 1823. Marmont was exiled from France in 1830 and spent some time in Vienna as tutor to Napoleon's son, the former King of Rome, later the Duke of Reichstädt, a sad young man who spent most of his life as a pawn in European politics and died in his early twenties. Soult became a Marshal of France again in 1820, a Republican following the Revolution of 1848, and died a very rich man in 1851. Oudinot remained loyal to the Bourbons during the Hundred Days and lived on until 1847, commanding the Royal Guard and leading a corps into Spain in 1823, when the former Prince Ferdinand, now King of Spain, sought French help to suppress his ever turbulent subjects, resenting the loss of liberties they had achieved under Bonaparte.

Marshal Masséna adhered to the Bourbons and refused to follow Napoleon after his return from Elba. He also refused to sit on the court martial which tried Ney for treason after the Hundred Days, and died two years later, in April 1817. Ney was given every chance to flee abroad after Waterloo, but declined to do so. His promise to King Louis that he would bring Napoleon back to Paris in an iron cage had not been forgotten, and his subsequent desertion to the Emperor was clearly treason. Ney was eventually brought to trial in Paris, sentenced to death, and executed by firing squad in the Luxembourg Gardens on 7 December 1815. This trial and execution was an entirely French affair. The Duke of Wellington let it be known that he was privately against bringing Marshal Ney to trial, and ordered that no officer under his command was to play any part in the matter. A British officer who went to watch the execution was cashiered.

The firing squad was also the fate of Joachim Murat. He returned to France in 1815 and offered his services to the Emperor but his previous treachery had not been forgotten and his offer was declined. After Napoleon's final overthrow he landed in Calabria with a small force aiming to regain his kingdom of Naples, but was taken, court-martialled, and shot on 13 October 1815.

As the years passed and the ranks of the survivors were thinned by old age, the memory of their great battles and desperate campaigns passed into history, but for the better part of two hundred years the merits of the opposing sides – and the opposing generals – have proved a source of debate. Between Wellington and Napoleon, the honours of war may be shared. On balance, and by the judgement of the battlefield, Wellington must be considered the greatest general of his age, though he himself chose to award that title to the Emperor. Napoleon's best memorial is to be found in the legal statutes of Europe, rather than in the plaques and stones that still stand on his battlefields. His campaigns are still studied by military academies, not for his tactics, but for his leadership. 'To learn that Napoleon won the campaign of 1796 by manoeuvring on interior lines is of little value,' said General Wavell in 1938, 'but if you can discover how a young, unknown man inspired a ragged, mutinous, half-starved army and made it fight, then you will have learned something.'

Those European dynasties who opposed Napoleon were right to fear the ideas that followed in the wake of his armies. Ultimately it was those ideas and ideals that brought about their downfall. Few of the kingdoms of Italy or the petty principalities that made up the Confederation of the Rhine outlived the nineteenth century, and by 1918 the Russian, Prussian and Austrian Empires had followed Napoleon's into history. The question of Poland was still being debated at Yalta in 1945, and border problems survive to this day. There were new creations – such as Belgium, which came to nationhood in 1830 – but most of the kingdoms and many of the countries which made up Continental Europe in the early years of the nineteenth century have now vanished from the map.

Napoleon saw the possibilities of a United Europe which may yet come to pass. On balance, the judgement of history has been kind to him, kinder perhaps than his record deserves. He is seen today as a man of vision, the first great European. In fact, he became the victim of his own ambition and he was not the last European conqueror to come to grief on the rock-like intransigence of Britain.

History has replaced Napoleon on his pedestal. Wellington defeated the armies of Imperial France whenever they came against him, and he defeated the Emperor himself at Waterloo, but most of those victories are forgotten outside the pages of British history books.

Visit the battlefield of Waterloo today and it is hard to know who was the victor of that three-day battle long ago, while in Eueope it is the name of Napoleon which endures, as the law-giver, the visionary, the Man of Destiny. As a final morsel of evidence, it is Napoleon, the defeated, and not Wellington, the victor, who gave his name to that twenty-year struggle history calls the Napoleonic Wars. From all the evidence, both generals would have preferred it that way.

Bibliography

Captain Robert Batty, *The Campaign of the Western Pyrenees* (Lionel Leventhal 1983).

Anthony Brett-James, *Wellington at War* (Macmillan 1961).

——, *1812* (Macmillan 1967).

Sir Arthur Bryant, *The Great Duke* (Collins 1971).

David Chandler, *The Campaigns of Napoleon* (Weidenfeld & Nicolson 1967).

—— *Waterloo: The Hundred Days* (Macmillan 1980).

Alfred Cobban, *A History of Modern France* (Penguin 1961).

Duff Cooper, *Talleyrand* (Cape 1964).

Vincent Cronin, *Napoleon* (Fontana 1990).

R. F. Delderfield, *Imperial Sunset* (Chilton Press 1968).

J. W. Fortescue, *History of the British Army* (Vols 5 & 8) (1899–1930).

Captain Charles François, *From Valmy to Waterloo* (Everett & Co. 1906).

David Howarth, *Waterloo* (Fontana 1972).

——, *Waterloo, A Guide to the Battlefield* (Pitkin 1980).

Philip J. Haythornthwaite, *The Napoleonic Source Book* (Cassell 1990).

Lawrence James, *The Iron Duke* (Weidenfeld & Nicolson 1982).

Henry Lechouque, *Napoleon's Battles* (Allan & Unwin 1966).

Georges Lefebvre, *Napoleon: From Tilsit to Waterloo* (Columbia Press 1969).

Elizabeth Longford, *Wellington: The Years of the Sword* (Weidenfeld & Nicolson 1969).

W. F. P. Napier, *History of the War in the Peninsula and in the South of France, 1807–1814* (1828–40).

John Naylor, *Waterloo* (Batsford 1960).

Nigel Nicolson, *Napoleon 1812* (Weidenfeld & Nicolson 1985).

Sir Charles Oman, *Studies in The Napoleonic Wars* (Methuen 1939).

——, *A History of the Peninsular War* (7 vols; Oxford 1902–30).

Ed. Helen Roeder, *The Ordeal of Captain Roeder* (Methuen 1960).

Edith Saunders, *The Hundred Days* (Longman 1964).

Eugene Tarlé, *Bonaparte* (Seker & Warburgh 1937).

Jakob Walter, *The Diary of a Napoleonic Foot Soldier* (Doubleday 1991).

Tom Wintringham & J. N. Blashford-Snell, *Weapons & Tactics* (Penguin 1973).

Index